THE CAMBRIDGE COMPANION TO
CHRISTIAN PHILOSOPHICAL THEOLOGY

This Companion offers an up-to-date overview of the beliefs, doctrines, and practices of the key philosophical concepts at the heart of Christian theology. The sixteen chapters, commissioned specially for this volume, are written by an internationally recognized team of scholars and examine topics such as the Trinity, God's necessary existence, simplicity, omnipotence, omniscience, omnipresence, goodness, eternity and providence, the incarnation, resurrection, atonement, sin and salvation, the problem of evil, church rites, revelation and miracles, prayer, and the afterlife. Written in nontechnical, accessible language, they not only offer a synthesis of scholarship on these topics but also suggest questions and topics for further investigation.

Charles Taliaferro is professor of philosophy at St. Olaf College in Minnesota. He is the author and editor of several books, including *Evidence and Faith: Philosophy and Religion since the Seventeenth Century* and *Consciousness and the Mind of God.*

Chad Meister is professor of philosophy at Bethel College in Indiana. He is the author, most recently, of *Introducing Philosophy of Religion* and *Evil: A Guide for the Perplexed,* among many other titles that he has authored, coauthored, and edited.

D0145380

THE CAMBRIDGE COMPANION TO

CHRISTIAN PHILOSOPHICAL THEOLOGY

Edited by
Charles Taliaferro
St. Olaf College

Chad Meister
Bethel College

CAMBRIDGE
UNIVERSITY PRESS

CAMBRIDGE UNIVERSITY PRESS
Cambridge, New York, Melbourne, Madrid, Cape Town, Singapore,
São Paulo, Delhi, Dubai, Tokyo

Cambridge University Press
32 Avenue of the Americas, New York, NY 10013-2473, USA

www.cambridge.org
Information on this title: www.cambridge.org/9780521730372

© Cambridge University Press 2010

First published 2010

Printed in the United States of America

A catalog record for this publication is available from the British Library.

Library of Congress Cataloging in Publication Data

The Cambridge companion to Christian philosophical theology / edited by
Charles Taliaferro, Chad Meister.
    p.   cm. – (Cambridge companions to religion)
Includes bibliographical references and index.
ISBN 978-0-521-51433-0 (hardback) – ISBN 978-0-521-73037-2 (pbk.)
 1. Philosophical theology.   I. Taliaferro, Charles.   II. Meister, Chad, 1965–
III. Title: Christian philosophical theology.   IV. Series.
BT40.C28   2010
230.01–dc22   2009022573

ISBN 978-0-521-51433-0 Hardback
ISBN 978-0-521-73037-2 Paperback

Contents

Contributors

William J. Abraham is Albert Cook Outler Professor of Wesley Studies and Altshuler Distinguished Teaching Professor at Perkins School of Theology, Southern Methodist University.

Brian Davies is Professor of Philosophy, Fordham University.

Stephen T. Davis is Russell K. Pitzer Professor of Philosophy, Claremont McKenna College.

Ronald J. Feenstra is Heritage Professor of Systematic and Philosophical Theology, Calvin Theological Seminary.

Gordon Graham is Henry Luce III Professor of Philosophy and the Arts, Princeton Theological Seminary.

John E. Hare is Noah Porter Professor of Philosophical Theology, Yale Divinity School.

Harriet Harris is Member of the Faculty of Theology, University of Oxford, and Chaplain of Wadham College, Oxford.

William Hasker is Professor Emeritus of Philosophy, Huntington University.

Brian Leftow is Nolloth Professor of the Philosophy of the Christian Religion, Oxford University.

Chad Meister is Professor of Philosophy, Bethel College.

Sandra Menssen is Professor of Philosophy, University of St. Thomas.

Paul K. Moser is Professor and Chair of Philosophy, Loyola University Chicago.

Katherin A. Rogers is Professor, University of Delaware.

Thomas D. Sullivan is Aquinas Chair in Philosophy and Theology, University of St. Thomas.

Charles Taliaferro is Professor of Philosophy, St. Olaf College.

William J. Wainwright is Distinguished Professor of Philosophy Emeritus, University of Wisconsin-Milwaukee.

Jerry L. Walls is Senior Research Fellow in the Center for Philosophy of Religion, University of Notre Dame.

Acknowledgments

We thank Andy Beck at Cambridge University Press for his enthusiastic support of this project, and we also thank Brigitte Coulton and Jason Przybylski for their outstanding work at Cambridge University Press. We are grateful to Tricia Little, Elisabeth Granquist, and Cody Venzke for their invaluable assistance in helping us prepare the manuscript for publication.

Charles Taliaferro
Chad Meister

Introduction

The field of philosophy of religion today includes a growing, ambitious range of projects. The main topics that have been at the heart of the field since the mid-twentieth century (What is the meaning of religious belief? Does God exist? What is the relationship between religion and science?) are all up and running, but are now considered alongside distinctive philosophical projects that are specific to religious traditions. Today, philosophers in the Jewish, Christian, Islamic, Hindu, and Buddhist traditions not only contemplate themes that are of shared interest across religions, but are also concerned with themes that arise within their religions. Many philosophers, for example, have taken up questions about the Trinity, incarnation, atonement, and the divine attributes, examining these topics and more from the Christian tradition. This enterprise is often described as *philosophical theology*, which may be seen as a branch of the overall field of philosophy of religion.

The subject matter of our Companion is Christian philosophical theology. It is Christian insofar as it concerns the Christian tradition, with its beliefs and practices, but the enterprise of Christian philosophical theology is not limited to Christian philosophers or inquirers. Not only are many of the tenets of Christianity shared by other religious traditions and so the study of Christian philosophical theology can contribute to philosophical reflection on other theistic faiths, but we should make clear that Christian philosophical theology is not the same thing as Christian apologetics. Any philosopher committed to thinking through topics such as the Trinity in the Christian tradition (critically examining different models of God's triune life) is practicing Christian philosophical theology even if her or his intention is to argue for the incoherence or implausibility of Christian traditional beliefs. Because of this, it should be clear that engaging in Christian philosophical theology is not, ipso facto, a project of convincing others of the truth of Christianity. Because the project of Christian philosophical theology is philosophically interesting only if there are plausible accounts of Christian theological convictions, each chapter in this volume seeks to demonstrate the consistency and plausibility of the theological claims addressed. However, it should be clear that such constructive accounts are an essential prelude to the project of developing rigorous counterarguments.

Our goal in this volume, then, is to put on exhibit some of the most exciting work being done today in Christian philosophical theology. Our hope is that this Companion may provide you with an accessible doorway into this growing field, irrespective of your own religious convictions (if any). Our claim, minimally, is that the work this Companion displays is deeply *philosophically significant*. It is also interesting socially and culturally insofar as readers are looking for ways in which philosophers have been developing a vocabulary and set of arguments that have a bearing on a very large, living religious tradition.

This Companion is divided into two parts. The first focuses on the being and attributes of God. Although other themes could have been included, those discussed in the first six chapters cover topics considered central to Christian theological discourse throughout the centuries. The second part includes ten chapters regarding God's activities with respect to creation, including God's actions through Christ, the church, revelation and prayer, and the natural world. We have chosen leading philosophers in the field to contribute their unique insights and analyses on the topics, and each of the chapters presents the authors' distinct views and approaches to the material. In addition, each chapter includes a list of further readings to enhance your studies of the subject at hand.

We hope that the chapters in this Companion inspire you to deeper reflection on God and God's relation to the world.

Part I

God

1 Trinity

RONALD J. FEENSTRA

INTRODUCTION

The doctrine of the Trinity is not only central to Christianity but one of its most distinctive teachings. Although the term "Trinity" never appears in the Christian Bible, Christians believe the doctrine to be grounded in Scripture. The doctrine developed during the first few centuries of Christianity, as early Christians began to reflect on Jesus' teachings, the writings of the apostles, the sacred writings that Christians came to call the Old Testament, and Christian practices such as worshiping Jesus and the Holy Spirit. Given the difficulties surrounding the doctrine, debates and disagreements inevitably arose, leading to a need for church councils to set agreed-upon teachings. Within the boundaries set by the conciliar decisions, Christians have discussed important issues related to the Trinity, including what a person is, what natures and substances are, and whether the Trinity has implications for the claim that humans are created in the image of God. Since the early twentieth century, Christians of various traditions have paid renewed attention to the doctrine of the Trinity.

BIBLICAL GROUNDING

How can someone affirm one of the central teachings of the Hebrew Scriptures – that there is but one God, Yahweh (Deut. 6:4; Mark 12:29) – and at the same time regard Jesus not only as Messiah (Christ) and Son of God, but also as God? If the Son is God (John 1:1), then what is the relationship between the Father and the Son? Is this in any way compatible with monotheism? Is God's Holy Spirit also a distinct divine agent, as Scripture seems to suggest? Although the New Testament includes brief glimpses into the relationship between Father and Son, as in Jesus' prayer to the Father (John 17:1–26), or among Father, Son, and Spirit, as in Jesus' farewell discourses (John 14–16), it leaves many unanswered questions regarding these persons and relationships.

Nevertheless, the New Testament's ascription of divine titles and functions to the Father and the Son offers significant grounds for Trinity doctrine. The New Testament identifies God as one, as Father, or as God and Father: "one God and Father of all" (Ep. 4:6; cf. Rom. 3:30; 1 Cor. 8: 4–6). Yet at the same time, it speaks of Jesus Christ as Lord (Acts 7:59; Rom. 10:9; 1 Cor. 8:6, 16:22; Phil. 2:11) and as God (John 1:1–2, 18; John 20:28). It also appears that early Christian worship spoke of Jesus Christ as Lord and God. The New Testament describes Jesus Christ as performing the divine functions of receiving prayer, and of creating, saving, and judging (Acts 7:59–60; Rev. 22:20; Col. 1:16; John 3:16–17; John 5:21–27).

Biblical descriptions of Jesus Christ's relationship to God the Father also raise important and complicated issues. On the one hand, the New Testament describes Jesus as having existed with the Father prior to his birth and as the "exact imprint" of God's being (John 8:58; John 17:5; Heb. 1:2–3). On the other hand, the New Testament suggests Jesus' subordination to the Father as the one sent by the Father and as one who will be subordinate to the Father at the eschaton (John 5:30; John 14:28; 1 Cor. 15:24–28). Although the Son, like the Father, has life in himself and deserves the same honor as the Father, nevertheless the Son can do nothing by himself, but only what he sees the Father doing (John 5:19–27). The complexity of biblical descriptions of Jesus Christ can be seen in a single passage that describes Jesus as "the firstborn of all creation" (suggesting creaturely subordination) and also as the one who is "before all things" and in whom "all things in heaven and on earth were created," and "all the fullness of God was pleased to dwell" (Col. 1:15–20). Passages such as these contributed to early Christians' struggle to understand and articulate Jesus Christ's status and relationship to the Father.

The New Testament's comments about the Spirit also lend support to the doctrine of the Trinity. Although some references to the Spirit might not suggest that the Spirit is personal, other passages do seem to imply that the Spirit is a person. Thus, according to the Gospels, Jesus describes the Spirit as guiding his disciples' speech when they are brought to trial (Mark 13:11) and as one against whom blasphemy is not forgivable – and by implication as one against whom blasphemy can be committed (Mark 3:29; Matt. 12:31; Luke 12:10).

The New Testament does not clarify the relationship between the work of the Spirit and the work of Christ. Jesus promises his disciples that when he leaves them, he will send the Spirit, who will be their advocate (John 16:7). But he sometimes speaks of himself and sometimes of the Spirit as coming to his disciples after he leaves them (John 14:18, 26).

Paul speaks of both the Spirit and Christ dwelling in and making intercession for believers (Rom. 8:9–11, 26–27, 34). Paul even seems to identify
Christ and the Spirit: "the Lord is the Spirit" (2 Cor. 3:17–18).

Given the ambiguous biblical evidence regarding whether the Spirit
is personal, as well as suggestions that the Spirit may be the ascended
Christ, one might have thought that Christians would seriously debate
whether there are two or three divine agents or persons. The lack of
such a debate follows from such biblical accounts as the story of Jesus'
baptism, at which three divine figures are present: Jesus as the one being
baptized, the Spirit as one who descends on him, and the Father as a
voice from heaven speaking of Jesus as "my Son" (Mark 1:9–11; Matt.
3:16–17; Luke 3:21–22; John 1:32–34). The New Testament also includes
triadic statements such as the baptismal formula ("baptizing them in
the name of the Father and of the Son and of the Holy Spirit" [Matt.
28:19]) and the closing benediction of Second Corinthians ("The grace of
the Lord Jesus Christ, the love of God, and the communion of the Holy
Spirit be with all of you" [2 Cor. 13:14]). Other passages also include
threefold references to Father (sometimes simply called God), Son, and
Spirit (1 Cor. 12:4–6; 2 Thess. 2:13–14; Titus 3:4–6; 1 Pet. 1:2). Taken
together, the descriptions of Jesus' baptism and these triadic statements
suggest that Father, Son, and Spirit are distinct in certain functions, yet
equal in status. These passages do not, however, clarify the relationships
among the three.

So the Christian doctrine of the Trinity is rooted in biblical affir-
mations of the divinity of Jesus Christ and the Spirit as well key triadic
texts. Still, the New Testament's lack of clarity about the relationships
among the three, especially given statements that suggest both the Son's
equality with and his subordination to the Father, left important issues
to be resolved by the early church.

THE EARLY CHURCH

Early Christians began to reflect on how their commitment to
monotheism fit with Jesus' teachings and the writings of the apostles,
as well as with their practice of worshiping Jesus and the Holy Spirit.
In the second century, Christian Apologists such as Justin Martyr and
Theophilus spoke about the unity of God, the divine preexistence of
the Logos, and the Triad (*trias*) of Father, Word, and Wisdom.[1] By the

---

[1] Eugene Fortman, *The Triune God: A Historical Study of the Doctrine of the Trinity*
(Grand Rapids, MI: Baker, 1982), 50–51; J. N. D. Kelly, *Early Christian Doctrines*, 3rd
ed. (New York: Longman, 1978), 109.

third century, two currents of thought developed. One current, known as monarchians and largely associated with Rome in the West, thought the emphasis on threeness threatened divine unity. Their belief in the oneness of God and the deity of Christ led the modalistic monarchians (notably, Sabellius) to speak of God as one being who appears first as Father and then as Son in the work of creation and redemption. The other current, initially associated with Alexandria in the East, empha-sized the divine threeness. Origen of Alexandria spoke of Father, Son, and Spirit as three persons or *hypostases*, distinct eternally and not just as manifested in their work. Origen also spoke of the Son and Spirit as pos-sessing divine characteristics derivatively from the Father and therefore as subordinate to the Father.[2]

At the beginning of the fourth century, amid a lack of agreement over how to think or speak about the divine threeness and oneness, Arius, a presbyter in Alexandria, provoked the church into resolving some central issues. Arius proposed that God the Father is the unique, transcendent, unoriginate source of everything that exists, including the Son, who was created out of nothing by the Father's will or decision and therefore had a beginning. He also held that, as a finite being whose essence was dissimilar to the Father's, the Word or Son "can neither see nor know the Father perfectly and accurately." His followers spoke of the divine Triad as three *hypostases* who did not share the same essence or nature.[3]

Arius's proposals generated much controversy, prompting the emperor to call the council of Nicaea in 325. This council composed a creed that affirms belief in "one Lord Jesus Christ, the Son of God, begot-ten from the Father, ... begotten not made, of one substance [*homoou-sion*] with the Father" and anathematizes those who "assert that the Son of God is from a different hypostasis or substance" than the Father.[4] Nicaea apparently used the term *homoousion* at least in part because the Arians found it unacceptable, but without clarifying what the terms *homoousion* and *hypostasis* meant.[5] For example, does the term *ousia* refer to an individual thing or entity (primary substance)

---

[2] Kelly, *Early Christian Doctrines*, 109–10, 121–22, 129–32.

[3] R. P. C. Hanson, *The Search for the Christian Doctrine of God: The Arian Controversy 318–381* (Edinburgh: T & T Clark, 1989), 143–44; Kelly, *Early Christian Doctrines*, 227–29.

[4] Kelly, *Early Christian Doctrines*, 232.

[5] Hanson, *The Search for the Christian Doctrine of God*, 181–202; Christopher Stead, *Philosophy in Christian Antiquity* (Cambridge: Cambridge University Press, 1994), 160–72.

or does it refer to an essence or substance common to several individuals (secondary substance)? As the debate took shape in succeeding decades, affirming "three hypostases" as distinct but consubstantial persons became accepted despite concerns by some Western theologians that it suggested three *hypostases* that were alien from one another and thus three gods. Debate during this period also clarified the Spirit's status as fully divine and equal with the Father and Son (such that some referred to the Spirit as *homoousion* with the Father and the Son).[6]

The Council of Constantinople (381) issued a new creed, sometimes known as the Nicene-Constantinopolitan Creed, both reaffirming and revising important teachings of Nicaea. It drops Nicaea's anathemas (including the anathema against saying the Son is of a different hypostasis than the Father) and it adds to Nicaea's mere mention of the Holy Spirit by affirming that the Spirit is Lord and life-giver, proceeds from the Father, is worshiped and glorified together with the Father and the Son, and spoke by the prophets.[7] The following year, a group of bishops in Constantinople wrote a synodical letter summarizing the true faith as belief in "one divinity, power, and substance of the Father and Son and Holy Spirit; and in their equal honor, dignity, and co-eternal majesty; in three most perfect hypostases or three perfect prosopa."[8]

The major figures engaged in the fourth-century discussions included Athanasius of Alexandria (ca. 296–373) and the Cappadocians – Basil of Caesarea (ca. 330–379), Gregory of Nazianzus (329/30–389/90), and Gregory of Nyssa (ca. 330–ca. 395). The Cappadocians spoke of the Trinity as three divine *hypostases* sharing one divine *ousia* and therefore as homoousios with one another.[9] Accordingly, Gregory of Nyssa describes the Father, Son, and Holy Spirit as being analogous to Peter, James, and John, who share one human nature yet are three distinct persons. Recognizing that some might accuse him of holding to three gods, Gregory offers two responses. His first response is based on his own Platonism: just as three persons who share divinity are one God, so, too, three persons who share humanity should be called "one human," although we customarily abuse the language by speaking of "many humans."[10] His second response appeals to the unity of operations or

[6] Kelly, *Early Christian Doctrines*, 253–63.

[7] Hanson, *The Search for the Christian Doctrine of God*, 816–19.

[8] Fortman, *The Triune God*, 85.

[9] Stead, *Philosophy in Christian Antiquity*, 162.

[10] Gregory of Nyssa, "On 'Not Three Gods': To Ablabius," in *A Select Library of Nicene and Post-Nicene Fathers of the Christian Church*, second series, ed. P. Schaff and H. Wace (Grand Rapids, MI: Eerdmans, 1979), 5:331, 336.

works of God as ground for the unity of the three divine persons as one God. The Father does not do anything by himself "in which the Son does not work conjointly"; nor does the Son have "any special operation apart from the Holy Spirit"; and therefore the "unity existing in the action" of the three divine persons prevents speaking in the plural of three gods.[11] In sum, Gregory argues, "The Father is God: the Son is God: and yet by the same proclamation God is One, because no difference either of nature or of operation is contemplated in the Godhead."[12] The views of Gregory and the other Cappadocians have been especially influential in Eastern Christian thought and in recent discussions of the Trinity.

In the Western church, Augustine's theology of the Trinity, like his work on many other topics, has been enormously influential. Like the Cappadocians, Augustine emphasizes the unity of will and work of Father, Son, and Spirit, who have "but one will and are indivisible in their working."[13] Similarly, Augustine rejects any suggestion that the sending of the Son and Spirit implies "any inequality or disparity or dissimilarity of substance between the divine persons."[14] Augustine's discussion of the Trinity is influenced by his understanding of divine simplicity.[15] Noting the difficulty of translating concepts from Greek to Latin theology, he says that the Greek formula of one *ousia*, three *hypostases* sounds to him as if it means one being, three substances, so he prefers to speak of one being or substance, three persons.[16]

Augustine's differences with the Cappadocians over terminology are expressed in his discussion of analogies for the Trinity. Augustine rejects the three human analogy, noting both the disanalogy that other humans could emerge with the same nature and that, if the image of the Trinity is realized in three human beings, then humans would not have been in God's image until there was a man, woman, and their child.[17] He offers instead a variety of psychological or unipersonal analogies for the Trinity. Therefore, when someone loves, the triad of the human mind, its self-knowledge, and its love is an image of the one substance of the Trinity. Alternatively, a person is one mind or substance, yet with a distinct memory, understanding, and will.[18]

---

[11] Gregory of Nyssa, "On 'Not Three Gods,'" 334–35.
[12] Gregory, "On 'Not Three Gods,'" 336.
[13] Augustine, *The Trinity*, trans., with an introduction and notes, by E. Hill (New York: New City Press, 1991), II.9, 103.
[14] Augustine, *The Trinity*, IV.32, 176–77.
[15] Augustine, *The Trinity*, VI.8, VII.1–3, XIV.22; 210–11, 217–21, 414–15.
[16] Augustine, *The Trinity*, V.10, VII.10–11, 196, 227–29.
[17] Augustine, *The Trinity*, VII.11, XII.5–9, 229–30, 324–27.
[18] Augustine, *The Trinity*, IX.2–18, X.17–18, 271–82, 298–99.

Still, Augustine does not completely avoid social analogies; and he sharply qualifies his commitment to unipersonal analogies for the Trinity. In discussing Jesus' claim that he and the Father are one (John 10:30) and his prayer that his disciples will be one as he and the Father are one (John 17:22), Augustine employs a social analogy: "just as Father and Son are one not only by equality of substance but also by identity of will, so these men ... might be one not only by being of the same nature, but also by being bound in the fellowship of the same love."[19] Then, in the concluding book of his work on the Trinity, Augustine notes that all images of the Trinity are inadequate: "So the trinity as a thing in itself is quite different from the image of the trinity in another thing." In particular, both social and psychological analogies ultimately falter: "while a triad of men cannot be called a man, that triad is called, and is, one God.... Nor is that triad like this image, man, which is one person *having* those three things; on the contrary, it *is* three persons, the Father of the Son and the Son of the Father and the Spirit of the Father and the Son."[20]

Augustine and the Cappadocians share broad areas of agreement on the Trinity as well as commitment to the language of the Nicene-Constantinopolitan Creed. Still, the differences between them mark out two distinct streams of Christian thought on the Trinity: one primarily associated with Western Christianity and the other primarily with Eastern Christianity.

MEDIEVAL THOUGHT

Western thought on the Trinity in the Middle Ages was influenced by Boethius (ca. 480–ca. 524), who defines a person as the "individual substance of a rational nature," which he takes to be equivalent to the Greek term *hypostasis*.[21] But in his treatise on the Trinity, Boethius speaks of divine persons as "predicates of relation."[22] Medieval Western thought also bears evidence of influence from the Cappadocians. For example, Anselm of Canterbury (ca. 1033–1109) echoes Gregory of Nyssa when he asks, "For in what way can those who do not yet understand how several specifically human beings are one human being understand

---

[19] Augustine, *The Trinity*, IV.12, 161.
[20] Augustine, *The Trinity*, XV.42–43, 428.
[21] Boethius, *The Theological Tractates* and *The Consolation of Philosophy*, trans. H. F. Stewart, E. K. Rand, and S. J. Tester, Loeb Classical Library (Cambridge: Harvard University Press; London: William Heinemann, 1973), 85–87.
[22] Boethius, *The Theological Tractates* and *The Consolation of Philosophy*, 27.

in the most hidden and highest nature how several persons, each of whom is complete God, are one God."[23] Like Gregory of Nyssa, Anselm considers the union of several human persons constituting one humanity to reflect the union of three divine persons constituting one God.

Differences over the doctrine of the Trinity became a significant point of contention in the eleventh-century schism between Eastern and Western Christianity. Although the Nicene-Chalcedonian Creed of 381 says that the Holy Spirit "proceeds from the Father," by the fifth and sixth centuries, under the influence of Augustine's thought, Western Christian thinkers held that the Holy Spirit proceeds from the Father and the Son (*filioque*).[24] Asserting the Spirit's procession from the Son as well as the Father had become an important means for Western theologians to affirm the Son's full equality with the Father. In contrast, Eastern Christian thinkers held that "the Spirit proceeded *from* the Father *through* the Son," but insisted that "the Father was the source or fountain-head of Deity."[25] For the East, "there could be no procession also from the Son, for whatever was common to two hypostases had to be common to all three, and then the Holy Spirit would proceed also from himself."[26] Although the church of Rome for a time resisted tampering with the creed, eventually it added the filioque, thereby provoking a dispute with the East.[27]

By the thirteenth century, using Boethius's definition of person as well as his understanding of divine persons as relations, Thomas Aquinas says, "a divine person signifies a relation as subsisting ... and such a relation is a hypostasis subsisting in the divine nature, although in truth that which subsists in the divine nature is the divine nature itself."[28] So Aquinas adds "heft" to Boethius's concept by defining a trinitarian person as a *subsistent* relation. Aquinas sees his position as occupying a middle ground between two opposite errors: Arianism and Sabellianism. To avoid Arianism, Aquinas speaks of a *distinction* between divine persons, but not of a separation or division; to avoid Sabellianism, he rejects both the phrase "the only God," since "Deity is common to several," and also the word "solitary," "lest we take away the society of the three

[23] Anselm of Canterbury, "On the Incarnation of the Word," in *The Major Works*, ed. B. Davies and G. R. Evans (Oxford: Oxford University Press, 1998), 237.

[24] J. N. D. Kelly, *Early Christian Creeds*, 3rd ed. (New York: Longman, 1972), 358–59.

[25] Kelly, *Early Christian Creeds*, 359.

[26] Jaroslav Pelikan, *The Spirit of Eastern Christendom (600–1700)*, vol. 2 of *The Christian Tradition* (Chicago: University of Chicago Press, 1974), 194.

[27] Kelly, *Early Christian Creeds*, 366–67.

[28] Thomas Aquinas, *Summa Theologica*, rev. ed., trans. the Fathers of the English Dominican Province (New York: Bengizer, 1948), I, Q. 29, a. 4.

persons."[29] Reflecting Western views, Aquinas holds that, if the Spirit did not proceed from the Son as well as from the Father, he could not be distinguished from the Son, since his relation to the Father would be identical to the Son's relation to the Father.[30]

RECENT PROPOSALS

The renaissance in work on the Trinity that began in the twentieth century in many ways is a response to the thought of the nineteenth-century theologian Friedrich Schleiermacher, who considers the Trinity only in the conclusion of his major work, *The Christian Faith*. Schleiermacher gives several reasons for putting the doctrine of the Trinity in what is essentially an appendix to this theology. First, based on his method of working from an analysis of the religious consciousness, Schleiermacher argues that this consciousness could never give rise to "the assumption of an eternal distinction in the Supreme Being."[31] Raising an issue that would become important in twentieth-century theology, Schleiermacher adds, "we have no formula for the being of God in Himself as distinct from the being of God in the world."[32] Second, he finds the church's doctrine inconsistent, affirming the equality of the persons while also making the Father superior to the other two persons. Finally, on the grounds that the Protestant Reformation offered no new treatment of this doctrine, but left the church vacillating between Tritheism and Unitarianism, he sees a doctrine due for "reconstruction."[33]

The "reconstruction" of the doctrine of the Trinity began in the first half of the twentieth century, initiated by Karl Barth but joined in by theologians of every theological and confessional stripe, including Karl Rahner, Leonard Hodgson, Jürgen Moltmann, Leonardo Boff, Catherine LaCugna, and John Zizioulas. In recent years, Christian philosophers as well as theologians have addressed important issues in the doctrine of the Trinity.

In the first volume of his *Church Dogmatics*, Barth develops the doctrine of the Trinity from his analysis of the event of divine revelation. In the event of revelation, says Barth, "God, the Revealer, is identical with His act in revelation and also identical with its effect" – a threefold reality that Barth describes as "Revealer, Revelation, and

[29] Thomas Aquinas, *Summa Theologica*, I, Q. 31, a. 2.

[30] Thomas Aquinas, *Summa Theologica*, I, Q. 36, a. 2.

[31] Friedrich Schleiermacher, *The Christian Faith*, ed. H. R. Mackintosh and J. S. Stewart (Edinburgh: T & T Clark, 1928), 739.

[32] Schleiermacher, *The Christian Faith*, 748.

[33] Schleiermacher, *The Christian Faith*, 742–49.

Revealedness."[34] Barth argues that the term "person" has a different meaning in modern thought than it did in the patristic and medieval periods, having acquired "the attribute of self-consciousness."[35] As a result, speaking of three divine persons based on this new concept of person, with the Trinity composed of "three independently thinking and willing subjects," seems inescapably tritheist; but speaking of divine "persons" as if the modern concept of personality did not exist is obsolete and unintelligible today. Therefore, replacing the term "person" with "mode (or way) of being," Barth restates the doctrine of the Trinity as follows: "the one God, i.e. the one Lord, the one personal God, is what He is not just in one mode but . . . in the mode of the Father, in the mode of the Son, and in the mode of the Holy Ghost."[36] Barth argues that this is not modalism, since he does not hold that the three modes are manifestations foreign to God's essence. Rather, just as "fatherhood is an eternal mode of being of the divine essence," so too Jesus Christ "does not first become God's Son or Word" and the Holy Spirit "does not first become the . . . Spirit of God, in the event of revelation."[37] For Barth, then, "Down to the very depths of deity, . . . as the ultimate thing that is to be said about God," God is Father, Son, and Spirit.[38]

One question at the heart of the doctrine of the Trinity has especially vexed contemporary theologians: how can we move from God's presence and action in Jesus Christ and the Spirit (that is, the divine "economy") to speaking of what God is in himself? Defending a position similar to Barth's, Karl Rahner states a thesis, sometimes called "Rahner's rule," that has become axiomatic for many: "The 'economic' Trinity is the 'immanent' Trinity and the 'immanent' Trinity is the 'economic' Trinity."[39] Catherine LaCugna notes one implication of this identification of the economic and immanent Trinity: "God has given Godself to us in Jesus Christ and the Spirit, and this self-revelation or self-communication is nothing less than what God is as God. Creation, redemption, and consummation are thus anchored in God's eternity."[40]

In contrast to Barth and Rahner, who favor unipersonal models, Jürgen Moltmann defends a social view of the Trinity. Moltmann argues

[34] Karl Barth, *Church Dogmatics*, I/1, ed. G. W. Bromiley and T. F. Torrance (Edinburgh: T & T Clark, 1975), 295–96.

[35] Barth, *Church Dogmatics*, I/1, 357.

[36] Barth, *Church Dogmatics*, I/1, 357–59.

[37] Barth, *Church Dogmatics*, I/1, 382, 390, 414, 466.

[38] Barth, *Church Dogmatics*, I/1, 414.

[39] Karl Rahner, *The Trinity*, trans. J. Donceel (New York: Seabury, 1974), 22.

[40] Catherine Mowry LaCugna, *God for Us: The Trinity and the Christian Life* (San Francisco, CA: HarperCollins, 1991), 209.

that, if there is just one divine subject, "then the three Persons are bound to be degraded to modes of being, or modes of subsistence, of the one identical subject," which would not merely revive "Sabellian modalism," but also "transfer the subjectivity of action to a deity concealed 'behind' the three Persons."[41] He argues that, on Barth's view, the "one divine personality" must be ascribed either to the Father or, like Sabellius, to "a subject for whom all three trinitarian persons are objective."[42] On Moltmann's view, "The unity of the divine tri-unity lies in the *union* of the Father, the Son and the Spirit, not in their numerical unity. It lies in their *fellowship*, not in the identity of a single subject."[43] Then, based on Jesus' prayer for his disciples in John 17:21, Moltmann concludes that, since the disciples are not only to have fellowship with one another that resembles the union of the Son and the Father, but also to have "*fellowship with God* and, beyond that, a *fellowship in God*," the unity of the Trinity implies the soteriological uniting of creation in God.[44]

Among recent scholars, Cornelius Plantinga, Jr. and Brian Leftow represent two main ways of understanding the Trinity. Plantinga develops and defends a social trinitarian view. He presents the Trinity as "a divine, transcendent society or community of three fully personal and fully divine entities: the Father, the Son, and the Holy Spirit," who are unified by sharing the divine essence and by "their joint redemptive purpose, revelation, and work." On this view, each member is "a distinct person, but scarcely an *individual* or *separate* or *independent* person," who has "penetrating, inside knowledge of the other as other, but as co-other, loved other, fellow."[45] Plantinga argues that this does not constitute tritheism on the grounds that important strands in the Christian tradition speak of three distinct persons. The pluralist Christian heresy is Arianism, which posits "three *ontologically graded* distinct persons"; whereas social trinitarianism does not affirm three autonomous or independent persons.[46]

Leftow articulates and defends "Latin Trinitarianism." Employing the concept of a trope as "an individualized case of an attribute," he notes that, although Cain and Abel "had the same nature, they had

[41] Jürgen Moltmann, *The Trinity and the Kingdom*, trans. M. Kohl (San Francisco, CA: Harper & Row, 1981), 139.
[42] Moltmann, *The Trinity and the Kingdom*, 143.
[43] Moltmann, *The Trinity and the Kingdom*, 95.
[44] Moltmann, *The Trinity and the Kingdom*, 95–96.
[45] Cornelius Plantinga, Jr. "Social Trinity and Tritheism," in *Trinity, Incarnation, and Atonement: Philosophical and Theological Essays*, ed. R. J. Feenstra and C. Plantinga, Jr. (Notre Dame, IN: University of Notre Dame Press, 1989), 27–28.
[46] Plantinga, "Social Trinity and Tritheism," 32–37.

distinct tropes of that nature," such that when Abel's humanity perished, Cain's did not. Leftow argues that "both Father and Son instance the divine nature (deity)," but, unlike Cain and Abel, "they have but one trope of deity between them."[47] Recognizing that this view seems to suggest that there is just one divine person, Leftow imagines a situation in which time-travel allows three distinct segments of one person's life to appear simultaneously (to us) as three persons side-by-side. Analogously, "God's life runs in three streams," with God as Father in one, as Son in another, and as Spirit in the third. Leftow argues that this account avoids Modalism because it can affirm a "Trinity of being" by saying that "the Persons' distinction is an eternal, necessary, non-successive and intrinsic feature of God's life, one which would be there even if there were no creatures," and because, although "the God who is the Father is crucified," he is crucified "at the point in His life at which He is not the Father, but the Son."[48]

Another recent debate focuses on whether the functional subordination of the Son to the Father and the Spirit to the Son has implications for other theological issues such as the inner life of the triune God or the relations between men and women. Some have argued, for instance, that just as the Son is eternally subordinate, yet equal, to the Father, so too women are permanently subordinate, yet equal, to men. Others reject this claim, either by rejecting the eternal subordination of the Son to the Father, or by rejecting the application of Father–Son subordination to male–female roles.[49]

Although the doctrine of the Trinity has generated much theological and philosophical discussion, this distinctive Christian doctrine has important implications for the Christian life: "The doctrine of the Trinity, which is the specifically Christian way of speaking about God, summarizes what it means to participate in the life of God through Jesus Christ in the Spirit."[50] As LaCugna observes, we cannot enter into the divine life without also entering into "a life of love and communion with others."[51]

---

[47] Brian Leftow, "A Latin Trinity," *Faith and Philosophy* 21(2004): 305.

[48] Leftow, "A Latin Trinity," 307, 319, 327.

[49] Kevin Giles, *Jesus and the Father: Modern Evangelicals Reinvent the Doctrine of the Trinity* (Grand Rapids, MI: Zondervan, 2006); Craig S. Keener, "Is Subordination Within the Trinity Really Heresy? A Study of John 5:18 in Context," *Trinity Journal* 20NS (1999): 39–51.

[50] LaCugna, *God for Us*, 1.

[51] LaCugna, *God for Us*, 382.

2 Necessity

BRIAN LEFTOW

Theories of divine necessity have had a checkered career. From Plotinus to Kant, it is hard to find a theist philosopher who considered the matter and denied one. In the dark night of post-Kantian Europe, it is hard to find a philosopher who considered the matter. Among twentieth-century analytic philosophers, one doctrine of divine necessity was once in such wide disrepute that J.N. Findlay could base on it a purported disproof of God's existence.[1] Things have changed again: that same doctrine is now the consensus view among "analytic" theist philosophers. I speak of doctrines of divine necessity because the sentence "God exists necessarily" is multiply ambiguous. In what follows, I first sort out the ambiguities, then indicate why divine necessity has been so popular for so long. I then consider some arguments for and against the strongest doctrine of divine necessity.

DIVINE NECESSITY DISAMBIGUATED

"God exists necessarily" can express claims of differing logical forms. It might assert that

1. necessarily, at least one thing is divine,
2. necessarily, at least and at most one thing is divine,
3. if anything is divine, it exists necessarily,
4. the individual who is actually divine exists necessarily,
5. the individual who is actually divine is necessarily divine and exists necessarily,

Or, indeed, that necessarily (3), necessarily (4), or necessarily (5). Further, "necessarily" can express many different concepts. Something exists

---

[1] J. N. Findlay, "Can God's Existence Be Disproved?" in *New Essays in Philosophical Theology*, ed. Antony Flew and Alasdair MacIntyre (NY: Macmillan, 1955), 49–55.

with nomic necessity just if, given the actual natural laws, it cannot fail to exist.[2] Something exists with real necessity just if, given the actual natural laws and the universe's initial conditions, it cannot fail to exist. Terence Penelhum suggests that God is "factually necessary," meaning that His existence is indispensable to other things and/or causally independent of all else.[3] Alvin Plantinga once suggested that God's necessity is His being such that the question of why He exists cannot sensibly be asked.[4] Richard Swinburne calls the Trinity ontologically necessary, meaning that it exists everlastingly with no active or permissive cause.[5] However, I deal here with the claim that God exists with the sort of necessity called "absolute," "broad logical," or "metaphysical." So the first thing I must do is explicate this concept.

ABSOLUTE NECESSITY

Nomic and real necessity are necessity *given* some condition. Because each deals in necessity relative to some condition, we can call these "relative" sorts of necessity. If we have the concept of a relative kind of necessity, we can also form the concept of a non-relative or absolute necessity, the concept of a necessity *not* relative to some condition, but *simpliciter*. More than this is, in fact, hinted even in the way I've explained nomic necessity, and so on. For I've said that what is nomically necessary is such that it is impossible that it not exist given the actual laws, and this is just to say that it is *necessary* that it exist given these. There was no modifier or condition on "necessary" in this second use: I explained a relative modality by using a modal term in a way not obviously relative. If this was a genuine analysis, relative modal concepts involve absolute ones. If it was at least a good explanation, perhaps our understanding of relative modalities depends on an understanding of absolute modalities. We can, at any rate, see that we can form the concept of an absolute modality as follows.

The sentence "it is physically necessary that P" asserts that

6. It is necessary that P, given that s_1 and s_2 and $s_3 \ldots$,

---

[2] This is not to say that the laws in any way explain or require its existence – merely that necessarily, if these laws obtain, it also exists.

[3] Terence Penelhum, "Divine Necessity," in *The Philosophy of Religion*, ed. Basil Mitchell, (Oxford: Oxford University Press, 1971), 189.

[4] Alvin Plantinga, "Necessary Being," in *Faith and Philosophy*, ed. Alvin Plantinga (Grand Rapids, MI: William B. Eerdmans, 1964), 106.

[5] Richard Swinburne, *The Christian God* (Oxford: Oxford University Press, 1994), 118–19, 181.

where s_1 etc. are sentences stating only and jointly stating all actual natural laws.[6] (6) instances a schema,

7. It is necessary that __ given that __ and __ and. . . .

Each relative-necessity phrase such as "it is physically necessary that__" in effect expresses the result of plugging the members of a different set of sentences into (7). Now, if we understand the result of plugging the members of one set of sentences into (7), we are just as able to understand the result of plugging the members of another set into (7). The null set, □ is a set (*inter alia*) of sentences. So we can understand the result of plugging the members of the null set of sentences into (7). This result would be, in effect,

> It is necessary that P, given the truth of the members of a null set of sentences, or
> It is necessary that P, given a null set of conditions, or simply
> It is necessary that P.

To say that *P* must be true given a null set of conditions is to say that *P* must be true, period.[7] A sort of necessity *P* given a null set of conditions is not really conditional on anything. It is absolute.

One family of what are clearly absolute modal concepts arises from the fact that what entails a contradiction just can't be true, period. This is not a matter to which any conditions are relevant. So the narrow logical modalities, built entirely on facts about entailing contradictions, must be absolute. We can define narrow logical modalities this way: *P* is narrow-logically (NL) impossible just in case *P* entails a contradiction. So *P* is NL possible just in case *P* entails no contradiction. *P* is NL necessary just in case ⌐*P* entails a contradiction. *P* is NL contingent just in case *P* is NL possible but not NL necessary. There clearly are theses that entail and theses that do not entail contradictions. So there are facts of narrow logical, and therefore absolute, modality.

Narrow logical modality is not the only absolute modality. Necessarily,

> R. nothing is red and green all over at once.[8]

---

[6] Merely possible natural laws would yield not nomic necessity, but a modality that *would* be nomic necessity were the laws different.

[7] Letters such as P abbreviate sentences. I adopt the convention that italicized sentence-abbreviations such as *P*, and italicized sentences, such as *God exists*, name the propositions those sentences express.

[8] At least, that (R) is necessary is plausible. But see C. L. Hardin, *Color for Philosophers* (Indianapolis, IN: Hackett, 1988), 124–26.

This necessity is more than nomic. The laws strictly imply (R): no matter what, if (e.g.) E = MC², (R) is true. But equally, no matter what, if E = MC³, (R) is true. This means that the necessity that (R) is stronger than nomic.[9] In fact, our intuition is that altering natural law, however greatly, cannot affect whether (R). This is a matter independent of natural law. This necessity does not seem relative to any further condition; it seems to rest solely on the nature of color itself and, therefore, to be absolute. However, though the matter has been controversial, ⌐(R) does not seem to entail a contradiction. Again, consider the claim that Hesperus is not Hesperus. This isn't of the right form to be a contradiction; hence it is not a self-contradiction.

As to entailing a contradiction, this presumably would be something on the order of "something which is Hesperus, isn't Hesperus" – that is, (x)(x = Hesperus and x ≠ Hesperus). But someone who said that Hesperus is not Hesperus presumably wouldn't hold that anything else is either: if Hesperus isn't Hesperus, nothing is. So I doubt that he would mean to be committed to (x)(x = Hesperus); the contradiction-yielding formulation doesn't express what he means to say. There is clearly an impossibility here, but it does not appear to be a form of self-contradiction. Again, mathematical statements seem to be necessary truths. So consider such contra-mathematicals as that 1 + 1 = 3 or that 2 = 3. These are impossible but, like "Hesperus ≠ Hesperus," the impossibility doesn't seem to involve self-contradiction. These are inconsistent with mathematical theses: it cannot be the case that 2 = 3 if, interpreting succession as a relation among the natural numbers,

every natural number has a successor,
no two natural numbers have the same successor,
2 = 1's successor and
3 = 2's successor.

[9] A necessary truth is one that would hold no matter what. "No matter what," in effect, means "no matter whether this or that or that . . . occurs." Different sorts of necessity differ by having a different "no matter what" – because there is a different range of situations such that they'd hold no matter whether this or that or that of them occurred. What is nomically necessary, for instance, would be true in any possible situation in which the physical laws were just like ours.

To say that a claim would be true no matter whether S_1 or S_2 or S_3 obtains is to say that it would be true in all of them. In effect, "necessarily" is a universal ("all") quantifier over possible situations, saying that the sentence it governs would express a truth in all of these, or that the predicate it governs would be satisfied in all of these. The more situations the quantifier quantifies over, the stronger the necessity it expresses. So if every situation with our laws is an (R) situation, but there are (R) situations with laws different from ours, the necessity that (R) is stronger than nomic.

These jointly entail that $2 \neq 3$. So $2 = 3$ entails their joint negation "$\neg$(every number has a successor • no two natural numbers have the same successor • $3 = s2$ • $2 = s1$)." However, this last isn't, in form, a contradiction and doesn't seem to entail any. Again, if mathematics is a body of necessary truth, the widely accepted claim that mathematics in some sense "reduces" to set theory[10] entails that the axioms of the set theory to which it reduces are also necessary. But it is unclear that the negations of any of these axioms entail contradictions. The Zermelo axioms assert that there are an infinite and an empty set. Is it a contradiction that there not exist an infinite set? An empty set?[11]

So there seems to be a kind of absolute modality that is not narrowly logical – not based on relations to contradictions. One could give still more examples, but the most basic point is this. Our account of narrow logical modality invoked entailment. On the best available account, this notion is modal; P entails Q just if it cannot be the case that P is true and Q false (and, perhaps, some further conditions are met). Our account also invoked the claim that contradictions can't be true. But how are we to explain these "can't"s? Swinburne suggests that a contradiction "is not conceivable by someone who begins to fill out what the world would be like in which it was true, and so . . . does not make ultimate sense."[12] Contradictions are (ultimate) nonsense, so they can't be true, and so they're false.[13] But this can't be right. Nonsense can't bear a truth-value. "The slithy toves did gambol in the wabe" isn't true, but it isn't false either. It just doesn't say anything. The function of "it is not the case that" is to reverse truth-value; that is, it is to generate a false sentence from a true one. It is not to generate nonsense from sense. (Swinburne holds that all necessary truths are necessary because their negations entail self-contradictions. What entails nonsense is nonsense itself.[14] So for Swinburne, in the case of necessary truths, "not" always generates nonsense from sense.)[15] I do not see how a logical operator could do that.

---

[10] For a selection of testimonials to this effect, see Stephen Pollard, *Philosophical Introduction to Set Theory* (Notre Dame, IN: University of Notre Dame Press, 1990), 1.

[11] It contradicts the axioms, of course. But if it sufficed to render P necessary that $\neg P$ contradict P, every proposition would be necessary.

[12] *Op. cit.*, 113; see also 111–12.

[13] *Ibid.*, 114.

[14] On an alethic account of entailment, nothing *can* entail nonsense. But on Swinburne's, this seems allowable.

[15] Swinburne presumably might also opt for something along the lines of "the rules do not permit that P be true but Q false" or ". . . that both P and *not-P* be true."

We can't appeal to nonsensicality to explicate these "cannot"s. However, it seems that any sort of relative modality involves some absolute modality.[16] So any appeal to a relative modality would simply bring us back to some sort of absolute modality. But it would be circular or infinitely regressive to explain the "can't"s in our account of narrow-logical modality in narrow-logical terms. A regress would not explain the "can't"s. It also doesn't seem satisfactory to rest with a circular account here. True, in some families of terms, one can't break out of such circles, and can only try to explicate terms in the family by making the circle as wide as one can and invoking examples – for example, moral terms. However, when it comes to the claim that

> it can't be the case that some contradiction is true,[17]

the circle involved seems unacceptably narrow, for this claim then amounts at once to

> that some contradiction is true entails that some contradiction is true,

which is hardly illuminating. Further, on a modal account of entailment, this in turn amounts to

> it can't be the case that some contradiction is true and no contradiction is true,

which includes our original

> it can't be the case that some contradiction is true

and so can't illuminate it, and in addition amounts to

> that some contradiction is true and no contradiction is true entails that some contradiction is true,

which still leaves us none the wiser. Again, in our definitions of the narrow-logical modalities, the right sides give the meaning of or explain

---

[16] Swinburne may seem to offer an account that does not when he says that the naturally necessary "is the fully caused" (*op. cit.*, 117). But a full cause just is a cause a statement of the activity of which entails the occurrence of its effect by way of statements stating appropriate natural laws. It is a fully explanatory cause, and explanation involves entailment.

[17] Robert Adams points to this as a problem case ("Divine Necessity," in *The Concept of God*, ed. Thomas Morris [Oxford: Oxford University Press, 1987], 43), but develops the problem differently.

the left sides. So if the impossibility with which it is impossible that contradictions be true is only narrow-logical, the claim that

C*. that some contradiction is true entails that some contradiction is true

gives the meaning of or explains the claim that

C. it is impossible that a contradiction be true.

(C) certainly doesn't *seem* like a case of P□P. Nor does (C) seem vacuous. But (C) is vacuous if (C) means (C*). Nor can (C*) explain (C). It's hard to see how a case of P□P could explain anything, but it seems that we need to bring in (C) again when considering (C*). For when we consider (C*), we think this tells us why (C) is true only if we're covertly accepting that (C): that is, (C*) only seems relevant to the question of why something is impossible if we suppose that contradictions can't be true and add this to the consequent. So we have a coherent, contentful concept of narrow logical modality only if we also have a coherent, contentful concept of at least one other sort of absolute modality, which we can bring in to explicate (C) and entailment.[18]

To avoid a circle, we must not explain this sort of modality in terms of entailment. To avoid a needless regress of kinds of absolute modality, we must not explain it in terms of any other sort of modality. Modal concepts of this sort must be primitive. Plantinga calls this sort of modality "broadly logical," Saul Kripke calls it "metaphysical."[19] The extensions of broad and narrow logical modalities are related this way. It is broad-logically (BL) impossible that contradictions be true. So whatever is NL-necessary is also BL-necessary. But there are (I've suggested) cases of BL-necessity that are not cases of narrow-logical necessity. If *P* is BL-necessary, but ⁷*P* does not imply a contradiction, ⁷*P* is narrow-logically but not BL-possible. As a result, not everything narrow-logically possible is BL-possible. For instance, that something is red and green all over at once is BL-impossible but narrow-logically possible. However, because whatever implies a contradiction is BL-impossible, BL-possibility implies narrow-logical possibility.

I use the term "absolute modality" for BL-modality henceforth, as narrow logical modalities will not concern us. Absolute modalities are

---

[18] That is, if entailment is an alethic relation.

[19] Alvin Plantinga, *The Nature of Necessity* (NY: Oxford University Press, 1974), Chapter 1, *passim*; Saul Kripke, "Naming and Necessity," in *Semantics of Natural Language*, ed. Donald Davidson and Gilbert Harman (Dordrecht: D. Reidel, 1972), 253–355.

objective. That is, whether a thing is (say) absolutely possible is independent of whether any of us do or can conceive, believe, or know it to be so. Absolute modal concepts are primitive, and I suggest that all other objective modalities are definable in their terms: for example, it is nomically possible that P just if it is absolutely possible that P and s_1, s_2, s_3 ..., nomically necessary that P just if it is not absolutely possible that ⁢P and s_1, s_2, s_3.... Thus, whatever is objectively possible in any other sense is absolutely possible, but perhaps not vice versa. So, too, absolute necessity is the strongest sort of objective necessity. Whatever is absolutely necessary is objectively necessary in every other sense: it holds no matter what possible thing occurs, and so holds in every possible situation that would include our natural laws.

Understandings of necessity vary widely across the history of philosophy, and philosophers have not always been sensitive to the logical differences among (1)–(5).[20] So philosophers who say "God exists necessarily" may well be making different claims. One generalization that seems to hold true is that pre-Kantian philosophers who assert some of (1)–(5) take "necessarily" to express the strongest necessity they recognize. It's difficult to say just when theist philosophers began to understand "God exists necessarily" in terms of absolute necessity. Anselm's *Reply to Gaunilo* asserts divine necessity and gives a modal argument for God's existence based on a thesis of modal logic now called the Brouwer axiom. This axiom is often seen as true of absolute modalities. But Anselm's own explanation of modal concepts makes it doubtful that he has these explicitly in mind.[21] Aquinas calls God's existence *per se notum* in itself, and so explains his reason for this as to suggest that he sees some proposition asserting that God exists as what we now would call an "analytic" truth.[22] Analytic truths are true by absolute necessity, and one can show that Thomas had a necessity concept very close to this and would apply it to analytic truths.[23] So I suggest that Thomas, at least, sees God's existence as absolutely necessary, though he also argued for God's existence in terms of a weaker necessity-concept.[24]

I now consider the historic roots of theories of divine necessity. In doing so I do not distinguish among (1)–(5), as the writers I discuss

---

[20] Particularly since given certain other assumptions (which many of them made), (1)–(5) turn out to be logical equivalents.

[21] See Eileen Serene, "Anselm's Modal Conceptions," in *Reforging the Great Chain of Being*, ed. Simo Knuutilla (Dordrecht: D. Reidel, 1980), 117–62.

[22] *ST* Ia 2, 1.

[23] See my "Aquinas, Divine Simplicity and Divine Freedom," in *Metaphysics and God*, ed. Kevin Timpe (London: Routledge, 2009), 21–38.

[24] In the Third Way (*ST* Ia 2, 3).

were not always clear on this. Thereafter, I discuss (5), which implies (1) and (4).

THE POPULARITY OF DIVINE NECESSITY

At least four strands contribute to the historical popularity of doctrines of divine necessity.

It is a primary Scriptural datum that God is eternal. Aristotle argued that whatever is eternal exists necessarily.[25] The thinking that underlay this argument was influential until well into the modern period.

Again, it is usual among theists to hold not just that God never will cease to exist, but that He is imperishable, being *unable* to cease to exist. Medieval Aristotelians tended to think that the past, once past, is absolutely necessary.[26] Before Socrates drank the hemlock, he was able not to. All the same, they argued, once he had drunk it, it was no longer possible in any sense that he did not; thereafter, "Socrates did not drink it" implies a contradiction.[27] On this account, though things now past could have gone differently when they were still to come, there is now just one possible past. Suppose then that there is just one possible past, and that in it, God existed and was unable to cease to exist. The latter implies that in no possible continuation of actual history does He do so. But if there is just one possible past, every possible world consists of the actual past plus some possible continuation of actual history. On these assumptions, in no possible world does God not exist at any time: God exists with absolute necessity.

Again, beginning with al-Farabi, Muslim philosophers developed versions of the cosmological argument from contingency, which contends that something exists, which explains the existence of all contingent beings. Such a being could not, itself, exist contingently, since it then would account for its own existence. It must exist necessarily, in some sense. The Bible tells us that God created the universe. The universe is the total assemblage of contingent beings. Creating it explains its existence. Theists will not accept that God shares universe-explaining honors with anything else. So if any cosmological argument from contingency is sound, theists must hold that God is identical with the necessary being whose existence the contingency argument infers. Theist

---

[25] *De Caelo* I, 12. It is difficult to sort out just what sort of necessity he means; for present purposes we need not address this.

[26] See e.g., Aquinas, *ST* Ia 25, 4.

[27] See again Aquinas, *loc. cit.*

philosophers from al-Farabi to Kant believed that some contingency argument was sound. Many still do.

Finally, Anselm argued in his *Response to Gaunilo* that because He is perfect, God exists necessarily. This sort of argument yields (I submit) the strongest case for divine necessity.

DIVINE NECESSITY: A CONTEMPORARY CASE

One can give many perfect-being arguments for divine absolute necessity. For instance,

I. Absolute necessity would make God's existence wholly inescapable, part of our ineluctable fate, a thing to which we must merely bow, like the existence of the universe.[28] Even numbers, if any, might deserve some awe for this property, of the sort we can have on catching sight of an imposing mountain. They would do so the more if they had an active impact on our existence, and plans for us. So God would deserve some awe for this as well. Anything rendering more awesome a being otherwise of the right sort to worship moves it more toward deserving worship, as deserving awe is one note of deserving worship. And something more deserves worship than another thing either because it has done more for us or because it is better – more perfect – in some way. Only the latter applies here.

II. Absolute necessity would lend God's existence the "hardness" of a logical truth, making it even more ineluctable than the universe's. This again moves Him toward deserving awe.

III. When young and healthy, we regret that we will cease to be. The old sometimes come to feel differently, but were they still biologically young and healthy, and moreover assured to remain so, they would continue to regret their eventual demise. Any regret-worthy property is an imperfection, *ceteris paribus*. Thus it would be more perfect to lack it. Again, our ever having existed was not assured. It depended on a lucky meeting of gametes. If our existence has been good, we can, in some moods, find this disturbing. Vulnerability to never having had a good existence seems to us a defect. A necessary God would be free of this defect. To be free of a defect is a perfection. So God would be more perfect if existing necessarily.

IV. God is the source of all concrete existents other than Himself. If (5) is true, in no possible world does any concrete thing not owe its

---

[28] Weaker modal properties would also do this – e.g., inability to cease to exist. But this does not entail that necessity does not do it.

existence to God. Nothing can exist independent of God. Every possible being other than God depends essentially on God for existence. This is an awesome status.

V. If He exists necessarily, God can be the ground of all necessary truth.[29] If He is, He is the sole ultimate reality in all possible worlds (rather than sharing that duty with whatever accounts for necessary truths). Again, this is an awesome status.

VI. If God grounds necessary truths, we can easily hold that God is the sole necessary being. If we do, God becomes the sole answer to the question "why is there something rather than nothing?" Again, this renders God more awesome.

These arguments are just a sample. And the standard divine attributes are compatible with divine necessity. So if it is appropriate to use perfect-being arguments to fill out our concept of God, and it is possible that a concrete being be absolutely necessary, (5) is true. I have defended the first thesis elsewhere.[30] Below I consider some arguments against God's being absolutely necessary that are equally arguments against any other concrete thing's being so. Blocking them goes some way to supporting the claim that a concrete thing could exist necessarily. If there turn out to be no good arguments against it, then we should be no worse than agnostic about this.[31] I also suggest that if God can be absolutely necessary, we should expect that no other possible concrete being can be. If this is correct, the only resources to settle the more general issue about concrete beings and necessity will be arguments about God – for example, (I)–(VI). So I suggest that if (I)–(VI) give reason to accept a conclusion about God, they are also reason to accept that some concrete being can be absolutely necessary and, so, accept (5).

I now say a bit about what divine necessity might consist in, then turn to what can be said against (5).

THEORIES OF DIVINE NECESSITY

To explicate God's necessity, I introduce the idea of a possible world. Possibilities come in many sizes. It is possible that I become Pope. It is also possible that I become Pope and my wife is surprised. It is also possible that I become Pope, my wife is surprised, and my students are (as ever) unimpressed. Possibilities have a natural largest size. Some are

---

[29] See my *God and Necessity* (Oxford: Oxford University Press, forthcoming).

[30] In the Introduction to my *God and Necessity*.

[31] For a case that we should be agnostic, see Peter Van Inwagen, "Ontological Arguments," *Nous* 11 (1977), 375–95.

so large that were they realized, for any proposition *P*, it would be true that P or else that ⌐P. These are the largest possibilities. A "possibility" π could be larger than one of these only by being such that for some *P*, were □ to be realized, both *P* and ⌐*P* would be true. A "possibility" like this would not be a possibility at all – it would not be something that could occur. Philosophers call largest possibilities possible worlds. Every smaller possibility is embedded in some possible worlds, and is their intersection. The possibility that Leftow become Pope, for instance, is part of the possibility that Leftow become Pope and his wife is surprised and so on, and part of the possibility that Leftow become Pope and his wife is unsurprised, etc.: it is what they have in common. Because every smaller possibility is the intersection of some possible worlds, giving a metaphysical account of possible worlds is one way to give a metaphysic for all possibilities.

Given the language of possible worlds, one can give an easy account of the absolute modalities. The basics are these: a proposition is true in a possible world just in case it would be true were that world actual, and an individual or property exists in a possible world just in case it would exist were that world actual.[32] A proposition is absolutely possible just if it is true in at least one absolutely possible world, absolutely impossible just if true in none, absolutely necessary just if it is true in all, absolutely contingent just if neither necessary nor impossible. Philosophers standardly treat the modal operators "necessarily" and "possibly" as quantifiers over possible worlds. As "(x)(Fx)" is true just if at least one object in the domain quantified over is F, they take "possibly P" to quantify over a domain of possible worlds, and to be true just if there is at least one object in the domain – one possible world – in which P. So the standard approach takes "possibly P" to assert "in some possible world, P," and "necessarily P" to assert "in all possible worlds, P." That is, the standard approach gives the semantics of modal talk in possible-worlds terms.[33] And so, on the standard approach, to explicate God's necessity, we need to speak of how God is related to possible worlds.

There are two broad approaches on this. One, which we can call Platonic, sees possible worlds as existing independent of God, and sees

[32] Plantinga, *Necessity*, 46–47.

[33] The *locus classicus* is Saul Kripke "Semantic Considerations on Modal Logic," in *Reference and Modality*, ed. Leonard Linsky (Oxford: Oxford University Press, 1971), 63–72. For alternate approaches, see e.g., I. L. Humberstone, "From Worlds to Possibilities," *Journal of Philosophical Logic* 10 (1981), 313–40; John Perry, "From Worlds to Situations,"*Journal of Philosophical Logic* 15 (1986): 83–107; Robert Stalnaker, "Possible Worlds and Situations," *Journal of Philosophical Logic* 15 (1986): 109–23.

God's existence as necessary because in each, God exists: it is necessary, then, because of the contents of independent possible worlds. This threatens to make God's existence derive from items independent from Him: the worlds are there independently, that He is in all of them entails that He actually exists, and so (one might think) worlds' contents explain God's existence. But surely nothing outside Him explains God's existence. Thus most who accept (5) have placed possible worlds somewhere in God. Leibniz, for instance, saw them as ideas in God's mind.[34] In addition, Leibniz thought that God's nature determines of what worlds God has ideas.[35] Thus for Leibniz, in the end, God's being absolutely necessary consists entirely in facts about the divine nature and its contents. Aquinas varied the picture slightly, holding that possible worlds exist in God's power, not His intellect.[36]

OBJECTIONS TO DIVINE NECESSITY: FINDLAY

I have so far taken a broadly realist approach to absolute modality, assuming that absolute-modal facts are discovered, not invented. Twentieth-century objections to divine absolute necessity tended to come from modal conventionalists, who held that if there are absolute-modal facts at all, we invent them. The logical positivists popularized the idea that necessary truths do not make claims about the world, but somehow are true purely because they say what they do. God's necessity, however, is supposed to be a fact about the world. If these things are true, then if (5) tells us how God would be, there is no God. This was Findlay's necessity-based argument against God's existence: Findlay thought that all absolute necessity is a function of human linguistic conventions, and so no real object can exist necessarily, since it would then (he thought) exist as a function of human linguistic conventions – that is, just because we choose to speak a particular way.[37]

However, here, several points are useful (apart from the obvious one that conventionalism is a tough sell these days). One is that languages are real things, parts of the real world, and exist solely because we choose to speak a particular way. Being real doesn't entail being convention-independently real; the adopting of conventions can bring real things to be. Nor is this sort of point limited to languages and their parts. The USA

---

[34] *Monadology*, #43–6, *Theodicy*, secs. 180–85, 335, 351, 380.

[35] Leibniz, "On Nature's Secrets," in C. I. Gerhardt, ed., *Die philosophischen Schriften von G. W. Leibniz* (Berlin: Weidmann, 1875–90), vol. vii, 310.

[36] See my "Aquinas on God and Modal Truth," *The Modern Schoolman* 82 (2005), 171–200.

[37] *Op. cit.*

is a real object. But there is such a country only because people speak and act as if there is – that is, only because some speak and act as if they themselves or others are its citizens. The USA came into existence because certain people adopted certain ways of speaking and acting (and got the British to adopt them as well). And the country could cease to exist simply by fifty states' declaring independence – which would be just a matter of no longer recognizing certain laws (conventions) and taking up others.

Still, it could be argued that non-linguistic objects the existence of which rests on the way we choose to speak aren't *ultimately* real – that all talk of the USA could be paraphrased into talk about people and their behavior dispositions, a particular land mass, and so on. So the important point is this: Findlay assumes that what accounts for a claim's being necessary must account for its being true (perhaps because its being necessary entails that it is true). This is why he thinks that if convention accounts for God's necessity, it accounts for His existence. But things could be the other way around. Perhaps truth helps account for necessity rather than vice versa. Thus some argue that whereas nature makes it true that water is H_2O, our conventional practices of individuating are what make it a necessary truth that water is H_2O.[38] The truth comes first; only because it is there can our practices lift it into the realm of necessity. So even if all necessity is conventional, perhaps some thing that exists independent of convention could exist necessarily. A conventionalist could allow that God really exists, His existence in no way depends on us, but our ways of speaking make His existence count as necessary. A conventionalist could even employ a modal ontological argument – one reasoning from implications of God's being a necessary being – to prove God's existence. This would not commit him/her to claim that our conventions account for His existence or that any principle we invoke to explain His necessity, or His necessity itself, accounts for His existence.

SCHRADER'S MARBLE

David Schrader claims that there is a case from modal intuition against divine absolute necessity:

> I can image a possible world in which there is only one green marble...in so imagining I need not fall into imaginative

---

[38] Mark Sidelle, *Necessity, Essence and Individuation* (Ithaca, NY: Cornell University Press, 1989), and Nathan Salmon, *Reference and Essence* (Princeton, NJ: Princeton University Press, 1981).

inconsistency...since I can image...possible worlds with
no green marbles at all...no single object (God or anything
else)...exists in...all...possible worlds.[39]

"Conceiving" how it would be if P is usually taken as *prima facie* evidence that possibly P, and imagining is one form of conceiving, which
sometimes provides such evidence.[40] But it seems to me that Schrader
is just wrong about what he can imagine. He can have an experience of a
green marble and (in effect) *title* it "world containing just a marble." But
a visual image, mental or not, cannot depict the nonexistence of God –
nor His existence. Visual depiction is based on how things look to us;
a painting depicts Churchill because it looks to us in some respect as
Churchill might from a certain perspective. So God can't be depicted,
because there is no way God looks. Nor can God's absence be depicted,
because there is no way His absence looks. One can no more visually
depict a world containing or not containing God than one can a world
containing or not containing the empty set. One can visually depict
the nonexistence of visible things: showing Churchill as a corpse, or an
empty chair in which he used to sit, with a grieving daughter nearby.
But this is because there is a way things look when they are present,
and so there is a way their absence looks. Perhaps existentialist plays
attempt to depict how the world would be if God did not exist. But even
if one succeeds, that is not the same thing as depicting God's nonexistence *in itself* – not least because for all we know, some ways the world
would look if God did not exist (if there could *be* a world without God)
might also be ways it could look if He did. Thus Schrader's mental image
really depends for its Godless content on its title. So it can have no more
modal-evidential force than is provided by the bare apparent coherence
(of which more anon) of "there is a possible world without God, and its
being actual would look like *this*."

EMPTY WORLDS

It is plausible that there could have been nothing physical.[41] If

NC there could also have been nothing concrete –

---

[39] David Schrader, "The Antinomy of Divine Necessity," *International Journal for Philosophy of Religion* 30 (1991): 51–52.

[40] But not always: see Robert Adams, "Has It Been Proven That All Real Existence Is Contingent?" *American Philosophical Quarterly* 8 (1971): 285.

[41] For a review of recent debate on this, see Geraldine Coggins, "Metaphysical Nihilism," *Philosophical Books* 49 (2008): 229–37.

that is, nothing with any causal power, God could have failed to exist. But if any concrete thing could be nonphysical, we can't simply infer the possibility of (NC) from the possibility of there being nothing physical. And if any concrete thing is invisible, we can't visually imagine its absence, any more than its presence, as just noted. Nor can we imagine the experiences we might undergo were there nothing concrete, for if that were the case, we would not exist, and so would have no experience.[42] "There is nothing concrete" does not immediately impress us as impossible. But neither does "there necessarily is some concrete thing or other," and we have no basis to privilege one intuition of possibility against the other. I suggest, then, that we simply have no source of modal intuition on one side or the other when it comes to NC. NC can't make a difference to the debate over divine necessity.

THE UNIQUENESS PROBLEM

Another point sometimes raised in this context is that if God exists necessarily, He is the only example of this: why would there be only *one* truth entailing the existence of something concrete that is necessary?[43] However, this is what one would expect from God, as (IV) above suggests. In any possible world, He has the traits that make Him free creator of every other concrete thing, free in the strong sense that it was up to Him whether it existed. In any possible world, God was free to bring it about that He existed alone; but if He were so even in one possible world, and it is also the case that nothing could exist if He had determined that nothing should, then God would turn out the only possible concrete necessary being. We might even suggest that if more than one concrete being were a necessary existent, that would be good reason to think none of them were God. God's modal uniqueness, then, is just His footprint on the rest of the modal realm.

There is more to say here, of course, but I suggest in sum that the doctrine of divine absolute necessity may well deserve the wide adherence it has found.

---

[42] Robert M. Adams, "Has it Been Proven that All Real Existence is Contingent?", *American Philosophical Quarterly* 8 (1971), 285.

[43] Swinburne raised this in correspondence.

3 Simplicity

BRIAN DAVIES

That God is entirely simple is a teaching that has been reiterated by generations of Christians. It is found in the writings of Augustine of Hippo, Anselm of Canterbury, and Thomas Aquinas. It was formally ratified by the Fourth Lateran Council and the First Vatican Council.[1] No historian of Christianity can plausibly deny that it has featured significantly in Christian discourse. Yet, recently, some Christian (and some non-Christian) analytic philosophers who have turned to the claim that God is simple have rejected it. Are they right to do so? I shall shortly suggest that they are not. To start with, however, I need to explain what the doctrine of divine simplicity amounts to, and I shall do so by focusing on the way it is presented in the work of its most systematic defender – Thomas Aquinas.[2]

AQUINAS ON SIMPLICITY

(a) Preliminaries

When it comes to divine simplicity, thinks Aquinas, everything hinges on the notion of God as Creator. What should we mean by saying that there is a God who creates? Some would reply that we should only take ourselves to be saying that something or other got the universe started. Though he believes that the universe had a beginning brought about by God, however, Aquinas also thinks that for God to create is to make something exist for as long as it exists. In his language, God is the cause of the *esse* (existence/being) of things. For Aquinas, to speak

---

[1] For the conciliar texts, see Norman P. Tanner, ed., *Decrees of the Ecumenical Councils* (London and Georgetown, VA: Georgetown University Press, 1990), I: 230 and II:805.

[2] For an account of Maimonides and Avicenna on divine simplicity, see David B. Burrell, *Knowing the Unknowable God* (Notre Dame, IN: University of Notre Dame Press, 1986) and David B. Burrell, *Freedom and Creation in Three Traditions* (Notre Dame, IN: University of Notre Dame Press, 1993). For Augustine on divine simplicity, see *The City of God*, XI, 10; *Confessions* I, vi, 10 and XIII, iii, 4. For Anselm on divine simplicity, see *Monologion*, 17 and *Proslogion*, 18.

of God as Creator is to speak of him as causally responsible for the sheer existence of anything other than himself. As he puts it in one place: "Among all effects, the most universal is being itself. Hence, it must be the proper effect of the first and most universal cause, which is God."[3]

Why does Aquinas think this? Because he finds it hard to believe that (a) something which does not exist by nature *has* to exist, and (b) it is in the nature of anything in the universe to exist. For him, the fundamental reason for supposing that there is a God lies in what he calls the distinction in creatures of essence (*essentia*) and existence (*esse*).

Here one needs to be careful to distinguish Aquinas's position from the familiar (and perfectly plausible) suggestion that one can understand what a noun means without knowing that there is anything that can be truly named by it. I can understand, say, what "wizard" means without it following that there are any wizards. Dictionaries tell us that a wizard is someone skilled in magic. But we cannot define wizards into existence on the basis of dictionary definitions. Aquinas would not deny this. He would, however, go on to suggest that knowing what something *real* is does not come with a knowledge that the thing has to exist.

My cat Smokey is not a definition. He is an *actual* cat, a thing of a certain kind, a thing with a distinct nature or essence (a nature or essence different from that of any dog or fish or strawberry). But does a knowledge of what Smokey is by nature or essence come with a knowledge that *he* exists? Aquinas thinks not. His line is that what the greatest experts on cats know about what it is to be feline does not allow them to conclude that Smokey exists. So he would say that Smokey does not exist by nature, or that his existing (his having *esse*) does not follow from what he is by nature (if it did, then Smokey would have always existed). And he would say the same of anything that is part of the universe. If Smokey's existing as a cat does not follow from what he is, to say that he might not exist (that is, might not be existing, might not be continuing to exist) is to say that he continually stands over and against the possibility of not existing. In that case, however, what accounts for him being something? And what accounts for there being anything, any universe, rather than nothing?

Obviously, it makes no sense to suppose that there is a mode of being called "being nothing" that something could possess. Yet if everything in the universe is such that its essence or nature does not guarantee its existence, then there might have been/might be no universe at all. Or

[3] Brian Davies and Brian Leftow, eds., *Summa Theologiae* (henceforth ST) *Questions on God* (Cambridge: Cambridge University Press, 2006), 1a,45,5.

so Aquinas thinks. For him, it makes sense to suppose that there might be or have been nothing that we could recognize as a world. According to Aquinas, we ought to raise causal questions until it no longer makes sense to do so. So, he holds, we ought to ask (the sensible question) how come there is any universe at all. This, he argues, is where God comes in. According to Aquinas, God, as Creator, is the cause of the existence of everything that does not exist by essence or nature.

In that case, however, what account can we give of God's nature? We can give an account of what Smokey is by nature since we can single him out as part of the universe and note how he resembles and differs from other things in it. In other words, we can give a scientific account of what Smokey is. But how can there be a science when it comes to what accounts for the sheer existence of the universe? It would seem that there can be no such thing. A scientific account of what something is would place it squarely within the universe. Aquinas is very much aware of this fact, so, having argued that God must exist as the cause of the *esse* of creatures, Aquinas regularly goes on to say that we cannot know what God is. "Having recognized that something exists," he writes, "we still have to investigate the way in which it exists. But we cannot know what God is, only what he is not. We must therefore consider the ways in which God does not exist rather than the ways in which he does."[4]

Aquinas does not mean that we can make no true propositions concerning God. He actually thinks that there are a number of propositions about God which we can know to be true (that, for example, God is perfect, good, infinite, omnipotent, eternal, and causally efficacious). In saying that we cannot know what God is, he means that we cannot have a scientific knowledge of what God is, that we cannot single him out as a member of the universe and then go on to document what he is as a thing of some kind rather than another. We can, thinks Aquinas, know what Smokey is. Not so, however, when it comes to God. With this thought in mind, Aquinas's development of the doctrine of divine simplicity leaves the runway and begins to take off.

(b) Details

To start with, says Aquinas, if God accounts for the being of the universe, then he cannot be something bodily. Why not? One answer Aquinas gives is: (a) anything bodily can undergo change (if only by being broken up somehow); (b) change derives from something causing

---

[4] ST, 1a, introduction to Question 3. I quote from Brian Davies and Brian Leftow, eds., *Summa Theologiae Questions on God* (Cambridge: Cambridge University Press, 2006), 28. Cf. *Summa Contra Gentiles*, I,14.

it, while God is the cause of the being of everything other than himself (and, therefore, of all change or coming to be).[5] For Aquinas, God cannot be something now in such and such a state but able to be in a different state later. Again, argues Aquinas, God cannot be a physical object since no such object can intelligibly be thought of as causing the being and goodness of everything other than itself (as Aquinas takes God to do when accounting for things existing or having *esse*).[6]

If God is not part of the material world, however, then there is something else that he cannot be, Aquinas says. For, not being material, God cannot, thinks Aquinas, be thought of as being an individual belonging to a class of which there could be many different members.

Smokey is such an individual, and he would be so even if he were the last cat alive. But what is it about Smokey that allows us to think of him in this way? What makes him the particular cat he is rather than some other particular cat? What, if you like, accounts for the fact that when another cat meets Smokey there are *two* cats as opposed to *one* cat?

Let's call the other cat Felix. When Smokey and Felix get together, we have two cats, two individuals of a particular kind (two felines). Now, in seeking to explain why we have two cats here, not one cat, we obviously cannot note what they are by nature (by, as Aquinas would say, noting what they are *essentially*). For they are identical on that score. Smokey is a cat, and so is Felix. Their feline nature is something they *share* or *have in common*, so it cannot *distinguish* them from each other.

One might be tempted to say that Smokey and Felix are different from each other since they differ in appearance or location or something like that (differ, Aquinas would say, *accidentally* rather than *substantially*). So one might suggest that Smokey and Felix are distinct since, for example, Smokey is gray whereas Felix is black and white, or since Smokey is sitting on a chair while Felix is sitting on a rug. This suggestion, however, simply *presupposes* that Smokey and Felix are different from each other (that we are dealing with two cats rather than one). Smokey and Felix cannot differ in the respects now in question unless they are already distinct to begin with.

With these thoughts in mind, Aquinas argues that the numerical difference between Smokey and Felix cannot be put into words. It is, he thinks, a matter of material (as opposed to formal) difference – of Smokey being *this* material object and of Felix being *that* one. Yet if God is not a

---

[5] Cf. ST, 1a, 3,1. For a more developed defense of the claim that God cannot be a body, see *Summa Contra Gentiles*, I,20.

[6] Cf. ST, 1a, 3,1.

body, Aquinas goes on to argue, we cannot get a purchase on the notion of him being one of a kind; we cannot take God to be something distinct from what he is by nature. God, says Aquinas, *is* what his nature is; God and whatever his nature is cannot be thought of as distinct; there is in God no distinction between *suppositum* and *natura*.[7] "The individuality of things not composed of matter and form," Aquinas reasons, "cannot derive from this or that individual matter. So, the forms of such things must be intrinsically individual and themselves subsist as things. Such things are therefore identical with their natures."[8]

As it happens, Aquinas does not believe that God is the only non-material thing (the only "spiritual substance," as he sometimes says). As well as believing that God exists, Aquinas believes in angels. So he concludes that angels, also, are not to be thought of as different from what they are by nature. For Aquinas, on the individual/nature front, angels are just like God. On another front, however, they differ dramatically, or so Aquinas thinks. For, and this is the final element in his doctrine of divine simplicity, in God (and in nothing else) there is no distinction of essence (*essentia*) and existence (*esse*). God, says Aquinas, "is not only his own essence, but also his own existence."[9]

The basic point Aquinas is making here is that God's existing is not an *effect*, not something brought about by something else; that God's existing is uncaused, that it is not something *created*. As we saw earlier, Aquinas wants to ask why anything exists at all, and his answer appeals to what causes everything else to exist without itself being caused to exist. Now can we think of such a cause as acquiring existence in some way? Hardly. So how should we think of it? Aquinas's answer is that we should think of it as something existing by nature, as something the nature of which is to exist, as something with respect to which there is no distinction of nature and existence (as there is, say, with Smokey).

---

[7] By *suppositum* Aquinas means what, I suppose, we would call "individuality" when saying, for example, that the individuality of Socrates is unique to Socrates, that Socrates is one individually existing thing and not another.

[8] ST, 1a, 3,3 (Davies and Leftow, p. 34). "Form" is the word Aquinas typically uses when thinking of what something can be said to be. He distinguishes between substantial forms and accidental forms. To say what something's substantial form is would, he thinks, be to say what it is by nature (e.g., a cat). To say what something's accidental forms are, he thinks, would be to say what something is without having to be like this given what the thing is by nature. My being a human being does not mean that I have to weigh 140 lbs or be sitting at a desk. My weighing 140 lbs or sitting at a desk would, in Aquinas's language, be accidental forms that I possess.

[9] ST, 1a,3,4.

(c) Summary

In short, Aquinas's development of the claim that God is simple amounts to three positions: (1) God is not something changeable; (2) God, in one sense, is not an individual; (3) God is not created or made to exist. This, of course, means that Aquinas's doctrine of divine simplicity is not offered as a *description* of God, or as an attempt to suggest that God has an *attribute* or *property* of simplicity. It is not a description since (in keeping with Aquinas's promise to note ways in which God does *not* exist) it consists entirely of negations, of attempts to say what God *cannot* be. It also is not ascribing simplicity to God as an attribute or property since it explicitly denies that, in a serious sense, God has any attributes or properties. Normally, attributes or properties can be distinguished from the things that possess them. Yet, as we have seen, Aquinas denies that God and his nature can be thought of as distinct. It is very important to bear all of this in mind if one's aim is to understand Aquinas on simplicity, for what his teaching amounts to is what might be called an exercise in *negative* theology. It is not concerned to paint a portrait of God. Its aim is to put up "No Entry" signs in front of certain roads into which we might turn when trying to think about God.

It has been said that error in philosophy largely consists in exploring in minute detail aspects of a path one should never have turned into in the first place. Aquinas, we might say, is concerned to warn theologians away from comparable explorations. Whatever we ask, think, or say about God, he believes, we should never start from the supposition that God is something material and changeable, an instance of a kind, or something that owes its existence to anything.

OBJECTIONS TO SIMPLICITY

As I have said, some philosophers reject the conclusion that God is simple. Why so? Here are a few notable lines of argument and some comments on them from me.

(a) God is not a property

In *Does God Have a Nature?* Alvin Plantinga famously says this in a discussion of Aquinas on divine simplicity:

> If God is identical with each of his properties, then, since each
> of his properties is a property, he is a property... Accordingly
> God has just one property: himself... This view is subject to a

difficulty both obvious and overwhelming. No property could have created the world; no property could be omniscient, or, indeed, know anything at all. If God is a property, then he isn't a person but a mere abstract object; he has no knowledge, awareness, power, love or life. So taken, the simplicity doctrine seems an utter mistake.[10]

But *does* Aquinas think that God is what Plantinga takes to be a property? And *is* there something wrong with denying that God is a person?

At this point I should explain that Plantinga takes a property to be an "abstract object," a nonmaterial thing that cannot fail to exist and is not created by God. Plantinga believes that there are many abstract objects. As well as properties, he takes propositions and "states of affairs" to be abstract objects, and he believes that all of these things exist independently of God and independently of what we would normally think of as any individual thing. I take Smokey to be an individual thing (an individual cat). Plantinga would agree that Smokey is, indeed, something individual, but, he would add, to say that Smokey is a cat, or that he is gray, or that he is agile, is to say that he "exemplifies" or "instantiates" properties ("being a cat," "being gray," "being agile") which exist necessarily and independently of him. From what he says in *Does God Have a Nature?* Plantinga seems to be asserting that Aquinas is wrong on divine simplicity since God is not an uncreated abstract object.

This line of thinking, however, does not engage with what Aquinas says as he develops his account of divine simplicity. Unlike Plantinga, Aquinas does not believe in uncreated abstract objects, so he is manifestly not trying to say that God is one of them. He would never say that there is an uncreated property called "being a cat" that preexists the coming to be of all cats. He would say that to call something a cat is to ascribe a nature to something that actually exists without having to exist by nature. So, when Plantinga suggests that Aquinas's teaching on God's simplicity is erroneous since it implies that God is what Plantinga thinks of as a property, he is just talking past Aquinas rather than addressing him.

Now, what about the problem with God being a person? According to Plantinga, if God is a property, he cannot be a person. I have tried to indicate why Aquinas, in his defense of divine simplicity, is not saying that God is a property in Plantinga's sense. Yet if Plantinga's claim that "God is a person" defeats what Aquinas says on divine simplicity, then

---

[10] Alvin Plantinga, *Does God Have a Nature?* (Milwaukee. WI: Marquette University Press, 1980), 47.

it might well be thought to be a really serious objection to Aquinas. For, surely, as a theist, Aquinas has to agree that God is a person, and how can he do that while maintaining what he says about divine simplicity? For are not persons anything but simple in the sense that Aquinas takes God to be? I am a person. But I am not immaterial, and I am not unchangeable, and I exist as an individual of a kind. I am not identical with my nature. Also, I do not exist by nature. So if I am a person, how can God be a person? And if the doctrine of divine simplicity denies that God is a person, should it not be rejected immediately, and in the name of theism?

Yet, *does* Aquinas have to agree that God is a person? Arguably not. The formula "God is a person" does not occur in the Bible. Nor, so far as I know, is it present in the writings of any Christian theologians from New Testament times to the end of the Middle Ages. As the Christian doctrine of the Trinity developed, the term "person" (*persona*) came to be used to speak about God, but it was never used to refer to the divine nature (what it is to be God). It was used to talk about God the Father, God the Son, and God the Holy Spirit (not thought to be three gods), and it never ended up in sentences like "God is three persons in one person." In short, far from it being obvious that a theist has to insist that God is a person, centuries of theists managed not to make the claim at all. Aquinas is one of them. In all that he writes about God (and abstracting from his discussions of the Trinity), he never asks us to believe that God is a person. This is hardly surprising, for the paradigm instances of persons are, presumably, human beings – animals with a particular way of functioning, things that learn and develop, things that talk and go through reasoning processes, things existing in a world of space and time, things that come to be and pass away, things (so Aquinas would say) that depend for their being on God. That God (the divine nature) is one of *those* things is not a suggestion that Aquinas could take seriously since, given his approach to creation, it looks as though it is assimilating God to a creature of some kind. This, I presume, is why he does not even single out the suggestion as a topic for discussion.

Plantinga, of course, might reply: "So much the worse for Aquinas. His position is just not theistic." However, that would seem to be a silly thing to say given that Aquinas stands in an ancient and long-standing tradition of theistic thinking of God. By saying that God is a person, perhaps Plantinga is merely concerned to stress that knowledge and will and agency can be ascribed to God, and here Aquinas would not disagree with him. In his view, knowledge, will, and agency most certainly can be ascribed to God. However, Aquinas would add, what it means to ascribe these things to God must be understood in the light of the teaching that God is entirely simple.

(b) Distinct properties cannot be identical

Another common criticism of the doctrine of divine simplicity boils down to the assertion that different properties are just different. Smokey is agile and inquisitive, yet his being agile is different from his being inquisitive. In that case, however, how could it be that God and his nature are not to be distinguished (that God *is* his nature)? Let's say that God is by nature both living and knowing. If there is no distinction in God between *suppositum* and nature, does it not follow that "is living" and "is knowing," when predicated of God, do not predicate different properties of him? And does not this leave us with an absurd result – that properties which are different are, when it comes to God, identical?

So the argument sometimes goes. And its merit lies in the evident truth that when things in the universe exhibit different attributes, the attributes in question are really distinct from each other. Smokey's inquisitiveness is a reality in him which might well survive his being agile. Aquinas, however, is not denying this. When he defends the claim that God is simple he is not telling us that there is something in which different attributes are actually one and the same attribute. As I have stressed, what he is doing (and what he says he is doing) is *denying* something of God; he is saying that God (unlike Smokey) is not a being with distinct attributes or properties. Aquinas, of course, is aware that theists often speak of God as if he were a being with different attributes. He is aware that they utter subject/predicate sentences such as "God is good" and "God is powerful" – sentences that would be naturally taken to be ascribing different attributes to something if they did not have the word "God" in them.

However, thinks Aquinas, what this should lead us to say is not that God has different attributes, but that the simple reality of God is often spoken of in a way that fails to capture the reality in question. Aquinas thinks that there are positive reasons for employing different words (and meaning them literally) when it comes to talking about God. He thinks, for example, that there are positive reasons for speaking of God as omnipotent and good. But, in addition, he thinks that there are positive reasons for not taking God to be an individual exhibiting a variety of attributes, and he wishes to give weight to all the reasons in question here. So he concludes – and I think reasonably – that goodness and power in God do not amount to different realities. One might, of course, therefore complain that Aquinas is making God seem terribly mysterious or terribly different from the things with which we are acquainted in day-to-day life. Aquinas would not regard this as undermining his position, for his final verdict is that God *is* terribly mysterious and *is* terribly different from the things with which we are acquainted in day-to-day life.

(c) God cannot be existence

As we have seen, Aquinas's teaching on God's simplicity includes the claim that there is no distinction in God of essence (*essentia*) and existence (*esse*), a point he sometimes makes by saying that God is *ipsum esse subsistens* (subsisting existence itself).[11] Yet is such a suggestion even coherent? Many would say that it is not since it displays deep confusion when it comes to the meaning of the word "exists." Take, for example, the late C. J. F. Williams. According to him, to say, for example, "Readers of Aquinas exist" is not to tell us anything about any particular reader of Aquinas. It is to tell us that "___ is a reader of Aquinas" is truly affirmable of something or other. Or, in Williams's language (which echoes what we find in the writings of Immanuel Kant), "existence" or "being" is not a property of individuals.[12] According to Williams, to say of some individual or thing that it exists is unintelligible. With this thought in mind, he savages Aquinas on simplicity. Williams argues that what Aquinas writes on this topic wrongly presupposes that existing is a property of individuals, and then, ludicrously, identifies this property with God in an attempt to tell us what God is.[13] The idea here is that Aquinas has no business saying that God creates by bringing it about that various individuals exist, and that he has no business identifying God with a property of existence had by these individuals.

One of Williams's main arguments for the view that it is nonsense to ascribe existence to an individual holds that if existence were attributable to individuals, then we could never (as we surely can) consistently say things like "Readers of Aquinas do not exist." Why not? Because, says Williams, if existence *were* intelligibly attributable to individuals, to say, for example, that readers of Aquinas *do not exist* would be to say that they lack a certain property, and to say this is implicitly to assert that they *exist*. In other words, according to Williams, if existence

---

[11] Cf. ST, 1a, 11,4.

[12] Cf. Immanuel Kant, *Critique of Pure Reason*, trans. Paul Guyer and Allen W. Wood (Cambridge: Cambridge University Press, 1997), A592–602.

[13] C. J. F. Williams, "Being," in *A Companion to the Philosophy of Religion*, ed. Philip L. Quinn and Charles Taliaferro (Oxford: Blackwell, 1997).

is a property of individuals, then statements such as "Readers of Aquinas do not exist" is true only if it is false.

This argument, however, wrongly assumes that negative existential assertions (such as "Readers of Aquinas do not exist") have to be taken as presupposing the existence of their subjects and to be denying something of them. To say that readers of Aquinas do not exist is not to suppose that existing readers of Aquinas lack a property of some kind. It is to deny that anything can be truly said to be a reader of Aquinas.

Williams also argues for his position by claiming that sentences ascribing existence to individuals are ones for which we have no use "outside philosophy."[14] He means that we just do not normally say things such as "I exist" or "New York exists." This also seems to be a poor line of argument. People would, doubtless, be puzzled were I to accost them and assert "I exist." They would probably be equally puzzled if, out of the blue, I announce "New York exists." But would anyone seriously take me to be talking nonsense were I to say, for example, "The great pyramid at Giza exists, but the Colossus of Rhodes does not," or "You and I exist, but we won't if a giant meteorite hits the earth"? Contrary to what Williams suggests, "exists," as affirmed of individuals, is hardly some esoteric piece of philosophical baggage. To be sure (and this is something of which Aquinas was acutely aware) what it is for one thing to exist might be different from what it is for something else to exist. For Smokey to exist is for him to be a cat. For me to exist is for me to be a human being. For a cabbage to exist is for it to be (what else?) a cabbage. Cats, humans, and cabbages are obviously things of different kinds, but individual examples of these kinds can surely, and as individuals, be sensibly thought of as existing.

Williams, I presume, would reply that it still makes no sense to say, in reply to the question "What is God?" that God is existence (or something like that). However, to repeat what is obviously my mantra in this chapter, Aquinas's account of divine simplicity is not offered as an account of what God is. It is offered as an account of what God *cannot* be. When saying that there is no distinction in God of essence and existence, Aquinas is asserting that, *whatever* God is, he *cannot* be something the existence of which is derived. And why does he say this? Because he thinks that there are things the existence of which does not derive from what they are (their essence), things which, therefore, have to be caused by what is distinct from them when it comes to essence and existence. Drawing on the biblical and patristic tradition, and

---

[14] C. J. F. Williams, *What Is Existence?* (Oxford: Clarendon Press, 1981), 79 ff.

thinking that nothing we take to be part of the universe exists by nature, Aquinas concludes that "God" is the obvious word to use so as to name what accounts for anything other than "it" existing. And why should he not?

(d) A simple God cannot be free

Let us suppose (as many have denied) that people have freedom of choice (at least sometimes). In that case, presumably, when they do such and such freely they are also freely not doing something or other. Suppose that I am free to brush my teeth before going to bed. Then, it would seem, I am also free not to brush my teeth. Freedom of choice seems bound up with the notion of different courses of action. Not only that; it seems bound up with different ways in which an agent can be described. If I choose to go to bed without brushing my teeth, then I would be different from what I would be had I chosen to brush my teeth. For one thing, I would be someone who had made a decision not to brush his teeth, and someone who chose to brush his teeth would not be that.

With this line of thinking in mind, it has been suggested that the doctrine of divine simplicity should be rejected since God is free to create or not to create, and that he is free to create worlds of many different kinds. The argument goes like this: (a) God has freedom to create or not to create; (b) God is free to create different kinds of worlds; (c) if (a) and (b) are true, then God could be different from what he is; (d) but if God could be different from what he is, then he cannot be simple, for to say that God is simple is to say that he and his nature are changelessly one and the same, which is to say that God cannot be different from what he changelessly is.

This argument is sometimes advanced using the notion of a "contingent property." When Smokey has had a good meal, he is not hungry. When I forget to feed him, he becomes hungry. We might put this by saying that being full or being hungry are contingent properties of Smokey. And we might add that many of Smokey's properties are not contingent since they are properties he has to have in order to exist at all. Since he is a cat, he is a mammal and, so some philosophers would say, being a mammal is a necessary property of Smokey. Now, so it is sometimes said, according to the doctrine of divine simplicity God has no contingent properties. Yet God must have contingent properties if he is free to create or not to create, and if he is free to create worlds of different kinds. Why? Because, without ceasing to be God, he is different from how he could be. If he had not chosen to create, he would have been different from what he is given that he chose to create. If he had chosen to create a world without cats, he would be different from what he is given that he has created cats. And so on.

The merit of this argument lies, I think, in the fact that freedom and difference (or freedom and contingent properties) do come together when we are thinking of people. I (and my teeth) would have come to be different from what I was last night had I chosen not to brush my teeth. In addition, my ending up with brushed teeth last night would have left me being what I did not have to be considered as what I am by nature (that is, human). The problem with the argument, however, lies in the fact that if God is, in Aquinas's sense, the Creator of the universe, then he cannot be thought of as something able to be different from what he is, and he cannot be thought of as having contingent properties. When Aquinas speaks of the created order he is thinking about everything involved in a world of being and becoming. So he resists the suggestion that God is to be thought of as a being who comes (or could come) to be different in some way as time goes by. For him, such a being would simply be part of the spatio-temporal universe, not that which accounts for anything having *esse*.

Aquinas certainly wants to assert that (a) God is free to create or not create, and (b) God does not have to create a world just like ours. By (a), however, he means that God's nature *does not* compel him to create, that he is *not* forced into creating given what he essentially is. He also means that there could be nothing distinct from God which, so to speak, pushes him into creating. Given what we are by nature (human) we cannot but sometimes urinate, or breathe. According to Aquinas, however, divinity has no need of creatures and does not come with an in-built compulsion to create (if it did, thinks Aquinas, then it would, contrary to fact, make no sense to say of any creature that it might not exist). As for (b), Aquinas's meaning here is just that, logically speaking, lots of things that do not exist could exist, and that they would exist only if God made them to be. I live in the USA. Could I live in Russia? There seems to be no logical impossibility in the suggestion that I might be living in Russia. So, thinks Aquinas, the world could be different in that I could live in Russia rather than in the USA. But he takes this point to mean no more than that there is no logical impossibility when it comes to my living in Russia.

Applying all of this to the objection to divine simplicity now in question, it seems fair to observe that, for Aquinas, to say that God is free to create or not create, or that he is free to create a world different from what we find ourselves in, is not to suggest that God might be different from what he essentially is, or that he might acquire "contingent properties."

Aquinas's "God is free to create" is a comment on what God *is not*. God is *not* something whose nature forces him to create. It is also a comment on what exists in the world and on what can be thought to exist without logical contradiction. An objector to Aquinas on simplicity might reply, "But if God had not created Smokey, he would be different from what he is now." But why suppose that God creating or not creating Smokey makes for any difference in God? To suppose that it might would be to think of God as a spatio-temporal individual who is modified as he lives his life and makes *these* choices rather than *those* choices. If Aquinas's approach to the notion of creation is right, however, to think of God in that way is just not to think of God. For, so Aquinas would say (and here note the following negations), God *is not* part of space and time, *is not* (in a serious sense) an individual, and *does not* live a life consisting of many changes. Given arguments of Aquinas that I have noted above, it seems to me that Aquinas would be right to say all this, and that it suffices as a response to the claim that God's freedom to create, and his freedom to create what does not actually exist, entails that God cannot be said to be what he changelessly is (as the doctrine of divine simplicity says that he can). If we had lived our lives differently, then we would be different from what we are now. But why suppose that the Creator of the universe is something with a life history which could have taken a different course?

CONCLUSION

In David Hume's *Dialogues Concerning Natural Religion* (1779) Demea says to Cleanthes that he would rather be a "mystic" than an "anthropomorphite." Cleanthes insists on thinking of God as very much like a human being. Demea resists this approach and, at one point, takes it to be incompatible with "that perfect immutability and simplicity, which all true theists ascribe to the Deity."[15]

It seems obvious to me that in this debate Aquinas would have sided with Demea against Cleanthes, for (like other classical defenders of the doctrine of divine simplicity) Aquinas thinks that, if there is a God who creates, if there is one who makes to be all that exists (apart from itself), one who exists by nature, then there have to be *radical* differences between God and creatures, some of which Aquinas tries to document when teaching that God is simple. Aquinas reasons that we cannot think

---

[15] David Hume, *Dialogues Concerning Natural Religion*, ed. Norman Kemp Smith (Indianapolis, IN: Bobbs-Merrill Educational Publishing, 1947), 159.

of God as being something material and changeable. We cannot think of him as being one of a kind of which there could be others. And we cannot think of him as owing his existence to anything.

One might resist these conclusions (which, I repeat, do not amount to a "description" of God) by appealing to what the Bible says. After all, it sometimes speaks of God as though he were a material individual belonging to some kind (a father, a husband who has been cheated on, a woman in labor, a judge, and so on). Medieval theologians always take such ways of speaking to be exercises in metaphor. Many contemporary theologians would agree with them, though many of them do not. Many of them (the dissenters here) deny that God is simple in the sense that Aquinas thinks that he is. Why so?

Could it be that they are mesmerized by the formula "God is a person"? I suspect that many of them are, and that by God is a person they mean that God is an invisible being (like Descartes's "I"), very like a human one, though lacking a body. If that is what they do mean, however, they are seriously out of step with what might be called the traditional Jewish/Islamic/Christian concept of God. If that is what they mean, perhaps we might also ask them if there is any reason at all to believe that God exists? You and I, corporeal things, things the essence of which does not guarantee our existence, things able to change in various ways as time goes on, things with attributes that come and go, are all, surely, things which raise the question, "And how come they exist at all?" The doctrine of divine simplicity is part of a complicated answer to this question.

4 Omnipotence, omniscience, and omnipresence

WILLIAM J. WAINWRIGHT

Among the attributes Christians have traditionally ascribed to God are omnipotence, omniscience, and omnipresence. They not only appear to follow from God's maximal perfection but seem presupposed by his providential governance of creation. Christians have not always agreed on how these attributes are to be understood, however.

OMNIPOTENCE

Almost no theists think that God can perform logically impossible tasks. States of affairs such as the interior angles of a Euclidian plane triangle equaling 170 or 190 degrees are logically impossible, and hence *no* one can bring them about. Some think that necessary states of affairs like 2 + 3 equaling 5, while logically possible, aren't "producible" – that is, they can't have causes. If they can't, then *no* agent can produce them. Other states of affairs are logically possible and producible but can't be produced *by God*. For example, the state of affairs consisting in my freely choosing to spend the evening at home can't be brought about by someone other than myself since, if it were, then either the action wouldn't really be *my* action or it wouldn't be *free*.

These aren't real limitations, though. Since the tasks in question (bringing about a logically impossible state of affairs, producing an unproducible state of affairs, bringing about another person's free action) can't be brought about by *any* possible being, no being could surpass God by possessing the ability to perform them. Hence, these tasks aren't included within the scope of maximally perfect possible power.

God's perfection also makes certain things impossible for him. For example, any being that could appropriately be called omnipotent would surely have the power to create and lift stones of any weight, size, texture, and the like. If it does possess this power, though, it can't create stones it is unable to lift. However, because its "inability" to create stones it can't lift is simply a consequence of its *unlimited* power to make and lift stones of *any* weight, magnitude, texture, and so on, it doesn't seem to be a real incapacity.[1]

Nor can a maximally perfect being have powers the possession or exercise of which entails a limitation or weakness. Thus, God can't destroy himself or divest himself of his knowledge or power. Why not? A maximally perfect being would be eternally wise and powerful. It would also seem to possess these attributes essentially – that is, have them in every possible world in which it exists. Now if a maximally perfect being *could* destroy itself or divest itself of its knowledge or power, there would be possible worlds in which it does so and, in those worlds, it wouldn't be *eternally* wise and powerful. But given that eternal wisdom and power are *essential* properties of any maximally perfect being that has them, a maximally perfect being would possess those properties in *every* world in which it exists. If so, it can neither destroy itself nor make itself ignorant or weak.

Can a maximally perfect being act wrongly? There are at least two reasons for thinking that it can. The first is that if it can't, then there are many other things one would think that an omnipotent being should be able to do that it cannot do. For example, it would seem wrong for God to cause or permit a flood, earthquake, or other natural disaster, *n*, when he had no morally sufficient reason for doing so. So if God can't act wrongly, he can't cause or permit *n*. But any being that deserves to be called "omnipotent" surely has the power to bring about *n* or *any* natural disaster. It appears to follow that if a maximally perfect being can't act wrongly, it isn't omnipotent.

The second reason is this. Theists believe that God is to be praised for his moral goodness. But moral praise is in order only when its object could have acted badly but did not, in fact, do so. So if God is morally praiseworthy, he is able to sin.

On the other hand, if God can sin, then moral goodness isn't an essential property of God and, in that case, there are possible worlds in which the being who is God in our world exists but acts wrongly. Furthermore, given that the title "God" is only properly applied to a sinless being, the possible worlds in which the being who is God in our world acts wrongly are also worlds in which the being who is God in our world isn't God. But a being that sins and thus isn't divine in some of the logically possible worlds in which it exists seems less perfect than a being who is God and sinless in every possible world in which it exists.

---

[1] C. Wade Savage, "The Paradox of the Stone," *The Philosophical Review* LXXVI (1967): 74–79.

Hence, a being that can act wrongly isn't maximally perfect. It seems, then, that if God is maximally perfect, he must be essentially morally good, and that his power is therefore limited by his goodness.

This limitation may not be as significant as at first appears, however. For example, while God can't bring about earthquakes or floods when doing so would be morally wrong, he can bring about earthquakes or floods of any magnitude or degree of destructiveness when it would not be wrong for him to do so. God's inability to bring n about isn't a consequence of a deficiency in his earthquake- or flood-producing powers but of his own inherent goodness. The limitation thus doesn't seem to involve real weakness or lack of power.

Nor does it follow that God's actions aren't morally praiseworthy. Jonathan Edwards believed that moral agency and freedom are consistent with metaphysical necessity. In choosing worlds, God can only do what is fittest and best. He is, nonetheless, free in the sense that he is aware of alternatives (the array of possible worlds), has the ability (that is, the power or skill) to actualize any one of them, is neither forced, constrained, nor influenced by any other being in making his selection, and does just what he wants to do. Edwards thought that this is the only kind of freedom that is either relevant to moral agency or worth having. Even if Edwards was mistaken about this, "compatibilist"[2] notions of freedom are more plausible with respect to God than with respect to creatures. As a classical theist, Edwards believed that the source of God's actions are found in himself. God is genuinely independent – neither determined nor causally affected by other powers. His activity is thus fully autonomous even if it is necessary. By contrast, if determinists are correct in thinking that the choices of human agents are causally necessary consequences of conditions that ultimately extend beyond their control, then those agents are *not* fully autonomous. Therefore, the two sorts of necessity significantly differ. Hence, that the second is incompatible with morally significant freedom and responsibility doesn't entail that the first is. God's essential goodness, then, isn't clearly incompatible with the appropriateness of moral praise.

OMNISCIENCE

Christian theists traditionally have thought that God is omniscient. Yet *can* God know all truths? There are reasons for thinking that he can't. In the first place, if God is timeless it seems that he can't know

---

[2] So-called because, on their view, freedom is compatible with determinism.

some things I know. For example, God can timelessly know that at
7 P.M. on July 2, 2010, I assert the true sentence "It is now 7 P.M." God
can also timelessly know that a thunderstorm occurs at my location at
7 P.M. on July 2, 2010. But it seems that he can't know that it is *now*
7 P.M. or that the thunderstorm is *now* starting, for knowing what time
it now is or that an event is now starting (or has started or will start)
presupposes that the knower is in time and, by hypothesis, God isn't.
But of course I *do* know things like these. It thus appears that I know
things that God can't know. If I do, God doesn't know everything and so
isn't omniscient.

Again, traditional theists believe that God can't experience pain or
guilt since the former is incompatible with his infinite joy and the latter
with his moral perfection. However, if he *can't* experience them, then
while God may know all *about* pain and guilt, he doesn't know what
pain and guilt *are like*. He thus doesn't know something I do know and
so, once again, doesn't know everything.

Although these difficulties could be escaped by denying that timelessness, infinite joy, and moral perfection are included among God's
essential attributes, traditional theists would be reluctant to do so. It
seems, then, that they should conclude that there are knowable things
that God cannot know. Several things help remove the sting from this
conclusion, however. Not knowing what time it now is is not knowing what one's position currently is in the temporal series – that is,
not knowing where one is now temporally located (at, before, or after
7 P.M., for example). This is clearly a limitation for temporal beings for
temporal beings have temporal locations. It isn't clearly a limitation *for
God*, though, because the God of traditional theism doesn't have a temporal location. Not knowing one's temporal location when one doesn't
have one isn't a cognitive limitation. Moreover, if the world is composed of substances, events, and the relations between them,[3] then a
timeless God's knowledge of the world's constituents and their relations
can be complete. The *mode* in which God knows temporal happenings
differs from that in which we know them, for we are in time and God
is not. But *what* we know (substances, events, and their relations) is the
same.

Again, since knowing what pain and guilt are like requires a direct
acquaintance with them (that is, actually *experiencing* pain or guilt),
and the latter is intrinsically bad, God's inability to know what pain and
guilt are like would seem to be *consequences* of his perfection rather

---

[3] Including relations of before, after, and simultaneity.

than detractions from it. Other difficulties have been thought to be more intractable, however.

Not only are some knowable things (for example, what time it now is, what pain is like) such that God cannot know them, there are things that it seems God *should* know if he is omniscient, which *no* one can know. Consider the power set of the set of all true propositions, S (that is, the set consisting of all of S's subsets). Since a distinct true proposition corresponds to each member of S's power set, and the power set of any set is greater in size than that set, there are more true propositions than there are members of S. However, because S is the set of *all* true propositions, this is impossible. Hence, there is no set of all true propositions. This has the following consequence: if there is no set of all true propositions, then, since the object of omniscience would presumably be such a set, not even God can be omniscient.[4]

How compelling is this argument? Note that it appears to assume that God's knowledge is propositionally structured, that it consists in an infinite set of justified true beliefs each of which corresponds to its appropriate counterpart in the infinite conjunction of truths that constitutes the divine knowledge's alleged object. But this assumption is questionable. Defenders of the doctrine of God's simplicity would reject the notion of a multiplicity of divine cognitive states. And even if God *isn't* simple, the objects of God's acts of knowledge may be *things*, rather than propositions, as Thomas Aquinas, William Alston, and others have argued.

Furthermore, the argument has a very counterintuitive consequence, as Alvin Plantinga points out. Let S* be the set of all propositions. A proposition corresponds to each member of the power set of S*. Since the power set of S* is greater in size than S*, some propositions are *not* included in the set of *all* propositions – which is absurd. The notion of a set of all propositions is thus as incoherent as that of the set of all true propositions. It follows that there are no coherent propositions about all propositions, and thus that propositions such as "All propositions are either true or false" and "No proposition is both true and false" are incoherent – which is highly counterintuitive.[5]

Finally, note that even if the argument were successful, it is unclear just how damaging it would actually be. For, in the first place, even if no set consists of all true propositions, there does appear to be an infinite hierarchy of sets of true propositions such that while no set

[4] Patrick Grim, "Logic and the Limits of Language," *Nous* 22 (1988): 341–67.
[5] Patrick Grim and Alvin Plantinga, "Truth, Omniscience, and Cantorian Argument: An Exchange," *Philosophical Studies* 71 (1993): 267–306.

at any level contains all true propositions, every true proposition is a member of some set at some level. Suppose that God's belief system was structured in a corresponding fashion. Then, even if there is no set of all the truths that God knows, there is (as Keith Simmons has said) no *particular truth* that God doesn't know.[6] Moreover, a divine epistemic structure constituted in this fashion would seem to *show* or *evince* that God knows all truths even if his doing so couldn't be coherently stated propositionally. (Compare Wittgenstein's *Tractatus* on language showing or evincing what cannot be stated in that language.)

In the second place, as George Schlesinger and others have suggested, the relevant *root* notion in discussions of God's omniscience is that of the most perfect possible knowledge. But if that is correct, and the knowledge of all truths is logically impossible, the knowledge of all truths isn't included in the concept of the most perfect *possible* knowledge. Its impossibility therefore doesn't pose a significant theological threat. Note that the key question is, "Could a possible being's knowledge be more perfect than God's?" There is a serious problem for the traditional doctrine of God's knowledge only if it can be shown that there is a possible being distinct from God whose knowledge is more perfect than his. The argument we have been discussing does not show this.[7]

---

[6] Keith Simmons, "On an Argument against Omniscience," *Nous* 27 (1993): 22–33.

[7] As we have seen, some knowable things (e.g. what time it now is) can't be known by God. Other seemingly knowable things (e.g., the set of all truths) can't be known by anyone. Some philosophers believe that God's knowledge of future contingents falls somewhere between these two classes. A future contingent is a fact or event that is logically contingent, but hasn't yet obtained or occurred and isn't necessitated by its causal history. If we are contra-causally free, the decisions we will make tomorrow are (now) future contingents. My future free decisions are knowable in the sense that *once they have been made and slipped into the past*, they can be known by me and others. But while my decision is still future, it can't (on certain views) be known by anyone – *including God*. Why not? If God is in time, the future isn't immediately present to him. Nor can God's knowledge of the future be grounded in his perfect knowledge of the past and of his own present intentions since, by hypothesis, future contingents aren't necessitated by the past or by God's decisions. There seems then to be no basis or ground for God's knowledge of the (contingent) future. It isn't clear how serious this difficulty is, however. For one thing, if God is timeless, there may be a sense in which what to us is future is immediately present to him. For another, God's knowledge of the future may not *need* a basis. Some knowledge, after all, is groundless. We are immediately aware of our own intentions, for example, and of the truth of simple necessary propositions such as $3 - 2 = 1$. Our knowledge of these things isn't based on something else such as inference, memory, or the use of our senses. The fact (if it *is* a fact) that God's beliefs about future contingents are groundless isn't, itself, sufficient to show that they don't constitute knowledge.

OMNIPRESENCE

Aquinas thought that God is present in all things by power, knowledge, and essence. He is in them "by his power inasmuch as all things are subject to his power"; by his knowledge inasmuch "as all things are bare and open to his eyes"; and "by his essence, inasmuch as he is present to all things as the cause of their being."[8] The third mode of presence is an instance of the first, however, since God's creation and preservation of being is one exercise of his power. The question therefore is: "How does God's power over, and knowledge of, everything entail his presence in or to all things?"

As for the second, Brian Leftow suggests that Aquinas may have implicitly argued as follows:

(1) All things are immediately present to God's knowledge. (Nothing God knows is known inferentially.)
(2) "Present to" is a symmetrical relation. Therefore,
(3) God's knowledge is present to all things. (From 1 and 2.) But
(4) God and God's knowledge are identical. (The doctrine of divine simplicity.) Hence,
(5) *God* is present to all things. (From 3 and 4.)[9]

As for the first, Aquinas distinguishes a "contact of power" from the "contact of dimensive quantity" exhibited by physical bodies that touch each other.[10] Aquinas shared Aristotle's view that there is no (direct) action at a distance. If there isn't, then if God is directly responsible for a thing's being, he must be present to it. Therefore, since God is the cause of *all* being, he must be directly present to all being.[11] Then, too, a thing's power is arguably present (felt) in the effects it produces. However, because God is simple, God and his power are identical. It follows that *God* and not just his power is present in his effects, and thus in everything.[12]

Note that the doctrine of simplicity plays a central role in these explications of God's omnipresence. If God is simple, though, he doesn't

---

[8] Thomas Aquinas, *The Summa Theologica* (New York: Benziger Bros., 1947), 1; A I, Q 8, 3.

[9] Brian Leftow, "Omnipresence," *Routledge Encyclopedia of Philosophy*, ed. Edward Craig (London and New York: Routledge, 1998), 106.

[10] Aquinas, *op. cit.*, A I, Q 8, 2.

[11] Note, too, that God is contiguous with everything in the sense that (being nonspatial) there is no distance between God and other things.

[12] Brian Leftow, "Anselm on Omnipresence," *American Catholic Philosophical Quarterly* (formerly *The New Scholasticism*) 63 (1989): 333–40. Cf. Leftow 1998.

participate in Beauty, Justice, Goodness, and the like, as creatures do, but is *identical* with them, and thus has "certain abstract object features." If God does, then perhaps he "is present to time and space as abstract objects are . . . God is present everywhere and in everything as if he were an abstract entity exemplified everywhere and in everything" (Leftow 1989: 340, 347). But notice that while the presence of a universal such as blueness does not vary extensively, it can vary intensively. It does not vary extensively because "the whole of [it] is present at each point of a blue surface." (Each part of a blue surface is no less blue than the whole surface is.) It can vary intensively, however, since one wholly blue surface can be a lighter or darker blue than another wholly blue surface. Similarly, "as wholly present in any space or thing, God is not more [extensively] present in a large area than in a small, but God is more [intensively] present in a saint than in a sinner" (Leftow 1998: 106).

Accounts such as these undoubtedly contain a significant measure of truth, but they also reduce omnipresence "to a metaphor for God's omniscience, creatorhood," and sovereignty, whereas (as Leftow points out) a number of things suggest that "something closer to literal spatial location is needed." When Jeremiah "declaims 'Can anyone hide in secret places so that I cannot see him? declares the Lord. Do I not fill heaven and earth? declares the Lord' (Jer. 23:24), the suggestion seems to be that God's knowledge rests on his omnipresence, not vice versa. Again, the religious (and even more the mystical) sense of God's presence seems to be not just that God knows us or creates us, but that God is in some sense here with us" (Leftow 1998: 106).

Can more be said about God's presence, then, that would illuminate the idea that God is, in some sense, literally with us? One suggestion is that God is present in the world in the intimate way that our souls are present in our bodies. Richard Swinburne, for example, has argued that God's direct control over any object, and immediate knowledge of "the qualities exemplified in any region [of space] at any time," involves a kind of embodiment. (Although the embodiment in question is "restricted" or limited. "God has no particular orientation or restricted point-of-view on the world" as we do. Nor is he "pained by disturbances in material bodies [or] affected in thought by states of those objects as we are." Similarly, Charles Hartshorne contends that the world is God's body because he "knows and controls it" in "a non-mediated way."[13]

---

[13] Hud Hudson, "Omnipresence," in *The Oxford Handbook of Philosophical Theology*, ed. Thomas P. Flint and Michael Rea (New York: Oxford University Press, 2009), 203.

Views like Swinburne's and Hartshorne's are problematic. For one thing, because both interpret God's embodiment in terms of his knowledge and power, they are in no better position to explain the "religious...sense of God's presence" than the medieval accounts we examined earlier. Their views also appear to some to have an intuitively unacceptable consequence. Because God "knows immediately what is happening at" any region of unoccupied space (namely, nothing) and is able to "control directly what happens there" (that is, if something happens there, he is able to control it), Swinburne's and Hartshorne's characterizations of omnipresence commit them to the conclusion that God is *embodied* in empty space.[14] Whether this conclusion really is counterintuitive seems doubtful, however. Our bodies, after all, aren't "material" through and through. They include empty spaces, and these empty spaces are as much a part of our bodies as the physical events that transpire in them.

A more telling consideration, however, is this. Direct knowledge or control is neither necessary nor sufficient for embodiment. They aren't necessary since human persons, for example, don't have direct knowledge and control over every part of their bodies. Much of what goes on in my body is a mystery to me, and there are "some small parts of my brain I can move only by moving my head."[15] Nor are direct knowledge and control sufficient for, as Leftow points out, if telepathy and telekinesis are logically possible, then "x can move directly and/or know y immediately" does not entail that x is embodied in y (Leftow 1998).[16]

Yet whether we can or can't isolate necessary and sufficient conditions of embodiment, we do have various coherent *models* of embodiment. Classical philosophical discussions in the West provide four of them: (1) Physicalists believe that mind and some part or aspect of the body such as the brain are identical. (2) Mind-body parallelists contend that mental and physical events occur in two causally unrelated but parallel series. Events in one series (a feeling of pain, for example)

---

14 Edward R. Wierenga, "Omnipresence," in *A Companion to Philosophy of Religion*, ed. Philip L. Quinn and Charles Taliaferro (Oxford: Blackwell, 1997), 289. (cf. Hudson, *op. cit.*)

15 Edward R. Wierenga, "Anselm on Omnipresence," *American Catholic Philosophical Quarterly* (formerly *The New Scholasticism*) 62 (1988): 39.

16 But might not direct knowledge of and control over *some parts* of x be a necessary and sufficient condition of embodiment in x? They might be necessary but they aren't sufficient, for, as Wierenga points out, I can directly move and know *parts* of a number of larger entities to which I belong (e.g., my family, the contents of the room I am writing in, the entire spatio-temporal complex of which I am a part) without being embodied in them.

correspond to events in the other (the appropriate neurophysiological event), but there are no causal interactions between members of the two series. (3) Epiphenomenalists maintain that events in the brain and nervous system cause mental (as well as physical) events but mental events cause nothing. Finally (4) mind–body interactionists believe that a person's mind and body are ontologically distinct but causally influence each other.

None of the four provides a satisfactory model of the God–world relation, however. By identifying God with the spatio-temporal complex, the first implies that God is contingent, mutable, and both spatially and temporally divisible. The second and third models imply that God doesn't act upon the world, and the third implies that God is causally dependent on it. Both implications are incompatible with any standard form of theism. The fourth model may initially seem more illuminating but is objectionable on two counts. According to classical theism, God acts upon the world but the world does not act upon God. Furthermore, by allowing a certain independence to mind and body, the model fails to accommodate the radical dependence of the world upon God which is so essential to classical Christianity.

A fifth model of the mind–body relation is more promising, however. In later Platonism, the soul creates or produces or emanates its own body. This body (or the lower self *cum* body) is an image or expression of the soul (or higher self) on a lower level. Moreover, Plotinus thought that the (higher part of the) soul is necessary, immutable, and impeccable. While later Neoplatonists refused to follow Plotinus on this point, they agreed that the body cannot act upon the soul. Vishishtadvaita Vedanta's view of the soul–body relation is similar. Ramanuja, for example, argued that a soul and its body are related as (1) support and thing supported (bodies are incapable of separate existence), (2) controller and thing controlled, and (3) "principal" (*sheshin*) and "accessory" (*shesha*) – something that can fulfill itself only in serving its principal.

To say that the world is God's body, on this view, is to say that God is the world's support, controller, and principal. Furthermore, the relations in question run only one way. Bodies depend on souls; souls do not depend on their bodies. Thus, the world is absolutely dependent on God; God is in no way dependent upon the world.

The Platonic–Vishishtadvaitin model is largely free from the defects of the other four. Just as, in this model, the body depends upon but does not affect the soul, so the world depends upon but does not affect God. God's absolute sovereignty and complete causal independence is preserved. Moreover, just "as the defects or deficiencies of the body do not affect the soul, so...the defects of [the world] cannot affect the nature of Brahman. Thus, though Brahman has a body, He is partless," immutable, not subject to contingency, and "wholly unaffected by all faults. [He] remains pure and perfect in himself."[17] The inference from "the body of x is P" to "x is P" is illegitimate on this model. Hence, on the Vishishtadvaitin view, that the world is God's body and exhibits various defects and limitations does not entail that God or some part of him does so.[18]

Note that for this model to be useful, it isn't essential that God be related to the world as our minds are, *in fact,* related to our bodies. All that is necessary is that the Neoplatonic–Vishishtadvaitin model is a conceptually possible description of a soul–body relation, for, if it is and God stands to the world in that relation, it is both legitimate and potentially illuminating to speak of the world as his body.

However, Leftow has two interesting objections that would, if sound, cut against *any* attempt to construe the world as God's body, including this one. The first is this. "The universe can be caused to exist; it is quite possible that the Big Bang had a cause. So if God does not exist save as embodied in a universe, God can be caused to exist – and cannot have created the universe *ex nihilo*" (Leftow 1998: 104f). Leftow's last point is correct but doesn't imply the truth of the notion that the doctrine of creation *ex nihilo* was designed to combat, namely, that in creating, God is confronted with some kind of independent "matter" or "stuff" the properties of which limit what he can do. On the Vishishtadvaitin view, at least, the "stuff" (*prakriti*) out of which the physical and ordinary mental universe is made, *isn't* independent of God but, on the contrary, is an aspect of God or his body. Again, on a Vishishtadvaitin view, such things as the Big Bang, as well as the basic physical laws and constants, *are* caused by God since they are features of the manifest universe that evolves from *prakriti* under God's direction. Nor is God caused on this

---

[17] Surendranath Dasgupta, *A History of Indian Philosophy* (Cambridge: Cambridge University Press, 1952),3: 200–01.

[18] This may become clearer if one notes that Vishishtadvaitins use "Brahman" ambiguously. Sometimes, as in the passage quoted from Dasgupta, "Brahman" refers to *Ishvara,* the ruling and controlling principle of things in their entirety. At other times, the term refers to the complex whole consisting of *Ishvara* (the "Lord") together with the individual souls and "matter" (*prakriti*) which depend upon him and comprise his body. This ambiguity is no more problematic than our sometimes using personal pronouns to refer to the soul–body complex and at other times to the soul alone. (Compare "Last year he was eating a hamburger at the corner diner but is now in heaven with God.") In the more inclusive sense, the defects of Brahman's body necessarily affect Brahman since the latter includes the former. In the narrower, and religiously more significant sense, they do not.

view. God has no cause or prior principle in *any* sense. Neither is *prakriti* caused since God isn't caused and *prakriti* is an aspect or "part" of him.[19]

Leftow's second, and most interesting, objection is the following. Some scientists think there can be universes that are neither spatially nor temporally connected with our own. Suppose there are two of them. If there are, then God is either embodied in both or in only one of them. He cannot be embodied in both for, if he were, then his thoughts in one universe would be spatio-temporally connected to his thoughts in the other, and so the worlds would not be spatio-temporally discrete after all.[20] On the other hand, if God were embodied in only one of them, he could not make or create another since, if he were to do so, the two universes would *not* be spatio-temporally disconnected – which is contrary to our initial supposition (Leftow 1998: 105).

It isn't clear that this will do, though. If God is aspatial and atemporal, as the tradition has generally maintained, then he doesn't stand in spatial or temporal relations to anything in universe 1 or in universe 2. Hence, the fact that God creates or causes these universes doesn't entail that they are spatio-temporally connected to each other.[21]

I think, then, that use of the fifth model goes some way toward deepening the account of God's presence in the world. Yet even if it does, it doesn't do full justice to the richness of the concept of divine omnipresence.

In discussing God's presence, Charles Taliaferro remarks that my friends "remain distant from me in so far as [they] find my projects and goals to be of little interest, neither delighting in my success nor grieving over my ills."[22] Conversely, one is present to another in so far as one knows him, loves him, embraces his projects, and shares his joys and sorrows.

One person can't be fully present to another, however, if the second isn't fully present to the first. (If the second distances herself from the

---

[19] It follows, on this view, that if the existence of God is necessary and God is necessarily embodied, then the existence of *prakriti* is necessary. It doesn't follow that any particular manifestation or development of *prakriti* is necessary, and hence doesn't follow that the Big Bang, the fundamental laws of physics, or the physical constants are.

[20] Could God's thoughts in one universe be unconnected with his thoughts in another? No, because "one being cannot have two spatio-temporally unconnected lifelong streams of thought." (?)

[21] Note, too: that A is causally connected to B and A is causally connected to C does not entail that B and C are causally connected to each other. That is: that I am the cause of my volition x and also the cause of my volition y does not entail that either x is a cause of y or y is a cause of x.

[22] Charles Taliaferro, *Consciousness and the Mind of God* (Cambridge: Cambridge University Press, 1994), 308.

first, the first is distanced from the second.) Now, omnipresence is one of God's perfections. Just as God's knowledge and power are perfect, so, too, is his presence. It seems to follow that the fullness or perfection of God's presence to creatures partly depends on their response to him.[23] Augustine hints at something of the sort in Letter 187. "Although God is everywhere wholly present, He does not dwell in everyone... God is everywhere by the presence of His divinity [by power, knowledge, and essence], but not everywhere by the grace of His indwelling." Moreover, not only does "He that is everywhere... not dwell in all, ... He does not even dwell equally in those in whom He does dwell." Even so, each redeemed soul is *a* temple of God, and the redeemed collectively (the Church or Body of Christ) is *the* temple of God. "The measure of our being" his temple, "is the measure of our belonging to His fellowship and His family of adoption" (or, alternatively, the degree of our holiness).[24]

Just how might these ideas be cashed out? I will conclude by briefly considering two attempts to do so.

The first is Jonathan Edwards's. Like his medieval predecessors, Edwards thinks that God is present to his creatures in virtue of his knowledge, causal activity, and substance. Yet because he is an occasionalist like Malebranche, an idealist like Berkeley, and a mental phenomenalist like Hume, God's presence, on Edwards's view, is more intimate than on more traditional accounts. What are "vulgarly" called causal relations are mere constant conjunctions. *True* causes necessitate their effects. Because God's will alone meets this condition, God is the only true cause. He is also the only true substance. Physical objects are collections of "corporeal ideas" (that is, ideas of color, for example, or solidity, resistance, and so on). Minds are series of "thoughts" or "perceptions." Now, any substance underlying perceptions, thoughts, and

---

[23] Does this imply that creatures can act in such a way that a divine perfection (perfect fullness or presence) is never fully exemplified? Perhaps, although not if all creatures will ultimately be saved.

[24] Saint Augustine, *Letters*, vol. 4 (165–203), in *The Fathers of the Church*, vol. 30, trans. Sister Wilfrid Parsons, S. N. D., 232–33 (New York: Fathers of the Church Inc., 1955). Compare Plotinus: Although Being, Goodness, and the like are omnipresent, "only the competent possess themselves of that presence which depends not upon situation [place] but upon adequacy; the transparent object and the opaque answer very differently to the light." (*Ennead* vi. 4, 11. trans. Stephen MacKenna, p. 597) Note that, for Augustine, God's indwelling isn't a function of our (present) knowledge of God, for God does *not* indwell some who know him (those, for example, whose knowledge of God is purely "speculative" or "historical" as the Puritans will say), and he *does* dwell in some who don't know him or are even unconscious of him – elect baptized infants, for instance, or spiritual infants who don't "recognize the Holy Spirit who [dwells] in them" and secretly "works in them... that they may be his Temple." (*Letter* 187: 237f, 241)

corporeal ideas would be something that "subsisted by itself, and stood underneath, and kept up" physical and mental properties. However, God alone subsists by himself, stands underneath, and keeps up thoughts, perceptions, solidity, color, and other corporeal qualities (ideas). Hence "the substance of bodies [and minds]" is "either nothing, or nothing but the Deity acting in that particular manner . . . where he thinks fit." The only real cause and the only real substance are thus God himself. "How truly, then is it in him that we live, move, and have our being."[25]

God's relation to his elect is even more intimate, however. The Holy Spirit "dwells" in the saints "as a vital principle in their souls [and] there produces those effects wherein he exerts and communicates himself *in his own proper nature*."[26] "True saving grace is no other than the very love of God; *that is, God, in one of the persons of the Trinity*, uniting himself to the soul of a creature as a vital principle, dwelling there and exerting himself by the faculties of the soul of man, in his own proper nature, after the manner of a principle of nature." The saints are thus "not only partakers of a nature that may in some sense be called Divine, because 'tis conformed to the nature of God; *but the very Deity does in some sense dwell in them*."[27]

Edwards is making two claims. First, the new spiritual dispositions and tastes that God bestows on the soul are divine. The difference between God's love and joy, and the love and joy he bestows on his saints, is a difference of degree, not of nature or kind.

Second, God does not act on the soul from without, but dwells within it, "as a principle of new nature," living, acting, and exerting itself in the exercise of the soul's faculties. What, though, is a principle of nature? Edwards sometimes describes it as a kind of "habit," a settled character or disposition, that leads one to exercise her faculties in a certain manner (*Religious Affections*: 206). The self-love of fallen humanity, for example, is a habit or second nature that disposes it to think, feel, and act in sinful ways. By analogy, the new divine principle would be a habit inherent in sanctified souls that disposes them to holy actions, thoughts, and feelings. However, even though Edwards's language often suggests this, the *Treatise on Grace* insists that it is misleading to speak of a habit of grace if, by that, we mean that, once it has been redeemed,

---

[25] Jonathan Edwards, "Of Atoms," in *Works of Jonathan Edwards* (New Haven: Yale University Press, 1980), 6: 215–16.

[26] Jonathan Edwards, *Religious Affections*, in *Works* (New Haven, CT: Yale University Press, 1959), 2: 201 (my emphasis).

[27] Jonathan Edwards, *Treatise on Grace*, in *Works* (New Haven, CT: Yale University Press, 2003), 21: 194 (my emphases).

the soul is, *itself*, capable of bringing forth holy thoughts, feelings, and actions. For "the giving of one gracious discovery or act of grace, or a thousand, has no proper natural tendency to cause an abiding habit of grace for the future; nor any otherwise than by divine constitution and covenant" (that is, by God's graciously promising to do so). Rather, "all succeeding acts of grace, must be as immediately and to all intents and purposes, as much from the immediate acting of the Spirit of God on the soul as the first; and if God should take away his Spirit out of the soul, all habits and acts of grace would of themselves cease as immediately as light ceases in a room when a candle is carried out." (*Treatise on Grace*: 196)

We saw earlier that God is the only real or true cause of ordinary material and mental phenomena. We now see that God is also the only real or true cause of spiritual motions. In the same way that his settled determinations to produce physical or mental effects in a certain order just are the natures of ordinary physical and mental phenomena, so, too, God's settled determinations to produce holy thoughts, feelings, and intentions in the redeemed in a certain order just are the new divine principles in the hearts of the saints. Edwards's occasionalism thus illuminates his doctrine of the Holy Spirit's indwelling.

However, it also creates a problem. If God is the direct and only cause of *everything*, then how does his gracious indwelling in the saints differ from his direct and continuous creation of the thoughts, feelings, and intentions of the ungodly? The *effects* are different of course, but Edwards clearly wants to say more – namely, that the *manner* of God's operation differs in the two cases. How, then, does it do so?

Miracles, "gracious operations on the mind," and other things of that sort are "done in the most general proportion [or "harmony"], not tied to any particular proportion, to this or that created being; but the proportion is," instead, "with the whole series of [God's] acts and designs from eternity to eternity."[28] Ordinary physical and mental events stand in "rule bound connections" to immediately surrounding events. Miracles such as the Resurrection do not. *All* the works of God are done with fitness and propriety, and ultimately form part of his grand design – the history of humankind's redemption from the world's beginnings in eternity to its final consummation. The harmonies into which natural events immediately fit are local, however, whereas the harmony to which the Resurrection and bestowal of the Spirit belong is "creation's

---

[28] Jonathan Edwards, "Miscellany 64," in *The "Miscellanies," a-500, Works* (New Haven, CT: Yale University Press, 1994), 13: 235.

total history."[29] "Common benefits," as well as other ordinary objects and occurrences, "are as much immediately from God as man's highest perfection and happiness; that is, one is as much by the direct present exercise of the power of God as the other. But there is this difference: common benefits are statedly connected with previous things in the creature, so that they are in a sense dependent on the creature" (that is, are uniformly or regularly connected with them in lawlike ways). However, "the excellency and blessedness of the soul is connected only with the will of God, and is dependent on nothing else"; it isn't a term in a natural regularity.[30]

Whether this fully disposes of the problem is doubtful, however. On Edwards's view, God is the immediate and only true cause of the thoughts, feelings, and intentions of the ungodly as well as those of the saints. To differentiate the latter from the former in the manner suggested earlier, Edwards must show that the mental acts of the ungodly "are statedly connected with previous things in the creature" in a way in which those of the saints are not. It is not immediately obvious how Edwards could do this, though, since on the face of it, the mental acts of the ungodly seem no more tightly bound up with local regularities than the mental acts of the saints.[31]

That being said, it remains true that occasionalism may provide one of the better accounts of God's presence in the redeemed soul. That is, even if occasionalism offers an inadequate picture of God's causal activity *in general*, its account of his intimate connection with the souls of the elect might be roughly on target.

---

[29] Robert W. Jenson, *America's Theologian* (New York: Oxford University Press, 1988), 69.

[30] Jonathan Edwards, "Miscellany 481," in The *"Miscellanies," a-500, op. cit.*, 523–24. In other words, it has no "occasional" cause. See, however, "Miscellany 1263" (in Edwards, *The Miscellanies, 1153–1360* in *Works* [New Haven, CT: Yale University Press, 2004] 23: 207), in which Edwards says that "spiritual operations ... are not altogether without use of means and some connection with antecedents and what we call (though improperly in this case) second causes." While God's grace is not bound to the study of scripture, confession, church attendance, prayer, and the like, there is a typical pattern of conversion and sanctification. These regularities are much narrower in scope than the laws of nature, however, and admit of many more exceptions. God's gracious establishment only applies to the elect, and his dealings with the saints are (from our point of view) not fully predictable.

[31] Neither can they be accounted for by purely empirical (i.e., scientific) regularities. The acts of the ungodly are, on Edwards's view, a necessary consequence of Adam's sin and God's decision to impute that sin to Adam's descendants. But similarly, the spiritual motions of the saints are a necessary consequence of Christ's obedience and sacrifice and God's decision to impute Christ's righteousness to the elect.

Another attempt to provide a richer account of God's omnipresence than that provided by Anselm, Aquinas, and other western mediaeval theologians is the Eastern doctrine of divine energies. Orthodoxy distinguishes God's essence or "nature, properly so-called" from "energies or... operations [or] forces [the *energeia*] proper to and inseparable from God's essence, in which he... manifests, communicates, and gives Himself."[32] It is only through these energies that we know God, for while they "descend to us... His essence remains unapproachable."[33] The Eastern church identifies the energies with Pseudo-Dionysius's "names" of God – "Wisdom, Life, Power, Justice, Love, Being, [Good, and even] God – and an infinity of other names which are unknown to us." The divine names are "an exterior manifestation of the Trinity which cannot be interiorized, introduced as it were, *within* the divine being, as its natural determination." For "God is not determined by *any* of his attributes" since "all determinations... are logically posterior to His being in itself" (Lossky: 80, my emphases). Even so, the divine energies *are God Himself*," although "not according to His substance"[34] (Lossky: 72, my emphasis).

Because these energies are essential to God, "God would... manifest himself beyond His essence" "even if creatures did not exist... just as the rays of the sun would shine out from the solar disk whether or not there were any beings capable of receiving their light"[35] (Lossky: 74).

It is in these beings "created from nothing," however, "that [the] infinite and eternal energies [contingently] abide, making the greatness of God to shine forth in all things" (Lossky: 76). "All creation is [thus] a gigantic Burning Bush, permeated but not consumed by the ineffable and wondrous fire of God's energies."[36] It is the "presence of this uncreated and eternal light," and not God's mere causal presence, "which is the real omnipresence of God in all things" (Lossky: 89). These energies are "the glory in which God appeared to the righteous in the Old Testament" (see, for example, *Isaiah* 6); and "the eternal light which shone through

---

[32] Vladimir Lossky, *The Mystical Theology of the Eastern Church* (London: James Clarke, 1957), 70.

[33] Saint Basil, quoted in Lossky: 72.

[34] The divine energies are thus essential properties of the divine essence or nature, and hence common to the three persons.

[35] That the divine energies necessarily and eternally flow out from the divine essence does not entail that the created world does so since the existence of the latter is "determined by a [free and contingent] decision of the common will of the three persons" (Lossky: 75).

[36] Timothy Ware, *The Orthodox Church* (Harmondsworth [England] and Baltimore, MD: Penguin, 1963), 78.

the humanity of Christ and manifested His divinity to the apostles at the Transfiguration." They are also "the uncreated and deifying grace" that is "the portion of the saints . . . in their life of union with God" (Lossky: 76). Grace is not a mere effect of the Supreme cause, therefore, but the divine energies themselves dwelling within us. Moreover, because these energies are common to the three *hypostases*, by their dwelling within us, the Trinity itself and thus God's very being, dwells in us. It is hard to see how God's presence to his creation could be more intimate than that.[37]

There are interesting similarities between the doctrine of the divine energies and Jonathan Edwards's animadversions on God's glory. Edwards distinguishes God's internal from his external glory. The latter is *God* manifest – not merely an image or representation or symbol of God (that is, not a *creature*) but God himself existing *"ad extra."* There are also differences, of course. Perhaps the most important is that Edwards's central contrast is between God's knowledge and love of himself, and joy in himself, and the saints' knowledge and love of God, and joy in him – not between God's unknowable essence and the names or operations that manifest it.

Other differences may be more apparent than real, however. For example, God's glory *ad extra* is principally identified with God's communication of his own knowledge, love, and joy to the saints and, as such, does not permeate the whole of creation, as do the divine energies. When Edwards is being more careful, though, he makes it clear that God's external glory includes "the exercise of [*all* of] God's perfections to produce a proper effect."[38] It therefore includes his production of the necessary conditions for the existence of the saints – namely, a proper "house" for the domicile of rational creatures. The orderly or beautiful frame of the cosmos is thus a *part* or *aspect* or *feature* of the emanation of God's glory *ad extra*.

[37] Barlaam and a few other Eastern theologians who were influenced by Aristotelianism and by medieval Western theology argued that the doctrine of divine energies was incompatible with God's simplicity. Given God's simplicity, the divine energies must either be identified with God's essence understood as "pure act" or with a created effect. Gregory Palamas responded that both alternatives preclude the deification, which is central to Orthodox thought and spirituality. Participation in and/or the reception of a mere creature can't deify us. And if the energies are identified with the essence, deification again is impossible since (according to Eastern theology) the divine essence is incommunicable. In any case, "simplicity does not mean uniformity or absence of distinction – otherwise Christianity would not be the religion of the Holy Trinity" (Lossky: 78).

[38] Jonathan Edwards, *Concerning the End for which God Created the World*, in *Ethical Writings, Works* (New Haven, CT: Yale University Press, 1989), 8: 527.

Another difference may also be more apparent than real. The knowledge, love, and joy of the saints, which constitute God's glory *ad extra,* are created *images* of his (internal) glory; unlike the divine energies, they are not, themselves, divine. However, this contrast is misleading. In the first place, for Edwards, God's glory *ad extra* principally consists in his *communication* of his own knowledge, love, and joy to the saints, not in their knowledge, love, and joy *per se.* Second (and more importantly), whereas the saints' knowledge, love, and joy are products of God's causal activity, they are identical in nature (although infinitely less in degree) with God's knowledge, love, and joy. So the saints are as literally divinized or deified as they are in Eastern Orthodoxy. On the other hand, like Edwards, the Eastern fathers clearly insist that the saints aren't one in essence with God (as are the Son and Spirit). Both their existence and participation in God's workings or operations (energies) are contingent effects of the will common to the three persons. The differences thus again turn out to be less significant than might at first appear.

References

Augustine. Letters, vol. 4 (165–203), in *Fathers of the Church,* vol. 30, trans. Sister Wilfrid Parsons, S. N. D. (New York: Fathers of the Church, Inc., 1955).

Dasgupta, Surendranath. *A History of Indian Philosophy,* vol. 3 (Cambridge: Cambridge University Press, 1959).

Edwards, Jonathan. *Religious Affections, The Works of Jonathan Edwards* vol. 2 (New Haven, CT: Yale University Press, 1959).

_____."Of Atoms," in *Scientific and Philosophical Writings,* vol. 6 in *Works* (New Haven, CT: Yale University Press, 1980).

_____. *Concerning the End for which God Created the World,* in *Ethical Writings,* vol. 8, *Works* (New Haven, CT: Yale University Press, 1989).

_____. *The Miscellanies, a-500, Works,* vol. 13 (New Haven, CT: Yale University Press, 1994).

_____. *Treatise on Grace,* in *Writings on the Trinity, Grace, and Faith, Works,* vol. 21 (New Haven, CT: Yale University Press, 2003).

_____. *The Miscellanies, 1153–1360, Works,* vol. 23 (New Haven, CT: Yale University Press, 2004).

Grim, Patrick. "Logic and the Limits of Language," *Nous* 22 (1988): 341–67.

_____ and Alvin Plantinga. "Truth, Omniscience, and Cantorian Argument: An Exchange," *Philosophical Studies* 71 (1993): 267–306.

Hudson, Hud. "Omnipresence," in *The Oxford Handbook of Philosophical Theology,* ed. Thomas P. Flint and Michael Rea (New York: Oxford University Press, 2009).

Jenson, Robert W. *America's Theologian* (New York: Oxford University Press, 1988).

Leftow, Brian. "Anselm on Omnipresence," *American Catholic Philosophical Quarterly* (formerly *The New Scholasticism*) 63(1989): 333–40.

———. "Omnipresence," in *The Routledge Encyclopedia of Philosophy*, ed. Edward Craig (London and New York: Routledge, 1998).

Lossky, Vladimir. *The Mystical Theology of the Eastern Church* (London: James Clark, 1957).

Plotinus. *Ennead* vi, fourth and fifth tractates, from *The Enneads*, trans. Stephen MacKenna (Burdett, NY: Larson Publications, 1992).

Savage, C. Wade. "The Paradox of the Stone," *The Philosophical Review* LXXVI (1967): 74–79.

Simmons, Keith. "On an Argument against Omniscience," *Nous* 27(1993): 22–33.

Taliaferro, Charles. *Consciousness and the Mind of God* (Cambridge: Cambridge University Press, 1994).

Thomas Aquinas. *The Summa Theologica*, vol. 1 (New York: Benziger Bros., 1947), Part I, Question 8.

Ware, Timothy. *The Orthodox Church* (Harmondsworth (England) and Baltimore, MD: Penguin, 1963).

Wierenga, Edward. "Anselm on Omnipresence," *American Catholic Philosophical Quarterly* (formerly *The New Scholasticism*) 62(1988): 30–41.

———. "Omnipresence," in *A Companion to Philosophy of Religion*, ed. Philip L. Quinn and Charles Taliaferro (Oxford: Blackwell, 1997).

5 Goodness

JOHN E. HARE

This chapter takes up the topic of goodness as it relates to Christian philosophical theology and proceeds by examining the central figures chronologically. An alternative would be to try to schematize the field under a series of types, but the usual type-names, often ending in "ism," tend to be vague in an unsatisfactory way. An author who attributes views to Kant, for example, can be held accountable to the texts of Kant. But an author is at liberty to characterize "deontologists" any way she likes.

Because the history of Christian philosophical theology is largely a history of the contact between classical thought (as represented especially by Plato, Aristotle, and the Stoics) and the Hebrew and Greek Scriptures (known within Christianity as "Old and New Testaments"), the chapter starts with sections on the classical philosophers and the Bible. It then describes the different approaches that have been taken to the relation between goodness and God in the philosophical and theological tradition over the past two millennia within Christianity. When limited to approximately 6,000 words, there is, inevitably, something absurd in such an undertaking. The article will have to be highly selective and take up only a few key figures. This selectivity is the cost that corresponds to the benefit of accountability.

THE GREEKS

Plato was already the inheritor of views about goodness and the divine from Homer, the Presocratics (especially Pythagoras), and his own teacher, Socrates. He writes his philosophy in the form of dialogues in which "Socrates" is usually one of the characters, and this makes it difficult to describe a systematic Platonic philosophy, since the views defended by "Socrates" in the different dialogues are not consistent with each other. Four dialogues in particular are relevant to this article – the *Euthyphro*, the *Republic*, the *Timaeus*, and the *Laws*. The *Euthyphro* is typical of the dialogues in which Socrates discusses the typically human forms of goodness or virtue with people who are supposed to be experts in them. Thus, in the *Euthyphro*, Socrates's interlocutor is a religious professional, and Socrates wants to talk about piety (or holiness), because he is about to face the charge of impiety, on which he will eventually be found guilty and condemned to death. Socrates makes it clear that he does not believe in those traditional stories about the gods that attribute immorality to them, and this gives rise to what is sometimes called "the Euthyphro Dilemma." Euthyphro says that holiness is what is loved by all the gods, and Socrates asks whether it is loved by the gods because it is holy, or whether it is holy because it is loved by the gods. His own answer is the former. His argument as stated (10a-11b) begs the question at a key point, but it can be reconstructed using a premise previously granted (at 7e), that the gods like what each of them considers beautiful, good, and just, and hates the opposites of these.

In the *Republic* Socrates develops a theory of Forms, which are proposed as answers to the questions such as "What is piety?" in the *Euthyphro*. The Form of Piety is what piety is, in itself. In the *Republic*, the Forms are said to be given their being and their intelligibility by the Form of the Good, which is, itself, "on the far side of being, exceeding it in seniority and power (509b)." The Form of the Good thus has the central role not only in ethics, but in metaphysics and epistemology as well. Although Socrates does not call it a god, he does say that it is king (509d) of the intelligible world as the divine sun is king of the visible world, that it begets this sun-god (508b), and that the contemplation of it is the contemplation of a divine or godlike as opposed to a merely human thing (517d, see also *Symposium* 212a on divine Beauty, and *Theaetetus* 176b, where our task is to become as like God as possible, which is to become just and holy with understanding). In the *Timaeus* (29e-30c) Socrates talks of a divine craftsman (a "demiurge") who is good, and therefore not jealous of anything, and therefore "wanted everything to become as much like himself as was possible." He formed the visible universe out of already existing stuff after the model of the intelligible universe, which is eternal and immutable. Finally, in the *Laws*, the main character, called simply "the Athenian," sets out to prove that the gods do exist, that they are good, and that they respect justice more than humans do (887b). Contrary to the views he attributes to "the sophists," he claims that goodness according to nature and goodness according to the law are not two different things, but that there is a natural standard of justice (889e), and that the whole domain of what moves and changes is under the control of soul (since this is the cause of good and evil, beauty and ugliness, justice and injustice, and so on) and of the best kind of soul (and so under the control of divinity), since the motions we observe are so orderly and beautiful. This does not prevent ghastly acts of impiety by humans who do not have the best kind of soul.

Aristotle was Plato's student for twenty years. His philosophical system is, to be sure, different in some key respects from his teacher's. For one thing, he denies (in *Nicomachean Ethics* I, 6) Plato's account of the Form of the Good (on the grounds that intrinsic goods are too various to allow helpful explanation by a single Form), and his metaphysical account of the Forms is that they are "in" material substances, rather than being in their own transcendent world. However, the two philosophers establish rather similar relations between goodness and the divine. In his *Metaphysics,* Aristotle affirms (XII, 7, 1072b29–31), "We say therefore that God is a living being, eternal, most good, so that life and duration continuous and eternal belong to God; for this *is* God," and this goodness explains how this God "moves everything else by being loved" (1072b3). God's life has, as it were, attractive force. The metaphor of a magnet comes from Plato's *Ion,* (536a, in the context of a discussion of poetic inspiration) where Socrates compares the drawing power of "the deity" to a magnet transmitting its force through a chain of iron rings. This attractive force is felt in human life more directly than elsewhere in the cosmos because humans have what Aristotle calls, in Greek, *nous.* This term is traditionally translated "intellect," but covers intuitive apprehension more broadly. Aristotle also calls God's activity *nous,* and since he thinks a thing becomes like what it contemplates, and God would therefore become less than God by thinking about anything other than God, the divine activity consists only in self-contemplation. Human *nous* thinks about God, but also about other things that do not change, such as the essences of material substances. This kind of contemplation is, Aristotle says at the conclusion of the *Nicomachean Ethics,* the focus of the best kind of human life (the best kind of happiness), even though there is another kind of good human life focused on activities in accordance with the ethical virtues (X, 7, 1178a9).

At the end of the *Eudemian Ethics* (VII, 15, 1249b12f), in a passage useful for comparison with Christian theology, he says that "whatever choice or possession of natural goods – bodily goods, wealth, friends, and the like – will most conduce to the contemplation of God is best: this is the noblest criterion. But any standard of living which either through excess or defect hinders the service and contemplation of God is bad." However, he says, this service of God should not be understood as being like the service of slave to master, because "God is not a superior who issues commands, but is that for the sake of which wisdom issues commands." Aristotle uses the term "ethical" to designate those virtues or excellences that we acquire by the forming of habit (*ethos*). In Latin, this term is translated *"mos"* from which we get the term "moral." This chapter does not distinguish "ethical" and "moral" goodness, though some philosophers make such a distinction (for example, Kant, and, differently, Hegel). The ethical virtues are those, such as courage, temperance (or moderation), generosity, and magnanimity, into which we are inducted by habituation of our passions under the control of reason. Ethical virtues are distinguished from intellectual virtues, such as practical and theoretical wisdom.

Finally, even though Aristotle rejects Plato's account of the Form of the Good, he accepts a theory of natural teleology, according to which every substance that exists is the actualization of the specifying potentiality of that kind of thing, and is, to that extent, good.

The Stoics disagreed with Aristotle in one way that is especially relevant to this chapter. They held that the only thing that is good is virtue. Other things that Aristotle held good – for example, the "natural goods" listed earlier – are indeed to be preferred, but only as material for virtue. Virtue itself, together with the knowledge that one is virtuous, is sufficient for happiness or the best life. Aristotle considers this view, and rejects it as unreasonable. For Cleanthes the Stoic, the connection with God is that, "our aim becomes living consistently with nature, that is, in accordance with one's own nature and that of the universe, being active in no way usually forbidden by the law common to all, which is right reason, which pervades everything and is the same as Zeus, lord of the ordering of all that exists. And this is the same as the virtue of the happy person" (Diogenes Laertius, *Lives of Eminent Philosophers* VII, 88). For the Epicureans, by contrast, the good is pleasure, and we see this from animals and children, who pursue pleasure by nature, before their inclinations are overlaid by misguided conventional beliefs about good and evil (Diogenes Laertius, *op. cit.*, X, 129, see also Irwin, Chapter 11).

THE BIBLE

The Hebrew Scriptures contain a set of terms that distinguishes this tradition sharply from the tradition we have so far considered. The God who appears in these books, unlike Aristotle's God, is a God who *commands*. In the first chapter of Genesis, God created by command, and (by the dominant interpretation) thus created the world from nothing. After the creation of animals, God commanded them, "Be fruitful and multiply," and repeated the command to the humans created in the divine image. After creating, God saw that the creation was good, and humans very good. God commanded Adam not to eat from the tree of the knowledge of good and evil, though he was free to eat from any other tree. When Eve and Adam disobeyed and ate of that fruit, they were expelled from the garden. God's commands set up a fundamental choice for humans, whether to obey or to disobey. God established a *covenant*, within which those who obey are blessed and those who disobey are not. Human disobedience is not explained in the Genesis text, except that the serpent says to Eve that they will not die if they eat the fruit, but will be like God, knowing good and evil, and Eve sees the fruit is good for food and pleasing to the eye and desirable for gaining wisdom. As the story goes on to describe Adam and Eve's descendants, Genesis says that wickedness spread to the whole human race, and calls this a corruption of the *heart*, a basic orientation away from obedience to God and toward evil. God wiped them out, except for Noah and his family, in a flood, and then made a covenant, which included the command not to shed human blood "for in the image of God has God made the human being" (9: 6). The sign of this covenant was the rainbow, and God made this covenant with "all living creatures of every kind on the earth."

Genesis continues with God's command to Abraham to leave his ancestral land and go to a land that God covenants to give him and his offspring. The sign of this covenant was circumcision of the males of the community at eight days old. Abraham's great-grandchildren ended up in Egypt because of famine, and became, through the generations, the people of Israel, who suffered under the Pharaoh's yoke. Under Moses, the people were finally liberated (an event they subsequently commemorated every year at the Passover), and during their wanderings in the desert, Moses received from God the Ten Commandments, on two tablets or tables. The first table concerned the obligations to God directly, to worship God alone, keep God's name holy, and keep the Sabbath day holy. The second table concerned the obligations to other human beings, and all the commands were negative (do not kill, commit adultery, lie, steal, or covet) except for the first, which required the honoring of fathers and mothers. God told Moses to tell the people, "If you obey me fully, and keep my covenant, then out of all nations you will be my treasured possession. Although the whole earth is mine, you will be for me a kingdom of priests and a holy nation" (Exod. 19:5–6).

Much of the first five books of the Hebrew Bible is concerned with *laws* that God gives to the people, and the idea of a holy *kingdom* or a kingdom of God is the idea of a realm in which these laws obtain. This raises a question about the extent of this realm. The Ten

Commandments are given in the context of a covenant with the people of Israel, though there are references to God's intention to bless the whole world through this people. The surrounding laws include prescriptions and proscriptions about ritual purity and sacrifice and the use of the land that seem to apply to this particular people in this particular place. But the covenant with Noah after the flood is applicable to the whole human race – indeed, to all living things – and universal scope is emphasized in the Wisdom books, which make a continual connection between how we should live and how we were created as human beings (for example, Prov. 8). One more pair of terms is important to the contrast with the tradition of Greek philosophy – namely, the terms "sin" and "forgiveness." The heart is sinful when it turns away from God and God's law, but the law also contains prescriptions for how the relationship with God, damaged by sin, is to be restored by God's mercy and forgiveness.

The terms contained in this set ("commandment," "covenant," "heart," "law," "kingdom," "sin," and "forgiveness") are understood in connection with each other, so that it is tempting to say that any one of them implies all the others, but they are also understood in connection with goodness. God's commandments and laws, themselves, are good (Neh. 9:13, Ps. 119:39, 68, Prov. 2:9). The covenant is one by which God promises to do good for God's people (Jer. 32:40), and to prosper them (Gen. 32:12, Deut. 6:24–5, 30:15). God's goodness is shown in God's love, mercy, and forgiveness of our sin (Ps. 86:5). God's kingdom is a kingdom of goodness and righteousness, in which God's love dwells with those who keep God's covenant (Ps. 103:17–19, Jer. 18:9).

The New Testament continues all these themes, but transmutes them through the figure of Jesus Christ. Jesus called his followers to obey God's law, but he accentuated the difficulty of doing so (Matt. 5:20–48), "You have heard it said that . . . , but I tell you that. . . . " For example, not only must we not murder, but anyone who is angry with his brother will be subject to judgment, and not only must we not commit adultery, but anyone who looks at a woman lustfully has already committed adultery with her in his heart. We have the two great commandments, to love God and to love our neighbor (see Deut. 6:5, and Lev. 19:18), but Jesus told us to love our enemies and pray for those who persecute us (see Luke 10: 25–37, the parable of the Good Samaritan). He summed up his commands, "Be ye perfect, therefore, as your heavenly Father is perfect." He announced that the kingdom of God had come with his own coming and his work (Matt. 12:28, Luke 11: 20), and he claimed the power to forgive sins, to the scandal of the Scribes and Pharisees (Luke 5: 21–26). At the commemoration of the Passover in Jerusalem, he applied to himself the language of the breaking of the bread and the shedding of the blood of the lamb, "This is my blood, which is poured out for many for the forgiveness of sins" (Matt. 26:28). After his crucifixion, he rose from the dead, and he now gives life to those who love and obey him (John 14:19–21).

In the letters attributed to Paul (Phil. 2:5–11 and Col. 1:15–23), we find two hymns that, perhaps, use older Greek material (though the extent of the borrowing is controversial among scholars). The hymn in Philippians says that Christ was in very nature God, but did not consider equality with God something to be grasped, but emptied himself, taking the form of a servant, being made in human likeness. We are to be like-minded, in humility considering others as *better* than ourselves. But after this humiliation, even to death, God exalted Christ to the highest place, and gave him the name that is above every name. The hymn in Colossians says that Christ is the image of the invisible God; all things were created by him and for him, and hold together in him; and that through Christ's blood shed on the cross, God reconciles all things to himself. Here, the goodness of the whole creation is seen in relation to Christ, both in origin and in destination. In our case, we were alienated from God but he has reconciled us by Christ's physical body through death to present us holy in his sight, without blemish and free from accusation. In these two passages we are given a pattern by which Christ first descends to his death and then, through this, is exalted and given the central role in the restoration of the goodness of cosmos.

THE MIDDLE AGES

The history of Christian theological reflection about goodness starts from these two traditions, the Greek and the biblical. There is a multitude of ways in which these traditions intersect. Augustine is a key figure, describing how he came to Christianity through the Platonists, whose work he calls "a preparation for the gospel." He describes this process through the metaphor of the people of Israel "despoiling the Egyptians" of their gold, and using it for vessels in the temple (*De Doctrina Christiana* II, 40. 60). Augustine says that the Platonists already understood the beginning of the prologue to John, that in the beginning was the Word and the Word was with God and the Word was God. But they did not understand the end, that the Word became flesh and dwelt among us (*Confessiones* VII, 9. 13–14). The central metaphysical move that allows Augustine's appropriation of Plato is the location of Plato's Forms in the mind of God, "the eternal and unchanging reason whereby

God made the world" (*Retractationes* I, 3. 2). As in Plato, priority is here given to the Form of the Good, and God ordains according to "right reason" the pattern that governs our being and our activities (*De Trinitate* IX, 7. 12). Human beings can participate in this eternal law by means of their reason, and Augustine sometimes refers to this participation as "natural law" (*Epistulae* 157. 3. 15). Our goal, which is also the goal of philosophy, is to achieve blessedness, a state of complete and ultimate fulfillment through union with God. Augustine starts his *Confessiones*, "You [O God] have made us, and in making us turned us toward yourself (*fecisti nos ad te*); and our hearts are restless until they come to rest in you." But even though all people desire happiness, they do not all reach it, because the way has not been revealed to them – namely, the way through the work of Christ in redemption. All of us have loves, which Augustine compares to weights, moving us in different directions. Our task is to order our loves so that they correspond to the order of goodness in the cosmos. We should only enjoy or love for its own sake (*frui*) God, and every other good we should use (*uti*) and not enjoy, although Augustine does sometimes allow a third class of good things – namely other people – which we should "enjoy in God" (*De Doctrina Christiana* I, 33. 36–37).

Of the philosophers of the later Middle Ages, sometimes called the scholastic period, Thomas Aquinas and Duns Scotus take different positions about goodness (though Scotus seldom refers to Aquinas, and the Franciscans at the time of his training were not allowed to read Aquinas's *Summa* without special license). Aquinas takes over from Augustine a robust connection between goodness and being. However, Aquinas is also heavily under the influence of Aristotle, many of whose works had recently been rediscovered through the Arabic commentators translated into Latin. "Being" and "goodness," Aquinas says, are the same in reference but differ in sense, and the formula (or definition) of good consists in this, that something is desirable (*Summa Theologiae* I, 5. 1; remaining citations all are from the *Summa*). Goodness and being are the same in reference because everything that exists is good since it is the actualization of the specifying potentiality of that type of thing, and he holds, following Aristotle, that no substance can exist without this teleological actualization. But the sense of "goodness" is different, because it means "desirable," not only in the sense "able to be desired" but in the sense "fit to be desired." The first principle of ethics, for Aquinas, is that the good is to be desired and the evil avoided. This can be specified for our own good, by the principle that we are to pursue our happiness or perfection and, in the case of the good of others, by the principle that we are to do no harm (II-II, 79.1). Aquinas, agreeing with Aristotle, says that "every man naturally wills happiness; and from this natural willing are caused all other willings, since whatever a man wills, he wills on account of the end" (I, 60.2). He also agrees with Aristotle that intellectual contemplation of God is the central component of the highest good. But in the detailed treatment of the virtues – for example magnanimity – he treats them very differently than Aristotle by bringing them into contact with the model of the life of Christ and with the Christian virtue of humility. Aquinas's account of natural law, a synthesis of Augustine and Aristotle, is that although everything participates in some manner in the Eternal Law (which is in God's mind), the rational creature "participates in divine Providence by providing for itself and others. Hence, it participates in the eternal plan through which it has a natural inclination to its due act and end. And this sort of participation in the Eternal Law by the rational creature is called the Natural Law" (I-II, 91.2). With the exception of the beatific object (which we contemplate in the next life), Aquinas does not think that any object determines the will, though an object can determine an inclination that is then used by the will. Because the beatific object *does* determine the will, he says that the priority of love that I Corinthians 13 describes is only in this life; in the next life, priority is given to a virtue of intellect.

Scotus, by contrast, gives priority to love also in the next life. Loving is an activity of the will, and the will is a faculty superior to the intellect (*Ordinatio* IV, 49. 9. 2). He agrees with the principle, endorsed by Aquinas, that nothing is willed except what has been pre-cognized. But in the case of our destination, which is to be co-lovers with God (*condiligentes*), the cognition is introductory to the loving. For Scotus, theology is a practical science, since its object is "God as one who should be loved...according to rules from which action can be chosen" (*Lectura* Prologue, 4. 1). Scotus takes from Anselm the doctrine that there are two affections of the will, the affection for advantage and the affection for justice (Aquinas does not have these terms). The affection for advantage is a pull toward one's own happiness and perfection. The affection for justice is a pull toward what is good in itself, independently of its relation to one's happiness and perfection. The human will contains both affections, and there is nothing wrong with this (it will be our state even in heaven), but the key question is the ranking. We should rank the affection for justice first, and the way to make this vivid is to imagine the counterfactual situation in which we had to sacrifice our own happiness. We should be willing to be damned for the sake of the glory of God (for similar language from Moses, see Exod. 32: 32, and from Paul, see

Rom. 9: 3). If we were motivated entirely by the affection for advantage, Scotus says our will would not be any more free than our intellect currently is (since it is determined by its object). The affection for justice is "the first checkrein" on the affection for advantage. It is only where there are two sources of motivation, and not just motivation by one's own happiness, that the question arises, "Why should I be motivated by the affection for justice?" A divine command theory gives an answer to such a question: "Because God commands it." Scotus also wants to deny the principle that the second table of the law can be deduced from human nature. It *fits* our nature, but it would be possible for God to command other laws that would also fit our nature. In this sense, too, Scotus is a divine command theorist, though he agrees that the second table is "natural law" in an extended sense. Scotus does not deny teleology – that natural things have ends – but he insists that the purposiveness is in the will of God, who makes the things, rather than in the things themselves. Finally, there is a kind of particularism in Scotus different from anything in Aquinas. He thinks that there is an individual essence that distinguishes each individual from others of the same species, and this essence is a perfection of the species, just as the species is a perfection of the genus. There is also a "particular happiness" toward which the natural will is directed, and it is "not something general or universal, but something singular" (*Ordinatio* IV, 49. 9).

THE MODERN WORLD

In the history of European philosophy after the Renaissance, there are two main lines of development – rationalism and empiricism – of which Gottfried von Leibniz is an example of the former and Thomas Hobbes of the latter. The rationalists constructed their system of human knowledge, as it were, from the top down, from principles self-evident to reason. For Leibniz, the true good is "whatever serves the perfection of intelligent substance," and he held that this world is the best of all possible worlds understood in this way. We know this because we know that this is the only world God could have sufficient reason to create. For the empiricists, by contrast, the system of knowledge is created from the bottom up, from what is evident to the senses. For Hobbes, all reality (including God) is bodily and human beings are machines moved by forces – either appetite (toward what is known by experience to be pleasant) or aversion (away from what is known by experience to be painful). What we call "will" is just "the last appetite in deliberating" (Lev. 1, 6). In Germany, Lutheran pietists objected to Leibnizian rationalism.

Christian August Crusius was the most important philosopher among the pietists, and defended human freedom against Leibnizian determinism. Like Scotus, he tied our freedom to the presence of a disinterested drive other than the drive to our own perfection, and he emphasized that there are actions that we ought to do regardless of any other ends we have – even the end of our own perfection. It is plausible to see here the origin of what Kant calls the categorical imperative. He also added a third drive, the drive of conscience, which is "the natural drive to recognize a divine moral law" and which is the capacity to be drawn toward what we recognize as divine command out of a sense of dependence on the God who commands us (*A Guide to Rational Living*, para. 132). In Britain, there was likewise opposition from the church to Hobbesian empiricism. One Presbyterian minister, Francis Hutcheson (himself accused of unorthodoxy), defended the existence in us of a moral sense, against Hobbesian psychological egoism. Hutcheson distinguished, like Scotus, objects that are naturally good, which excite personal or selfish pleasure, and those that are morally good, which are advantageous to all persons affected. "That Action is best," he said, "which procures the greatest Happiness for the greatest Numbers" (*Inquiry* II, III, VIII, 177–78). Because a possible gap opens up, on this picture, between one's own advantage and the morally good, Hutcheson thought we needed some assurance that morality and happiness coincide, and he thought God (who is impartially benevolent) had given us a moral sense for this purpose. When we intend the good of others, we "undesignedly" end up promoting our own good as well, because we get the unique kind of pleasure that comes from approving our own benevolence. Hutcheson is plausibly seen as the first utilitarian.

Crusius and Hutcheson are important partly because of their influence on Immanuel Kant. One standard interpretation of Kant in the twentieth century has been John Rawls's claim that Kant gives "priority to the right over the good" (*A Theory of Justice*, p. 31). Kant does not express himself this way. In fact, he says that right action has to be directed toward the highest good, which is the union of virtue and happiness. He is opposed to any view that reduces happiness to virtue (as he thinks the Stoics did) or sees virtue as the means to happiness (as he thinks the Epicureans did). Of these two different components of the highest good, he says that only the first (virtue, or the good will) is good without qualification. However, as creatures of need, he thinks we are bound to seek happiness in everything else that we seek. This is why, he says, "morality inevitably leads to religion" (*Religion within the Bounds of Mere Reason* 6: 6) since in order to believe in the real (as opposed to merely logical) possibility of the highest good, we have to postulate the agency of a supersensible being who is the author of nature as well as the author (though not creator) of our duties. Kant says throughout his corpus that we have to recognize our duties as God's commands (see, for example, *Religion* 6: 154). There was a tendency in the secondary literature of the twentieth century to downplay this "vertical" dimension of Kant's thought, but the tendency is beginning to be reversed. God is the sovereign of the "kingdom of ends" of which we are also members, and which is the kingdom under the law (the Categorical Imperative), which requires us to treat humanity in our own person and in the person of any other always at the same time as an end and never merely as a means (*Groundwork of the Metaphysics of Morals* 4: 429, 433–34). Kant does not, in any of this, reduce religion to ethics. However, he does give priority to the practical access to God over the access through the theoretical use of reason. His project is to "deny knowledge in order to make room for faith" (*Critique of Pure Reason* B xxx). Theoretical cognition is limited to *phenomena* (things as they appear to us) and their transcendental conditions, but Kant thinks we have justified beliefs about *noumena* (things as they are in themselves) that go beyond these limitations. Kant is also allergic to the use of religion as a substitute for the moral life, and he ends *Religion* by saying, "the right way to advance is not from grace to virtue but rather from virtue to grace" (*Religion* 6: 202).

G. W. F. Hegel took himself to be defending Christianity, as a second Luther, but he held, against Kant, that there was finally no need to make the separation between our knowledge and the thing-in-itself beyond our knowledge; in the final stage of absolute knowledge and freedom toward which history is moving, Spirit understands that reality is its own creation and there is no "beyond" for it to know. The distinction between "continental" and "analytic" schools of philosophy in the twentieth century can be seen as different responses to Hegel: the continental school reads him, and the analytic school (with a few exceptions) does not. Another somewhat idiosyncratic defense of Christianity was offered by Hegel's contemporary, F. D. E. Schleiermacher (who had a pietist education), who emphasized our dependence on God (like Crusius): "The consciousness of being absolutely dependent, or, which is the same thing, of being in relation with God" (*The Christian Faith*, sec. 4). "Sin" is resistance to this God-consciousness, and "salvation" is its awakening and "steady flame." Christianity was also attacked, for example by Friedrich Nietzsche, who announced the death of God, and hoped for a corresponding decline in mankind's feeling of guilt. He urged that we return from a Christian slave-morality, centered on the distinction between good and evil, back to the ancient Greek master-morality, centered on the distinction between noble and base. In the twentieth century, Jean-Paul Sartre developed an "existentialist" ethics, which is like Kant in that "in choosing myself, I choose man" (*Existentialism and Human Emotions*, 17), but unlike Kant in that it is atheist, and "there can no longer be an *a priori* Good, since there is no infinite and perfect consciousness to think it.... If God does not exist, we find no values or commands to turn to which legitimize our conduct" (*ibid*. 22–23).

At the end of the twentieth century, continental philosophy developed a "post-modernism" that is like Nietzsche in its distrust of any "meta-narrative" that could provide an overall system, but which is also unlike Nietzsche in that it does not require wholesale rejection but is hospitable to bits and pieces of Christianity and other religions. Finally, in continental and also analytic philosophy, there has been a return by some to Thomism (named for Thomas Aquinas) and natural law theory. The work of Jacques Maritain and, more recently, Alasdair MacIntyre and John Finnis spans the distinction between the analytic and continental schools. There has also been a revival of divine command theory in analytic philosophy, starting with Philip Quinn's *Divine Commands and Moral Requirements*, and continuing with Robert M. Adams's *Finite and Infinite Goods*. The present writer's own work has followed this line (John Hare, *The Moral Gap* and *God and Morality*), treating the good as what draws us and deserves to draw us, which is finally God and union with God, and treating the obligatory as that part of the good that God requires of us.

Returning to the nineteenth century in Britain, Hutcheson's utilitarian system was taken over by John Stuart Mill and Henry Sidgwick, both of whom (like Hutcheson) recognized that the gap between happiness and morality requires postulating some divine agency if hope in the coherence of our aims is to be preserved (Mill in *Three Essays on Religion* and Sidgwick in *Methods of Ethics*). G. E. Moore defended an intuitionist theory of the good, according to which goodness is a simple non-natural property to which we have access by the faculty of intuition. He condemned what he called "the naturalistic fallacy" by which "good" is defined by a natural property, such as "causing pleasure," or a supernatural property, such as "commanded by God" (*Principia Ethica* II, 29). Moore argued that these definitions cannot be right because it still remains an open question whether what causes pleasure or is commanded by God is good. R. M. Hare's theory, universal prescriptivism, explained why goodness could not be reduced to a natural or supernatural property; evaluative language has the function of expressing the will and, thus, prescribing how we should act or live. Goodness, he said, is supervenient on descriptive properties (the strawberry is good because it is red, sweet, and so on), but because of the expressive function of "good," someone who makes the judgment that something is good is not committed to the judgment that it has those descriptive properties unless he has made the decision to treat those properties as the criterion of goodness. The debate between realists and expressivists about goodness has continued to the present, as has the development of utilitarianism. One opponent of utilitarianism, John Rawls, held that utilitarianism is inconsistent with respecting the distinctness of persons, required by the notion of justice as fairness. He thought that this notion also required citizens with substantial conceptions of the good, including religious conceptions, to leave these behind in public discourse. Finally, one feature of contemporary analytic ethics is the attempt to relate ethics to contemporary science, whether this is neurophysiology, or evolutionary psychology. This does not, in itself, require abandoning a connection with religion, since there may be neurophysiological sites for God-consciousness and our evolutionary ancestors were almost certainly religious. However, following Moore and R. M. Hare, it is important to note that no value-free description of states of the brain or hunter-gatherer societies is going to entail the truth of any particular conception of the good.

References

Adams, Robert M. *Finite and Infinite Goods: A Framework for Ethics* (Oxford: Oxford University Press, 1999).

Aquinas, *Summa Theologiae, Blackfriars Edition* (London: Eyre and Spottiswode, 1964–73).

Aristotle, *Nicomachean Ethics, Metaphysics, Eudemian Ethics* in *The Complete Works of Aristotle*, ed. Jonathan Barnes (Princeton, NJ: Bollingen Series, 1984).

Augustine, *De Doctrina Christiana, Confessiones, De Trinitate, Epistulae, Retractationes*, in *Patrologia Latina*, vols. 32–46.

Crusius, Christian August. *A Guide to Rational Living*, in *Moral Philosophy from Montaigne to Kant*, ed. J. B. Schneewind (Cambridge: Cambridge University Press, 1990).

Finnis, John. *Natural Law and Natural Rights* (Oxford: Clarendon Press, 1980).

Hare, John E. *The Moral Gap* (Oxford: Clarendon Press, 1996).

Hare, John E. *God and Morality* (Oxford: Blackwell, 2007).

Hare, R. M. *Moral Thinking* (Oxford: Clarendon Press, 1981).

Hobbes, Thomas. *Leviathan*, ed. Michael Oakeshott (New York: Collier, 1962).

The Holy Bible. Genesis, Exodus, Leviticus, Deuteronomy, Nehemiah, Psalms, Proverbs, Jeremiah, Matthew, Luke, John, Romans, I Corinthians, Philippians, Colossians.

Hutcheson, Francis. *Inquiry into the Origin of Our Ideas of Beauty and Virtue,* ed. Wolfgang Leidhold (Indianapolis, IN: Liberty Fund, 2004).

Irwin, Terrence. *The Development of Ethics,* vol I (Oxford: Oxford University Press, 2007).

Kant, Immanuel. *Religion within the Bounds of Mere Reason, Groundwork of the Metaphysics of Morals, Critique of Pure Reason,* in *Cambridge Edition of the Works of Immanuel Kant* (Cambridge: Cambridge University Press, 1996–1998).

Laertius, Diogenes. *Lives of Eminent Philosophers,* trans. R. D. Hicks (London: Loeb Classical Library, 1925).

MacIntyre, Alasdair. *Dependent Rational Animals* (Chicago, IL: Open Court Press, 1999).

Maritain, Jacques. *Man and State* (Chicago, IL: Chicago University Press, 1951).

Mill, John Stuart. *Three Essays on Religion* (London: Henry Holt, 1974).

Moore, G. E. *Principia Ethica* (Cambridge: Cambridge University Press, 1993).

Plato. *Euthyphro, Ion, Symposium, Republic, Timaeus, Theaetetus,* in *Plato, Complete Works,* ed. John M. Cooper (Indianapolis, IN: Hackett, 1997).

Quinn, Philip L. *Divine Commands and Moral Requirements* (Oxford: Clarendon Press, 1978).

Rawls, John. *A Theory of Justice* (Cambridge, MA: Harvard University Press, 1971).

Sartre, Jean Paul. *Existentialism and Human Emotions* (Secaucus, NJ: Citadel Press, 1957).

Schleiermacher, F. D. E. *The Christian Faith,* trans. H. R. Mackintosh and J. S. Stewart (Edinburgh: T & T Clark, 1989).

Scotus, Duns. *Lectura, Ordinatio* in *Duns Scotus on the Will and Morality,* trans. A. B. Wolter (Washington, DC: The Catholic University of America Press, 1986).

Sidgwick, Henry. *The Methods of Ethics* (Indianapolis, IN: Hackett, 1981).

6 Eternity and providence

WILLIAM HASKER

The doctrine of divine providence asserts that time is governed by eternity. This assertion provokes the two questions that will occupy us in this discussion: What is eternity? What is it for time to be governed by eternity? Eternity in this context is conceived as the mode of existence of the theistic God, a personal, active, and creative being capable of forming and executing intentions concerning the created world. There are, however, two quite different conceptions of eternity on offer. On one conception, that God is eternal means that God has always existed, with no beginning, and will always exist hereafter, with no end. Traditionally this has been termed "sempiternity"; in recent discussion, the preferred term has been "everlastingness." This is the notion of eternity that by far predominates in ordinary religious discourse, and also in the Jewish and Christian Scriptures. It has, however, been a minority view in the history of theology, with preference rather for the claim that God is timeless, outside of time altogether. Since this is the view that has been dominant historically, and also the view that presents the greater conceptual and metaphysical challenges, I address it first.

What is it for God to be timelessly eternal? Augustine provides a powerful statement of the idea:

> It is not in time that You are before all time: otherwise You would not be before all time. You are before all the past by the eminence of Your ever-present eternity: and You dominate all the future in as much as it is still to be: and once it has come it will be past: but *Thou art always the Selfsame, and Thy years shall not fail* [Psalm 102: 27]. Your years neither go nor come: but our years come and go, that all may come. Your years abide all in one act of abiding: for they abide and the years that go are not thrust out by those that come, for none pass: whereas our years shall not all be, till all are no more. Your years are as a

single day; and Your day comes not daily but is today, a today which does not yield place to any tomorrow or follow upon any yesterday. In You today is eternity...[1]

The words are both clear and elegant, but the thought may be found perplexing. God's today is eternity – what does this mean? What is being taught is that God's life does not consist in a sequence of events, one after another. Rather, *all* the events of God's life occur together, as if in a single moment, and this moment is eternity. Furthermore, God's "eternal now" does not occur either before, or after, or simultaneous with any particular moment of our time. (If it did, God would eternally be thinking such things as "It didn't rain yesterday, but it will rain tomorrow," but such thoughts are not suitable for a timeless being.) Yet God, in some way, is both the source of temporal events and the sovereign Lord over them.

It is clear that these views have no real anchorage in Scripture. Even the little that has been said in the last two paragraphs goes far beyond anything said in the Bible on this topic – and of course a great deal more needs to be said if we are to grasp the idea in anything like a satisfactory way. The Bible as a whole is perfectly content to represent God as living, and acting, and reacting in time – but if so, why has the notion of God as timeless gotten itself so firmly entrenched in much of theology? A full answer to this question would be lengthy and complex, and would include large stretches of the history of ancient and medieval philosophy and theology. The story begins early in the history of philosophy with Parmenides, who was convinced that true reality must be not only changeless but absolutely indivisible, containing no distinguishable objects of any kind. (Thus the experienced world, containing a plurality of changing objects, was ultimately an illusion.) Parmenides' views were not adopted in their entirety by later philosophers, but they remained influential in the thinking of Plato and, later, of the neo-Platonists such as Plotinus. Augustine, in turn, was deeply influenced by Plotinus; he was a neo-Platonist before he became a Christian, and retained much of Plotinus' thought in his mature theology. For Augustine, it was axiomatic that what is truly real, that which most truly exists and has being, must be absolutely changeless.

An argument that a perfect being must be changeless goes back to Plato and is still invoked today: A perfect being cannot change, because any change would be either for the better or for the worse. A being that

---

[1] Augustine, *Confessions*, 2nd ed., trans. F. J. Sheed (Indianapolis, IN: Hackett, 2006), 242.

can change for the better is not yet perfect, and a being that changed for the worse would no longer be perfect. Furthermore, a perfect being that cannot lose its perfection is superior to an otherwise perfect being that is able to lose its perfection. And where there can be no change, there is also no time. God, rather, is the timeless reality that is the source of all that changes, all that comes into being and passes away. As for the exegetical issue, it turns out that when the Scriptures are read in the light of this conviction, a few passages can be interpreted as teaching the doctrine of divine timelessness, *provided that* the doctrine has already been made available from other sources.[2]

The doctrine of divine timeless eternity brings a number of problems with it. Can a timeless being act in time, as God is said to do? The answer given is that God's acts, considered as his acts, are timeless – or better, there is a single timeless act comprising everything God does – but that the effects of this act appear in time. It is more difficult, however, to see how a timeless God can *react* to temporal events: a causal "feedback" from time to eternity poses serious metaphysical problems. Perhaps the most intractable problem of all, however, is that a timeless God cannot know what is happening *now*. It is true, as this sentence is being typed, that a few seconds ago I concluded the previous sentence with the word "now" – but a timeless God cannot know this, for in order to know such facts God would have to change.[3] (A few minutes ago the proposition in question was not yet true, and so could not have been known by God to be true; and by *this* time it is no longer true, since the time-span since I typed the word "now" has grown longer.) More importantly, according to the liturgy, "Christ *has* died, Christ *has* risen, Christ *will* come again" – these are things Christians believe to be true, but a timeless God, unlike us, neither believes them nor knows them.

A solution – and most likely the only solution – to this last problem may be found by adopting the theory of time known variously as the B-theory, four-dimensionalism, eternalism, or the stasis theory. On this theory, to simplify a bit, *all* objects and events exist timelessly, in the four-dimensional continuum or "block universe" of spacetime. "Now" is an indexical word, used to single out events contemporaneous with a

[2] Texts that have been so interpreted include Gen. 1:1, Exod. 3:14, and John 8:58. Contemporary biblical scholarship, however, does not support reading these texts in terms of divine timelessness. For a full discussion, see Alan G. Padgett, *God, Eternity, and the Nature of Time* (New York: St. Martin's Press, 1992), Chapter 2.

[3] To be sure, God can know that *at the time when I was typing that sentence*, the preceding sentence had been concluded a few seconds ago. What a timeless God *cannot* know is that I am typing the sentence in question *right now*.

speaker's utterance; every time is "now" to the persons inhabiting that time, just as every place is "here" to the persons at that place. So just as there is no objective fact of the matter as to which place is "here," there is no objective fact of the matter as to which time is "now," and it is no defect in God's omniscience that he does not know what time it is now. This solution, however, comes at a heavy price. For one thing, it undercuts the motivation that inspired the doctrine of timelessness in the first place. Augustine is very clear that neither past nor future events exist; that is a prime source for the puzzles that drive his inquiries about time in the *Confessions.* (So he must be read as holding the "A-theory," or a "dynamic" view of time.) In addition, it is evident in the quotation given that divine timeless eternity is praiseworthy, especially because of the contrast it draws between the timeless and immutable God and the fleeting, evanescent reality of creatures. This contrast, however, virtually disappears if each of the events of time exists timelessly and unchangeably at its own point in the four-dimensional continuum. Furthermore, four-dimensionalism is inconsistent with libertarian free will, which is important to many defenders of divine timelessness. If the events of my future timelessly exist in the inalterable four-dimensional continuum, the "alternative possibilities" needed for free will simply are not there; it is categorically impossible that I should perform any action different than the one that exists timelessly in the space-time continuum.

The doctrine of God as everlasting faces challenges of its own, though, arguably, they are less severe. This doctrine affirms that God is unchangeable in his essential nature and, in particular, in his loving and just character; thus God is maximally reliable in his dealings with us and with his creation. To the argument that a perfect being cannot change, it is replied that there is change that is neither for the better nor for the worse, but that is needed in order to maintain an unchanging state of excellence. (A wristwatch that was "unchanging" in that it always registered the same time of day would hardly be maximally excellent. Most of us have a few such watches in a back drawer somewhere!) The changelessness that should be affirmed of God is the sort of changelessness that pertains to a *personal being,* not the changelessness of a mathematic formula. Time is not an independently existing reality with which God simply has to cope; rather time, in the sense of a changeful succession of states, is inherent in the nature of God. (On the other hand, clock time, measured by repeated physical processes, is indeed created, since it begins only with the creation of physical reality.) Above all, it is clear that the dynamic interaction with the world and with created persons that is so characteristic of the biblical God is far more readily understandable if God is conceived as everlasting rather than timeless.

One of the more interesting problems for this view was suggested by Augustine: What was God doing before he created the world? (Augustine mentions but rejects the answer that God was preparing hell for those who pry into such mysteries!) This is a nonissue for divine timelessness, since on that view, time begins with creation and so there was no "before" creation. However, the view of God as everlasting must confront the issue. Actually, several answers are possible. It may be sufficient to observe that we simply have no resources for knowing what God may have been doing in the fellowship of the Trinity, quite apart from any created reality. To the objection that God would have no reason to create at one time rather than another, it may be replied that a rational agent who sees that something would be good to do, but has no special reason to do it at one time or place rather than another, will choose arbitrarily and, none-the-less, be rational for doing so. Another possibility, though one not favored by mainstream theology, is that creation, like God, has been going on literally forever. (So that prior to *our* "big bang" there was another, and another before that, and so on...) Some have objected to divine everlastingness on the ground that an actually infinite past is impossible – indeed, that any actual infinity (as opposed to a potential infinity, such as the infinity of years that are yet to come) is impossible. These arguments do not seem to be logically compelling, but an infinity of past years can be avoided on the supposition that prior to creation God was in a state of rest or stasis that does not consist of measurable intervals. It may not be clear which of these answers is preferable, but the problem does not seem to be an insuperable one.

PROVIDENCE

How do these two doctrines of divine eternity bear on the doctrine of providence? Perhaps surprisingly, the differences in this respect are not great, with one proviso: the two doctrines are very similar in their application to divine providence *if and only if* several outstanding problems for divine timelessness have adequate solutions. These include the ability of a timeless God to act in time and to respond to temporal events, the ability of a timeless God to enter into intimate personal relationships with created, temporal persons, and the compatibility of divine timelessness with divine omniscience and with libertarian free will. At this point, I will not discuss further whether such solutions are, in fact, available; rather, I will assume provisionally that solutions are possible in order to get on with the discussion of divine providence.

Broadly speaking, there are four major types of variables that determine the shape of a doctrine of providence. There are the divine intentions – what God is doing or trying to do. There is divine power, God's ability to bring about what he desires. There is divine knowledge, the kind and extent of which conditions the exercise of his power. And there is human freedom: to what extent do human beings (and other rational creatures, if there are any) possess the capacity either to freely respond and cooperate with God's intentions, or to resist them?

Views about God's more particular intentions vary with the specific theology under consideration; one might say that this question belongs more properly to revealed theology than to philosophical theology. In a general sense, it can be said that God's intention is to bring his creation to its proper fulfillment and, in particular, to bring created persons into a relationship of worshipful love toward himself and a state of loving harmony with other persons. Concerning divine power, the main varieties of standard theism are able to agree on a conception that can be stated roughly as follows: God is able to do anything that is logically consistent, and consistent with God's perfect nature. The main exception to this generalization is process theism, which holds a view that is often expressed by saying that God has "persuasive power" over his creatures but not "coercive power." This means that God can "lure" creaturely agents in the direction of the greatest good by presenting it to them as an option to be chosen, but God cannot act in any directly efficacious way, either in the natural world or in the lives of persons, to ensure that his intention is carried out. The detailed arguments concerning this need not concern us now; what is clear is that, given this limitation, God's ability to bring about the results that he desires in the world is much more limited than traditional theists have conceived it to be.

The two remaining variables, then, are divine knowledge and human freedom. It seems likely that the disagreement concerning the nature of free will marks the deepest rift among the adherents of traditional theism. On one side are the theological determinists, here termed "Augustinians" after the first well-known exponent of the view. The line beginning with Augustine continues with Aquinas (though his case is contested), Calvin, Luther, and Jonathan Edwards. These writers held what is now termed a compatibilist view of free will: free will and moral responsibility are entirely compatible with causal determinism, so long as the proximate cause of the action is the agent's own desire and intention. (Some refinements are needed to insure that the desire/intention is not itself the result of unacceptable manipulation or control by another agent.) The consequence of this view for theology is that human freedom is consistent with absolute, unilateral divine control of everything that takes place, including the free actions of created persons. God will simply do whatever is necessary to insure that the created persons have the appropriate desires and intentions that will lead them to "freely" do exactly what he wants done. This also implies that everything that occurs is exactly what God desired and intended to occur; this consequence, however, is often muted because of the numerous Scriptural passages that imply that things have happened that are *not* as God intended them to be. It is often felt that theological determinism is confronted with an intractable problem of evil; those who hold this view sometimes say that the relation between God and evil is an impenetrable mystery.

On the other side of the divide are those who attribute to human beings free will in a broadly libertarian sense.[4] This group includes many of the early Fathers, the entire Greek church, Ockham, Molina, Arminius, and Wesley, among others. On this view, in order to be free, an agent must be really able, under exactly the same circumstances, to perform some other action or at least to refrain from the action she actually performs. This means that when an agent acts freely, God is permitting her to decide between *alternative possibilities*, and God cannot determine for her which possibility is chosen without removing her freedom. This clearly lessens the scope of God's control, as compared with that permitted by theological determinism; this limitation is, however, *self-chosen* on God's part, assumed by God when he decided to create free creatures and permit them to exercise their freedom. This opens the way for a "free will defense" for the problem of evil, a possibility of which many proponents of this view have gladly availed themselves.

It is at this point that divine knowledge enters the picture as an important variable. It is generally agreed that God possesses comprehensive knowledge of the world's past and present, but what of the future? For determinists, divine knowledge of the future presents no problem; God knows the future in virtue of knowing his own intentions, as well as the causal processes that he has put in motion. For libertarians, or "free will theists," on the other hand, divine knowledge of the future may seem problematic. The future does not exist (we are assuming a dynamic view of time), and the causal processes already set in motion are not sufficient to determine what will come about through the free

---

[4] The terms "compatibilist" and "libertarian" are of recent origin, but I believe they can be applied retrospectively in the way done here without excessive distortion.

choices of rational beings. This becomes important for the doctrine of providence for the following reason: If God knows, prior to his own decisions concerning the providential governance of the world, exactly what human choices will come about in consequence of God's own choices, this brings with it a remarkable degree of security and certainty with regard to the execution of God's plan. God may not, on this account, get everything he wants, because human beings may choose in ways different from what God desires for them. (Both Scripture and experience suggest that this is extremely common.) But God, nevertheless, can be sure of getting exactly the result that he plans for; in making his decisions he anticipates exactly what the human responses will be, and crafts his plan accordingly. But suppose God, in making his decision, is *not* guided by precise knowledge concerning how humans will respond? God will, of course, have a great deal of general knowledge concerning the human beings in question, enabling him to anticipate their responses far more accurately than any other human is capable of doing. However, that is not the same as absolute and certain knowledge of what will actually be chosen. In this case, a degree of riskiness in God's plan becomes inevitable; his planning must allow for the various contingencies. As Thomas Oden has stated, "If Eden is Plan A, and Eden does not work out, due to the self-determining volatility, frailty, and fallibility of human freedom, then God has a Plan B and a Plan C."[5]

Whether this element of risk-taking on God's part is a bad thing is open to question, but many people would like to avoid admitting anything of the sort into their picture of divine providence. In that case, the question may be raised, "What conception of divine knowledge is required, in order to avoid any element of risk in God's plan?" It might be supposed (in fact, it often is supposed) that it is sufficient if God knows the future – that is, he knows exactly what will happen. This, however, is a mistake: *Knowledge of the actual future is of no use whatever to God in devising his plan for the world.* To see this, ask yourself what God could do if, looking into the future, he were to see something occurring that was contrary to his desire and intention. The answer is, God could do *nothing whatever* to prevent such an event, because (by hypothesis) he knows this as an event of the *actual* future, and it is contradictory to suppose that God foresees that occurrence in the actual future, and yet acts with the result that the event is *not* part of the future.[6] Furthermore,

[5] Thomas C. Oden, *The Living God, Systematic Theology* (San Francisco, CA: Harper, 1987), 1: 306.

[6] For more extended argument on this point see William Hasker, *God, Time, and Knowledge* (Ithaca, NY: Cornell University Press, 1989), 59–61; *Providence, Evil, and the*

this same reasoning applies to God's timeless knowledge of the future, if God is timeless; such knowledge also would be of no use to God in his providential governance of the world. (Both Thomas Oden, quoted earlier with regard to God's "alternative plans," and Eleonore Stump are adherents of timelessness who admit that God's plan involves an element of risk.)

There is, however, a kind of knowledge concerning the future that, if it exists, would be of great use for divine providence. This sort of knowledge was first clearly articulated by the sixteenth-century Jesuit Luis de Molina, and it is generally termed "middle knowledge."[7] Middle knowledge is not, as such, knowledge of the actual future; rather, it is knowledge concerning what actions free creatures *would perform* under any conceivable circumstances in which they might exercise libertarian free will in choosing a course of action. Thus, God, preparing to test Job's allegiance to him, does not need to "wait and see" whether or not Job will remain faithful. Rather, he knows in advance exactly how Job would respond to any particular misfortune that might come to him. Armed with this knowledge, God knows with absolute certainty, *prior to his own decisions concerning what situations he will bring about,* just how creatures will react to those situations.[8] God has no need of a Plan B or a Plan C; he makes a single plan and is certain of its exact realization. Thus Molinism, the theory of providence that incorporates middle knowledge, gives God the maximum amount of control that is possible, consistent with libertarian free will for the creatures.

In spite of these apparent advantages, Molinism remains a seriously controversial theory. In the view of many philosophers, the "counter-factuals of creaturely freedom" (propositions of the form, "If A were in circumstances C, she would perform action X") that God knows according to this theory *do not exist to be known*. This is because, in the case of genuine counterfactuals (those whose antecedents are false), there is nothing whatever in the actual course of the world that could "ground" them or account for their being true. All of the antecedent circumstances are fully compatible with the agent's making either of

---

Openness of God (London: Routledge, 2004), 188–93; and John Sanders, *The God Who Risks: A Theology of Divine Providence*, rev. ed. (Downers Grove, IL: InterVarsity Press, 2007), 209–17.

[7] Middle knowledge is so called because it is viewed as intermediate between God's "natural knowledge," by which he knows all necessary truths, and his "free knowledge" of his own decisions and what follows from them.

[8] Here and elsewhere, the priority in view is a priority of logical and explanatory dependence, not (or not necessarily) a temporal priority.

the possible choices; otherwise the action would not be free. In addition to this "grounding objection," it has been argued that the kind of control afforded by middle knowledge would actually be undesirable: God's interaction with his creatures, given this knowledge, would not be a genuine interpersonal relationship but, rather, a kind of manipulation. In addition, the fact that God has specifically planned for each of the evil things that occur means that Molinism is confronted with a formidable problem of evil, albeit less severe than the one implied by Augustinianism.

These objections are not necessarily conclusive, to be sure. But if one finds them persuasive, the remaining option is one that has already been briefly indicated: God makes his plans without knowing, prior to the actual decisions, how free creatures will respond to the choices given them to make. This is true, as we have seen, for the theory of divine timeless knowledge and also for the theory of "simple foreknowledge" (foreknowledge without middle knowledge), though proponents of these views do not always recognize the fact. This conception of providence has been most extensively and consistently developed, however, in the view that has come to be known as "open theism." The name, open theism, is meant to imply that God is "open" both to his creatures and to the future, which is, itself, open in the sense of not yet being wholly decided. Since the future is intrinsically indeterminate, it is not knowable in full detail to anyone, even God. God knows, however, a vast amount about the future, including the probabilities for various responses in cases in which creaturely action is not predetermined. God has the wisdom, power, and resourcefulness to accomplish his ultimate purposes in the world, even in the face of creaturely resistance. God's "plan for our lives" takes the form, not of a detailed blueprint, but of his loving purposes for human beings that he will enable them to achieve through faithful, trusting, and obedient reliance upon him. God willingly assumes the risk that his creation of the world will result in evil as well as good; however, the specific instances of evil that occur are neither intended nor approved by God, even though he can and does work in the world to bring good out of evil. (Thus the problem of evil is less severe than for either Augustinianism or Molinism, though it is still by no means negligible.) This view, even more than the other libertarian options, maximizes the dynamic relationship between God and human persons that is so prominent in the biblical text. Insofar as the future is not fully determined, the efforts of human beings in cooperating with God, in prayer and in active service, assume an importance that other views cannot readily match.

Between the divergent views of divine eternity, it is clear that in recent years timelessness has lost ground to the view of God as everlasting, though both views continue to have able defenders. Among the options concerning providence, process theism has dwindled among philosophers nearly to the point of extinction, though it remains viable in some theological circles. Augustinianism remains the view of a small but determined minority. The most active discussions, on the other hand, are going on between Molinists and open theists. It seems likely that in the future these will take the form mainly of developing more thoroughly the theological implications of the two views in comparison with each other and with Augustinianism. All of these questions are likely to be impacted by ongoing discussions in the philosophy of time. The nature of past, present, and future, and the relationship of each of these to the others and to whatever may exist timelessly, are crucially important for both eternity and providence. Also relevant is the discussion concerning the doctrine that "truth supervenes on being." That doctrine, if accepted, is often seen as putting pressure on the dynamic or "presentist" view of time, and it also creates a problem for the counterfactuals of freedom that are central to Molinism. Final resolutions of these questions are not in sight – but in philosophy, we have learned not to expect them.

Part II

God in relation to creation

7 Incarnation

KATHERIN A. ROGERS

INTRODUCTION

Charity has compelled the Christian community to engage in some serious metaphysics. The Christian is told to spread the Good News, and the Good News is that God has become a human being in order, by his death and resurrection, to free us from our sins and bring us to life eternal. Good News indeed! But difficult philosophically. How could the omnipotent, eternal, and immutable source of all possibly "become" a human being? And why in the world, given divine omnipotence, would God choose such a messy and complicated process for the salvation of mankind, when, presumably, he could save us by divine fiat?

Christian theologians and philosophers have unanimously agreed that the Incarnation is a mystery that we cannot hope to fully grasp. Yet, for two millennia, they have struggled to meet the challenge of the unbeliever who says that the Incarnation is worse than a mystery: it is an impossibility. From the beginning of Christianity, the charge has been made that the Incarnation is, at best, demeaning to God: It is unthinkable that divinity would submit to the biological nastiness involved in Incarnation! At worst, it has been argued, the key claim of Christianity is just logically contradictory.

In this chapter I defend the traditional understanding of the Incarnation. By the traditional understanding, I mean the view that was proclaimed to be the correct one, as against a legion of heresies, at the Council of Chalcedon in 451. I support the Chalcedonian understanding by looking at the work of one of its great defenders, Saint Anselm of Canterbury (1033–1109). Anselm, in his unmatched optimism regarding the ability of reason to explain and defend the Christian faith, proposes to prove that the Incarnation *had* to happen. And it had to be just what Chalcedon said it was in order to do what it was meant to do. I offer a brief sketch of Anselm's argument, and then I defend Chalcedon against the charge of involving impossibilities. Chalcedon allows that Christ can be said to have both divine and human properties, but these can conflict. For example, how can the same person be both omniscient and not omniscient? I introduce a new analogy that tries to make plausible the traditional "*qua*" move – saying, for example, that Christ is omniscient *qua* God, limited in knowledge *qua* man.

Before offering an outline of Chalcedon, a quick sketch of what the Council and most Christian intellectuals for the subsequent millennium meant by "God" and "man" is in order. God, according to what I will call "classical theism," is perfect being and the absolute source of all.[1] There is nothing that is not either God or made by God. Even propositions about what is necessary and what is possible in some way depend upon or reflect the nature of God.[2] Classical theism holds that God's creative activity sustains everything in being from moment to moment. This immediate creation is especially associated with the Second Person of the Trinity, the Word "through Whom all things were made," as it says in the Nicene Creed. God is omnipotent, meaning he can do everything logically possible for a Perfect Being to do. He is omniscient, meaning that he knows everything past, present, and future. And He is perfectly good. Not only does he always do what is good, His nature is the absolute standard for value.

Unlike many contemporary philosophers of religion, classical theists held that God is absolutely simple, eternal, and immutable. In this chapter I use the example of omniscience as a property Christ has *qua* God and not *qua* man, so these more difficult properties can be bracketed for present purposes.

What of "man"? Those attending the Council would have thought of human *nature* as not identical to an individual human being, but as something which *becomes* individuated. They also would have thought of a human being as composed of a material body and an immaterial soul.[3] This is not Platonic dualism. For Plato, the *real* you is your soul. The body, in Plato's view, is a prison from which the real you should be happy to escape at death. The Christian consensus on the nature of man was quite different, though many of the heresies that troubled the Early Church were rooted in a too-Platonic understanding of the world.

---

[1] For more on the God of classical theism, see my *Perfect Being Theology* (Edinburgh: Edinburgh University Press, 2000).

[2] Anselm holds that the free choices of created agents are not up to God, but nonetheless everything in them that qualifies as a real "thing" must be caused by God. See Chapter 6 of my *Anselm on Freedom* (Oxford: Oxford University Press, 2008).

[3] There are many variants on this basic position. For example, Augustine seems to allow more independence to the two aspects of the human being than does Thomas Aquinas. Still, the basic outline holds for both.

The human being, in the classical Christian view, is a unity of soul and body.[4] The soul, as the thinking part, is superior, but the body is good as well. True, for fallen man the appetites of the body inevitably cause trouble, but that is a result of sinfulness, which originates in the soul. *You* come into being when your living body begins to exist and death is a terrible thing as it rips apart what ought to have been joined together. Happily (at least for the blessed) there is a resurrection of the body and you will spend eternity as a whole human being, with a human soul and body.[5]

CHALCEDONIAN CHRISTOLOGY

And so to Chalcedon. Scripture and tradition had said that God sent his only son, the Second Person of the Trinity, the Word, to assume flesh for our salvation. But what could that mean? The Early Church saw many competing analyses and spawned innumerable heresies with intriguing, polysyllabic names: Apollinarianism, Nestorianism, Monophysitism, and on and on. Once we have outlined the decision at Chalcedon, we will do well to mention some views it rejected, and why. This is no trivial matter. For one thing, some of these heresies are with us today. Moreover, many of the heresies were rooted in discomfort with the thought that God – *God!* – could be joined to a human body. Too gross. Even worse, the Blessed Virgin Mary could truly be *Theotokos*, the God-bearer. What could be nastier than the thought that God could grow inside a woman? Chalcedon will have none of this demeaning attitude toward the body. The view that bodies are bad or unimportant, and not really essential to the good and ever so *spiritual* human person, is roundly rejected. Chalcedon saw to it that the traditionally minded Christian, at least, would have to grant that Christ takes on a human body and grows inside a woman, and thus demonstrates irrefutably the great worth of the human being, soul and body. The practical consequences of this on Western thought are incalculable.

Here, then, is what Chalcedon taught:

> ... we all with one voice teach the confession of one and the
> same Son, our Lord Jesus Christ: the same perfect in divinity
> and perfect in humanity, the same truly God and truly man,
> of a rational soul and a body; consubstantial with the Father

[4] St. Augustine defines the human person as a rational substance consisting of soul and body (*De Trinitate* 15.7.11).

[5] See, for example, Augustine, *City of God* 22.5.

as regards his divinity, and the same consubstantial with us
as regards his humanity; like us in all respects except for sin;
begotten before the ages from the Father as regards his divinity,
and in the last days the same for us and for our salvation from
Mary, the virgin God-bearer as regards his humanity; one and
the same Christ, Son, Lord, only-begotten, acknowledged in two
natures which undergo no confusion, no change, no division, no
separation; at no point was the difference between the natures
taken away through the union, but rather the property of both
natures is preserved and comes together into a single person and
a single subsistent being; he is not parted or divided into two
persons, but is one and the same only-begotten Son, God, Word,
Lord Jesus Christ, just as the prophets taught from the beginning
about him, and as the Lord Jesus Christ himself instructed us,
and as the creed of the fathers handed it down to us.[6]

There are, then, all sorts of relationships that the Incarnation is
not. It is most emphatically not the case that in Christ God chose some
unusually nice human being and spoke especially clearly to him. Nor did
God merely *appear* as a man. He did not, remaining unsullied by flesh,
produce a lesser divinity that could then join with human nature. It is
not that God and man are two separate things, coexisting side-by-side
in Christ (Nestorianism). Nor is it the case that the divine and human
natures *fuse* such that man is transmuted into God, or the two natures
become some third thing, neither God nor man (Monophysitism). Chalcedon was especially concerned with these last two.[7] Pope Leo the Great,
whose letter to Flavian, patriarch of Constantinople, spelled out the doctrine Chalcedon would adopt, insists that none of these views can possibly do justice to Scripture, wherein Christ is clearly seen as fully God
and also as fully man.[8]

Chalcedon would also conflict with a recently conceived understanding of the Incarnation known as kenoticism, which holds that God,
to be Incarnate, must be diminished. The Word must either relinquish

---

[6] Available online at http://www.piar.hu/councils/ecumo4.htm.

[7] For a thorough overview of these heresies (and *more!*), see Thomas Weinandy, *Does
God Change?: Studies in Historical Theology*, vol. IV (Still River, MA: St. Bede's
Publications, 1985), xxii-63.

[8] Letter XXVIII (commonly called "The Tome") in *The Letters and Sermons of Leo the
Great, Bishop of Rome*, trans. Rev. Charles Lett Feltoe, M.A., in vol. XII of *Nicene
and Post-Nicene Fathers of the Christian Church*, Second Series, ed. Philip Schaff and
Henry Wace (Grand Rapids, MI: WM. B. Eerdmans Publishing Company, 1976), section
V, 41–43.

or somehow cease to exhibit his divine powers before he could be joined with man.[9] There are numerous problems with this position. Perhaps the most important is this: on the understanding of the activity of the Word assumed by Chalcedon, it is through the Word that all things are sustained in being from moment to moment. If the Word were to set aside his power, the created universe would blink out of being – an unfortunate consequence.

THE NECESSITY OF THE INCARNATION

The Chalcedonian teaching, then, is that Christ is one person with two natures, the Word having "assumed" or "taken on" a human nature. This is an extremely difficult doctrine, and yet Chalcedon held that Scripture and tradition could admit no other. However, cannot Scripture be interpreted in other ways? Perhaps tradition should not be assigned much weight. Might we not do well to abandon Chalcedon? This leads us to Anselm of Canterbury at the beginning of the twelfth century. Chalcedonian Christology was firmly established within the Church by then, but it had not ceased to be a puzzle, and it met with ridicule from those outside the Christian faith. Thus Anselm writes his *Cur Deus Homo (Why God Became Man)*.[10] In setting out the problem, Anselm explains that the Jews and the Muslims claim that it is denigrating to God to suppose that he could somehow really become man. Anselm starts his list of demeaning human properties with the same one that had partially motivated the call for the Council of Chalcedon: It is just nasty to suggest that God might have grown inside a woman![11] Moreover, if God is omnipotent, he could have saved mankind just by willing it so. Therefore, it is doubly unseemly that he would go through the biological rigmarole of Incarnation.[12]

Anselm sets out to prove, by necessary reasons and setting Scripture aside, that the Incarnation *had* to happen.[13] He does expect his readers

---

[9] Weinandy, pp. 102–18. See also Thomas V. Morris, *The Logic of God Incarnate* (Ithaca, NY: Cornell University Press, 1986), 90–101.

[10] The following is only the thinnest sketch of the argument of *Cur Deus Homo* and does not come close to capturing the richness and complexity of the actual work.

[11] *Cur Deus Homo* (hereafter CDH) Book I, Chapter 3 (hereafter noted as 1.3), 268. Page numbers refer to the recent translation, *Anselm of Canterbury: The Major Works*, ed. Brian Davies and G. R. Evans (Oxford: Oxford University Press, 1998), though translations will be my own from the critical edition of Anselm's *Opera Omnia* by F. S. Schmitt.

[12] CDH 1.6: 270–71.

[13] CDH Preface: 261–62.

to allow a number of assumptions. First, there is a God such as we have described. The Jews and Muslims of Anselm's day would likely have been willing to grant that assumption. Secondly, the God of classical theism must do the best with the assumption that there is a best to do.[14] Anselm explains that if some action seems the least bit inappropriate, it cannot be attributed to God. And if we have the least reason to think that one action is preferable to another, so long as it is not overridden by another reason to the contrary, then we should conclude that that is the action God will – indeed *must* – take.[15] Yet another assumption, which would have been widely accepted by Christians and non-Christians alike, was that God made man for happiness. We do desire happiness and God would not have created in us a desire which was not to be fulfilled. God will not abandon the work he has begun and so he will see to it that we may arrive at everlasting happiness.[16]

However, we now come to a related assumption that Anselm's Jewish and Muslim readers may not accept. Anselm holds that we do not deserve to be happy and indeed *cannot* be happy in our current state because of sin.[17] He seems to assume the doctrine of Original Sin, the view that at the dawn of human history our first parents turned against God in a way that has infected all of us. This strikes me as an extremely plausible claim looking at the empirical evidence, but it is not one Jews and Muslims need embrace. However, one who denied Original Sin might still be persuaded that we are all, in fact, sinful and cut off from God, and that is probably enough for Anselm's argument to proceed.

With these assumptions in mind, Anselm argues that it is the nature of sin to "rob" God of his honor. In order for human beings to reach happiness, they must make some sort of restitution or payment to God.[18] The interlocutor, Boso, asks the obvious question: Why can't God simply forgive the sin and make us happy? He's omnipotent, after all. Anselm responds with two arguments. First, to simply forgive the sin, without recompense, would be to treat the sinful in the same way as the sinless, which is injustice. God, as the source and absolute standard of justice, cannot engage in the least injustice. Were he, *per impossibile*, to do

---

[14] According to Anselm, divine freedom does not require open options. See Chapter 10 of my *Anselm on Freedom*.

[15] CDH 1.10: 282.

[16] CDH 2.1: 315–16.

[17] CDH 1.10: 282.

[18] CDH 1.11: 282–83.

so, the entire moral order would be destroyed.[19] Further, it is better for human beings that they be permitted to make payment for the sin. Recognizing the sin and the injustice of failure to make recompense, man will either want to pay for it or not. If he does not, then he is unjust and should not and cannot be happy. But if he wants to make payment and there is no way for him to do so, he still cannot be happy.[20] The best, then, is that God should not simply forgive sin, but rather should provide some way for mankind to repay the debt.

But the debt is *enormous* and must be counterbalanced by a payment of equal or even greater value.[21] The debt is so huge that only God can pay it. And yet it is man who owes the debt. Hence the necessity for a God-man.[22] But not just any God-man will do. Anselm is very explicit that the unity which allows Christ to pay the debt for us all is the unity of a literal, biological *family*. On Anselm's understanding, the oneness of a biological family is something *real*, and the only one who can pay the debt must be descended from Adam. And that explains the need for all the biological mess which so worried those for whom Anselm was writing, and which also concerned those subscribing to a number of the pre-Chalcedonian heresies.[23] (Just how, in Anselm's view, Christ's death pays our debt for sin, and how human freedom is factored in, is a complex story which need not be told here since it is not central to the Chalcedonian claim.[24]) He sums up his Chalcedonian conclusion this way:

> If we should say that these two intact natures are joined in some way so that the human is one thing and the divine another, and it is not the same thing which is God that is man, it is impossible that the two should do what must be done. For God will not do it, because He ought not [He is not the one in debt], and man will not do it because he is not able to. So in order that it should be done by a God-man, it is necessary that one and the same be perfectly God and perfectly man, who can make this payment, because only true God is able to do it, but only true man ought to do it. Because, therefore, it is necessary that a God-man be found in whom the integrity of the two natures is preserved, it

---

[19] CDH 1.12–13: 284–87; 23: 309; 24: 311.

[20] CDH 1.24: 312.

[21] CDH 1.21: 305–07.

[22] CDH 1.25: 313.

[23] See my "Christ Our Brother: The Importance of Family in Anselm's Thought," in *Saint Anselm: A Legacy of 900 Years*, ed. Ralph McInerny and John Fortin O.S.B. (Notre Dame, IN: Notre Dame Press, forthcoming).

[24] CDH 2.18–19 explain how Christ's death may function as the payment for the debt.

is not less necessary that these two intact natures should come together in one person...[25]

A VIDEO-GAME ANALOGY

Anselm takes it that he has shown the Chalcedonian understanding of the Incarnation to be, in some sense, necessary. But the philosophical difficulty is just beginning. Is it really possible that one person should be both God and man? How, for example, could the same person be both mortal and immortal? Anselm himself does not address this question at much length, and he tends to follow the line set out by Pope Leo the Great, whose views were ratified at Chalcedon.[26] We can attribute a property to Christ because of his divine nature that we would deny to human nature, and vice versa, or even attribute contrary properties to the two natures. For example, as Anselm puts it, Christ is mortal according to (*secundum*) his human nature, immortal according to his divine nature.[27] Today, this approach is sometimes referred to as the *qua* move, in that it attributes a property to Christ *qua* God, and a different, perhaps even contrary, property to Christ *qua* man. But how could a single, unified *person* possess contrary properties? For example, if Christ is one person, must we not say that he is either omniscient or not?[28]

This is an extremely difficult issue that has exercised theologians for centuries. We must suppose the Council of Chalcedon intended the Greek term we translate as "person" (Latinized as *prosoperon*) to refer to a being that is unified, yet not *so* unified as not to admit two natures. In addition, the Word is a person, with or without the added human nature, whereas the human nature *per se* is not a person and does not exist except as assumed by the Word. Much has been written on how this might work, and contemporary philosophers have contributed to the discussion, introducing some interesting analogies for the union of God and man in Christ. However, contemporary analogies often fail to recognize that God and man exist in different orders of being, and this is important for understanding the *qua* move. God is the absolute source of all. He is not just another thing among things. He is not a citizen of the created universe but its author and sustainer from moment

---

[25] CDH 2.7: 321 (p. 102, lines 11–21 in the Schmitt edition).
[26] Sermon XLVI in *Letters and Sermons*.
[27] CDH 1.8: 275.
[28] Thomas Senor raises the issue this way in "The Compositional Account of the Incarnation," *Faith and Philosophy* 24 (2007): 52–71.

to moment.[29] Early Christian thought was imbued with Neoplaton-
ism, and the Neoplatonic way of stating this would be to talk about
degrees of existence (with some capitalization). God is the Really Real,
the Truly Existent. Our world is just the barest reflection or image of the
Creator.

Here I would like to propose an analogy that points to the importance of the difference in orders in a way that often has been lacking in
the contemporary discussion.[30] Say that there is a fifteen-year-old boy,
Nick, playing a character in a video game. Here, Nick is (very distantly!)
analogous to the Word, the Second Person of the Trinity, who becomes
Incarnate. We will refer to Nick when he's playing this particular character in this particular game as "Nick Playing." I propose that Nick
Playing is analogous to the Word assuming human nature and becoming
Incarnate. So Nick Playing is analogous to Christ.

In this game, the character Nick plays does not preexist, but rather is
made by Nick as he starts to play. Say that Nick is playing a human character named Nick in the game. Call him Virtual Nick. Virtual Nick, the
two-dimensional image on the screen, is analogous to the human nature,
the human soul and body that the Word assumes. The ontological status
of Virtual Nick is a little tricky. He is not an independent individual,
even virtually in the game, because he has no existence at all except
as the character being played by Nick *while* Nick is playing. But this
is appropriate for the analogy. Jesus *is* the Christ, and not some human
individual apart from the Word Incarnate. The locution of "taking on"
or "assuming" could suggest that there is a preexistent individual thing
there to be assumed, but that is a mistake. The Word, the Second Person
of the Trinity, takes on human nature, not a human person.[31] Were there
any sense in which Jesus is an individual human being separate from the
Word, we'd be back with Nestorianism.

What I want to suggest is that Nick Playing is a unity of Nick
engaged in the activity of playing and Virtual Nick, and that this unity is
analogous to the unity of personhood ascribed to God and man in Christ.
Nick Playing involves something added to Nick, but Nick is a person,
and Nick Playing is the same person. Ordinary usage supports the claim
that there could be a unity between Nick and Virtual Nick. If I come

[29] Robert Sokolowski captures this important point in *The God of Faith and Reason*
(Notre Dame, IN: University of Notre Dame Press, 1982), and applies it to the Incarnation (pp. 36–40).

[30] Moviegoers may recognize some similarities between my analogy and the Disney film,
Tron (1982).

[31] Anselm, *De Incarnatione Verbi* 11.

home from work and see Nick in front of the television in the living room intent on his game I might ask, "Where are you?" If he were to respond, "In the living room," I'd think he was being a smart aleck. I'm expecting an answer more like, "Just outside Berlin in 1945." I might well ask, "Did you get killed?" Obviously I refer to the character that Nick is playing. But ordinary usage assumes the sort of unity that allows me to ask these questions of Nick.

Granted, Nick Playing may seem an odd sort of unity. It should be noted, though, that mereology, the study of the relationship of parts to wholes, including what constitutes individual objects, is incredibly difficult. There is no philosophical consensus even on ordinary things such as living bodies and cell phones. Nick Playing is not much odder a unity than that we ascribe to other things we more commonly take to be unified.[32] One thing that does set the unity of Nick Playing apart from the unity of, say, a living body or a cell phone (assuming there is some unity there) is that the "parts" of Nick Playing exist on two very different levels. There is Nick, who would be the same fifteen-year-old boy whether or not he was "part" of Nick Playing, and then there is Virtual Nick, who would not exist at all if he were not "part" of Nick Playing. A Neoplatonist considering Nick Playing would say that Nick is far more *real* than Virtual Nick. He is a three-dimensional citizen of a three-dimensional world. He has a history and life that extend far beyond the minimal, wholly Nick-dependent existence enjoyed by Virtual Nick. They inhabit different orders of being. This is an advantage of Nick Playing as an analogy for God Incarnate because it points to the – much vaster – difference between God and creation. It is this difference in orders that allows for the unity of Nick Playing. If Nick and his friend D. J. are side by side in the living room, there seems to be an irreducible twoness about them. If Virtual Nick is teamed up with Virtual D. J. in the game, then we have a two-character team. But the relationship of Nick to Virtual Nick, which requires that they occupy very different orders of being, allows that, although Nick and Virtual Nick can be distinguished, we may still ascribe unity to Nick Playing. (Some mereological theories would have it that there can be a Nick-and-D.J. object that is sufficiently unified to be considered one thing. If

---

[32] Here, I am assuming a whole-part analysis of Christ and His human nature. An alternative is to see the human nature more as a quality of the whole. The medieval debates over these two approaches insist that neither of them is more than an analogy. An in-depth discussion of this issue can be found in Richard Cross, *The Metaphysics of the Incarnation: Thomas Aquinas to Duns Scotus* (Oxford: Oxford University Press, 2002).

so, that counts in favor of my analogy, because Nick Playing certainly seems a *more* unified thing than Nick and D.J.)

The analogy helps underscore the mistake in the kenotic approach. Nick does not "empty himself" and become lesser in order to become Nick Playing. Nick does not need to try to "fit into" the virtual world at all. His presence there as joined to Virtual Nick does not crowd out or displace anything. Presumably, if he gave up some of his essential abilities and properties – if he became two-dimensional, for example – he would not be able to play Virtual Nick at all. There is no hint of Nestorianism. That Nick is real, and that Virtual Nick is also real, though with a much "thinner" and completely dependent reality, does not destroy the unity of Nick Playing. However, certainly, there is no danger of Monophysitism. Intent though he may be on his game, there is no danger of Nick and Virtual Nick merging into some third, half-virtual being.

As long as the unity of Nick Playing is allowed, I think this analogy can help defend and clarify the *qua* move. The question is: Must we say that Christ is, for example, either omniscient or not-omniscient? Or can he be omniscient *qua* God and not-omniscient *qua* man? For our analogy, we can discuss a Nick-property related to knowledge. Nick has Internet access. Nick's game is set in the 1940s. No character in the game, *qua* character in the game, has Internet access. There is no Internet, not even a virtual Internet, in this virtual world. Now suppose that Virtual Nick gets into trouble. Nick can't figure out what to do. He knows there's a way out of the predicament, but he can't seem to come up with it. When all else fails, you go to the Internet and consult a Strategy Guide that can tell you that you need to push the third brick above the trash barrel, and the trap door will open. Nick is extremely deft and can play a video game and consult the Internet simultaneously, so Nick Playing has access to the Internet. That means that Virtual Nick "knows" to push the third brick above the trash barrel. We can say that Virtual Nick has access to the Internet. But Virtual Nick has this property only as "part" of Nick Playing, and only because Nick can access the Internet. It is correct to say that Nick Playing *qua* human boy has access to the Internet, whereas Nick Playing *qua* virtual character does not have access to the Internet. If the other characters in the game are NPCs (nonplayable characters), then none of them has or could ever have Internet access in any sense. Again, Virtual Berlin in 1945 just doesn't get the Internet. Still, it is correct to say that Virtual Nick does have Internet access. That's how he "knew" to push that third brick. Analogously, Anselm holds that it is correct to say that Christ is omniscient. He was omniscient even in the womb. But his omniscience comes from being the Word, not from being human.[33]

On the other hand, we can attribute to Nick Playing certain attributes associated with Virtual Nick. As I mentioned earlier, ordinary usage would allow me to ask Nick whether or not "he" had been killed. We might say that Nick Playing has been killed, while the actual boy, Nick, is fine. It is only Virtual Nick who has been killed within the game. Nick Playing has experienced virtual death, but only *qua* Virtual Nick. Nick, the living boy existing outside the video game, does not and could not possibly experience virtual death. Only video-game characters die virtual deaths. Analogously, the Word as divine does not suffer pain or hunger or death. Yet we say that Christ, the Word assuming human nature, suffers pain and hunger and death. The *qua* move allows us to hold that Christ, the Person, experiences suffering and death, but only in his human nature.

Needless to say, the analogy here is radically distant from the Incarnation, and I would like to conclude by noting some of the disanalogies. In proposing analogies, we make progress by appreciating differences as well as by seeing similarities. One obvious disanalogy is that Nick is not the creator of the virtual world inhabited by Virtual Nick. Even if Nick were the designer of the video game, he would not be a creator in the way God is. Nick might take preexistent elements and rearrange them into this particular game, but rearranging is all any created "creator" ever does. This would be the case even if, *per impossibile*, Nick were to make the game and keep it in existence just by wishing. He would still be dealing with properties, things, and natures, that preexist. Even if Nick wishes a material brick wall into being, the materialness, the brickness, and the wallness already exist independently of him. This would be a pretty amazing feat, but it would not be creation as God does it. God is an absolute Creator in a way that Nick could not be. This means that there is an even greater ontological distance between God and human nature than between Nick and Virtual Nick. That, in turn, may suggest that "adding" human nature to the Word entails even less multiplicity than adding Virtual Nick to Nick.

A second disanalogy is that, as I described Virtual Nick, he does not have an intellect or a will. He is a two-dimensional image. The Chalcedonian understanding was that, in taking on human nature, the Word, already a person with will and intellect, adopted a human soul with its will and intellect, along with the human body. Now it might

---

[33] CDH 13.

seem that Christ's consciousness is getting a bit crowded with two wills and two intellects. Would the two wills make conflicting choices? Would the divine intellect know things the human intellect did not? Some Scriptural passages might suggest this, in which case it is difficult to see how Nestorianism is to be avoided. Anselm's solution is to insist that, although Christ has a human intellect and will, these are *Christ's* human intellect and will. Christ, the Word Incarnate, is omniscient and necessarily good. The human soul and body are "part" of Christ and so are omniscient and necessarily good – not *qua* human, but as "part" of Christ. Divine omniscience does not exactly need to "fit" into Christ's human brain, any more than Nick's Internet access needs to "fit" into Virtual Nick, the two-dimensional video image.

I do think a problem remains, though, with the question of how Christ's human nature is "joined" to the Word. Nick is simply manipulating Virtual Nick. The Word is not just the manipulator for Christ's humanity. The Word is really *being* Christ. He has entered more fully into creation than Nick can enter into the video game. The "joining" of Nick and Virtual Nick in Nick Playing does not really adequately capture the closeness of the "joining" that must be involved in the Incarnation. I did warn at the beginning that the Incarnation is a mystery. Anselm believes he has proven that the Incarnation must happen, and it must happen under the Chalcedonian description. I hope, with my video-game analogy, to suggest that it does not necessarily entail any obvious contradictions. That is, the *qua* move, whereby Christ can be said to be one thing *qua* divine, and its contrary *qua* human, allows us to analyze Chalcedonian Christology in a way that avoids contradiction. If we cannot fully understand *how* the Incarnation happens, even with analogies drawn from our most up-to-date technology, we should not be surprised or dismayed. A being whose greatness did *not* exceed our capacities would hardly be God, after all.

8 Resurrection

STEPHEN T. DAVIS

I. THE CHRISTIAN VIEW OF RESURRECTION

Resurrection is the notion that after death our bodies will disintegrate but at some future point God will miraculously raise them from the ground and reconstitute us as persons. Christians believe that resurrection comes in two stages. The first stage is the Resurrection of Jesus; the second (the "general resurrection") is the resurrection of all dead human beings (Acts 24:15).

The Christian view of resurrection is based on four assumptions. (1) The existence of a God who has the ability and the intention to raise the dead. (2) The miraculous nature of resurrections; they occur only because God makes them occur. Human persons do not naturally live after death. (3) The existence after death of embodied persons. Resurrection is not an immaterial existence in a world of pure mind or spirit.[1] Raised bodies will be changed (transformed, glorified, made fit for the kingdom of God) but are bodies nonetheless. (4) The identity of those persons with the persons who lived previously. The one who will be raised is the same person as the one who died, not a replica or a "closest continuer."

II. JESUS' RESURRECTION

The Resurrection of Jesus Christ on Easter morning is taken by Christians as the model and guarantee ("first fruits") of the general resurrection (see Rom. 8:11; I Cor. 15:20, 23; Phil. 3:20–21). Accordingly, the ability of Christians to defend the plausibility of the general resurrection depends, in part, on their ability to defend the plausibility of the Resurrection of Jesus. Four main views on the Resurrection are current today. All of the following theories have their contemporary defenders in Christian circles, although the first is not advocated by any scholars.

---

[1] As is envisioned in H. H. Price's "Survival and the Idea of Another World," *Proceedings of the Society for Psychical Research*, 50 (1953), 1–15.

1. *Bodily Resuscitation.* This theory affirms that Jesus was, indeed, genuinely dead and later genuinely alive and that the tomb in which Jesus was buried was empty. Jesus' body was restored in the Resurrection to its old condition of life. Jesus' raised body, in all important respects, had the same properties as his premortem body. The Resurrection, in effect, continued his once-interrupted life. Interestingly, this theory is frequently attacked by critics, but it is difficult to find examples of scholars who defend it. This doubtless is because the New Testament does not support it. There are, indeed, resuscitations in the New Testament (for example, the raising of Lazarus), but the idea is not that Jesus was restored to his old manner of life, only inevitably to die again at some time later. Rather, Jesus was raised in a transformed body to a new and exalted condition of life, never to die again.

2. *Bodily Transformation.* This theory likewise affirms that Jesus was genuinely dead and later genuinely alive and that the tomb was empty. However, it denies that Jesus was resuscitated. When he was raised, his earthly body was transformed into a new "glorified" body that was, indeed, physical but possessed strange new properties as well. There was material continuity between the old body and the new body; the first was changed into or became the second. However, the new body no longer was bound by at least certain of the laws of nature, as was the old body.

3. *Spiritual Resurrection.* This theory also affirms that Jesus was genuinely dead and later genuinely alive, but it is not committed to holding that the tomb was empty. What was raised, on this view, was Jesus' spirit or soul or self, quite apart from his body. His bones doubtless decomposed long ago in Palestine – so its defenders can say – but nevertheless he lives.[2] The theory is motivated by doubts about bodily resurrection, as well as by a nonbodily reading of I Corinthians 15. The concept of spiritual resurrection can be interpreted variously, and one problem is that friends of the theory almost never discuss the mind-body problem. Perhaps the most natural interpretation is to view the theory in terms of Platonic or Cartesian mind-body dualism: Jesus' body permanently died but his soul lives forever. But the problem with that idea is that many contemporary scholars don't think that classical mind-body dualism corresponds to the Bible's view of human nature.[3]

[2] See Hans Küng, *On Being a Christian*, trans. Edward Quinn (New York: Pocket Books, 1976), 351.

[3] For a work that does list such scholars, see John Cooper, *Body, Soul, and Life Everlasting: Biblical Anthropology and the Monism – Dualism Debate*, new edition (Grand Rapids, MI: Eerdmans, 2000).

4. *Reductive Resurrection Theories.* These sorts of theories affirm that Jesus genuinely died but deny that he was later genuinely alive; accordingly, no claim is made about the tomb being empty. The Resurrection appearances are explained psychologically, in terms of the disciples' inner states of mind. They are classified as visions or even hallucinations. The Resurrection was something that happened to the disciples, not Jesus. What the Easter affirmation, "Jesus is risen," really means is _____, where the blank is filled in with something like, "The cross of Jesus still saves people today" or "Jesus' work in the world goes on" or "The source of my faith is Jesus." These theories can be called reductive because they deny that the dead Jesus lived again.[4]

III. RECENT SCHOLARSHIP ON JESUS' RESURRECTION

Christian scholars have written notable works on the Resurrection of Jesus in recent years. Among them are New Testament scholar N. T. Wright[5] and philosopher of religion Richard Swinburne.[6] Both are defenders of what we are calling bodily transformation.

Wright sees his book as an exercise in ground-clearing (xvii, 717); he contests crucial claims of historical-critical scholars who defend either spiritual resurrection or reductive theories. For example, he challenges theories that claim that: (1) Exaltation talk (and perhaps ascension talk) antedated resurrection talk in the early church, and that the latter is simply an elaboration of the former (pp. 227, 233, 455, 573, 625). (2) By the "Resurrection of Jesus" the New Testament church meant only that Jesus was now present with God in some nonbodily sense (pp. 322, 330). (3) The general resurrection similarly meant that we will one day be present with God in some spiritual sense (p. 33). (4) Paul viewed the Resurrection as nonbodily (p. 247) or perhaps even as nonreal, merely symbolic (pp. 317–18). (5) The hypothetical document Q and the actual document of Thomas show that nonresurrectional Christian movements existed in the earliest times (pp. 429–34, 541, 547–51, 554–57). (6) There are several mutually inconsistent views of the Resurrection of Jesus to be found in the New Testament (p. 476). (7) Early Christian Resurrection talk was really a metaphorical way of talking about something else, such

---

[4] See, for example, Gerd Lüedemann, *The Resurrection of Jesus* (Minneapolis, MN: Fortress Press, 1994).

[5] N. T. Wright, *The Resurrection of the Son of God* (Minneapolis, MN: Fortress Press, 2003).

[6] Richard Swinburne, *The Resurrection of God Incarnate* (Oxford: Oxford University Press, 2003).

as the victory of the cross or the continuing influence of Jesus in our lives (pp. 646, 656–57, 666, 690–91).

Despite the length of Wright's book (some 738 pages) and the deep learning that it shows, the overall argument is disarmingly simple. It is something like this: The earliest Christians undoubtedly believed that God had raised Jesus from the dead. But where did this belief come from? The concept of resurrection existed in second-Temple Judaism, but the Christian view was so importantly different that it could not have generated spontaneously out of Judaism. The early Christians explained their belief by two facts: The tomb in which Jesus was buried was found to be empty and the resurrected Jesus appeared to many of them. Neither fact by itself could have generated Christian Resurrection belief: An empty tomb would have been a puzzle that could have been explained in any number of naturalistic ways and the appearances could have been explained as visions or hallucinations. Moreover, the skeptical explanations of what happened after the death and burial of Jesus and of early Christian belief in the Resurrection of Jesus – from Celsus to Crossan – are entirely unconvincing. Accordingly, Wright concludes that there is a high degree of historical probability that Jesus really was raised from the dead.

One possible objection to Wright's argument concerns metaphysical world views. Let us define two of them: *Naturalism*, let us say, is the theory that holds that physical matter is all that there is, that the physical universe in some form has always existed, that true natural laws are never violated, and that, accordingly, every event can, in principle, be explained by methods similar to those used in the natural sciences. *Supernaturalism* is the theory that holds that something else besides physical matter exists – *viz.* God – that the universe, with its natural laws, exists because God brought it into existence, that God has the power and occasionally the intention to set aside natural laws and bring about events that would not otherwise have occurred, and that, accordingly, not every event can be explained by scientific methods.

Wright recognizes the importance of worldviews to the issue of resurrection, but he does not factor in the question of which worldview his reader is committed to. The sorts of arguments that Wright cites in favor of the Resurrection may be convincing for supernaturalists. For such people, perhaps he is right that the probability that God raised Jesus from the dead is so high as to amount to virtual certainty (p. 710). However, for someone who is committed to naturalism, the conclusion does not follow. Such a person can always respond: "I do not know what happened after Jesus' crucifixion and burial – it was, after all, long ago – but I am sure that it was not a resurrection because dead people stay dead." Such a person will assess the probabilities quite differently than Wright does.

Wright's basic strategy in the book is an argument to the best explanation (see p. 706). He is right that most of the skeptical theories about what happened immediately after Jesus' death are feeble. However, the way in which one assesses the probabilities will always be a partial function of what worldview one accepts. So unless naturalism can be defeated, the "I don't know what happened" position seems to be rational.

Despite this point, one must conclude by lauding Wright's achievement. *The Resurrection of the Son of God* is comprehensive, authoritative, and, in its basic argument, convincing. It doubtless will be the standard work about the Resurrection of Jesus among biblical scholars for years to come.

In *The Resurrection of God Incarnate*, Richard Swinburne applies the methods of analytic philosophy of religion to the question of the believability of the Resurrection of Jesus. He holds that it is, indeed, believable, and he uses arguments from the probability calculus to reach that conclusion. It is important to note that the argument of the book is an exercise in natural theology; he argues entirely on historical-critical and probabilistic grounds. With his usual sagacity and common sense, Swinburne covers ground that has been covered by other apologists for the Resurrection – for example, the probability of theism, the possibility of miracles, and the believability of the New Testament empty tomb and appearance traditions. Swinburne, however, brings new insights to bear on the debate as well.

Two of them especially deserve mention. The first, as noted, is his use of the probability calculus, and especially Bayes' theorem. Swinburne helpfully explains for nonphilosophical readers how probability arguments work, and only gets into technicalities in a brief Appendix. The notion from Bayes' theorem that is crucial here is the idea that a given hypothesis h is probable if the evidence that we encounter is what we would expect to encounter if h were true. Swinburne wields this principle effectively.

The second is the fact that Swinburne ties together the Resurrection and the Incarnation. He believes that the case that God raised Jesus is strengthened by the claim that Jesus was God Incarnate, as is the case that Jesus was God Incarnate if God raised him. The two notions are mutually supportive. This is because – as Swinburne argues – if Jesus was indeed God Incarnate, we would expect God to validate his person and ministry ("put his signature" on Jesus). In other words, if some person were indeed God Incarnate, we would expect certain minimal things from him. We would expect him to lead a morally perfect life, to reveal to us otherwise unknowable truths, to make atonement for our sins, to be vindicated by God by some sort of "super miracle" like raising him from the dead, and to found an institution the purpose of which is to pass on his teachings to future generations. Jesus Christ – so Swinburne argues – satisfies these criteria. Indeed, he is the *only* candidate that we know of in human history who has done so.

The book's central conclusion is that, based on background evidence and the historical evidence, it is "probable that there is indeed a God who became incarnate in Jesus Christ and [raised him] from the dead on the first Easter morning" (p. 5). Although *The Resurrection of God Incarnate* amounts to a powerful argument, there are a few sunspots.

First, Swinburne argues that Jesus lived "a perfect life" (see pp. 83–91). This is so that he could provide for us an example of how life is to be lived and so that his life could be offered as reparation for our sins. However, on historical-critical grounds alone, we are not able to demonstrate this point. Christians certainly accept that Jesus lived a perfect life, but they do so on the authority of Scripture rather than on historical-critical grounds (see II Cor. 5:21; Heb. 4:15; 5:8–9; 7:26–28). We do find evidence in the gospels that Jesus resisted temptation, cared lovingly for the welfare of others, and was obedient to the divine will. He certainly lived, as Swinburne claims, "a good and holy life" (p. 89). But did he lead a "sinless" and "perfect" life? To argue as much seems to go beyond the evidence.

Second, at the end of the book, in a long footnote, Swinburne replies to an objection from Alvin Plantinga. This is the problem of "dwindling probabilities" that plagues any inductive argument that amounts to a long chain of probabilistic inference. Suppose we argue for a hypothesis h as follows: "p therefore very probably q, q therefore very probably r, r therefore very probably s, and s therefore very probably h." Now, if the probabilities are all extremely high, this could be a powerful argument for h. However, because at each step in the argument the probabilities must be multiplied and thus will diminish, the final conclusion may, indeed, be that h is *im*probable. Swinburne recognizes that this point could constitute a serious challenge, but it is not clear that his reply is satisfactory.

He notes first that the numbers might remain high throughout the argument (say, around 0.9 for each item in the chain), in which case the probability of h might still end up higher than the probability of *not-h*.

Second, he points out that there might be other routes to *h* than via the argument that he deploys, and that the case for *h* would be strengthened if other routes also tended to confirm *h*. Both these points are certainly true. As to the first point, however, it seems dubious in this case that the numbers will be high enough throughout the argument – given the fact of diminishing probabilities – to sustain a probability of greater than 0.5 for the Christian Resurrection claim. Certainly Swinburne has made a probable case for most of his various subconclusions. But do they possess a probability high enough to sustain the probability of 0.97 that Swinburne estimates for his overall conclusion (p. 214)? As to the second point, Swinburne is correct that other routes might be found for supporting the Resurrection of Jesus, but he does not mention what they might be.

Despite these points, *The Resurrection of God Incarnate* is an excellent and ground-breaking book, very much up to Swinburne's usual high standards. This book introduces new and important issues into the debate about the Resurrection of Jesus.

IV. THE GENERAL RESURRECTION

Let us turn to the general resurrection. This item has been discussed throughout Christian history, but contemporary Christian philosophers have suggested several interesting theories about the physics and metaphysics of resurrection. We will consider several issues that have divided Christian interpreters of the resurrection.

The Patristic Theory and the Modern Theory. The church fathers, along with many other theologians (for example, Aquinas), assume that our resurrection bodies will consist of the same stuff – that is, the same molecules or atoms (we will simply speak of particles) – as did our premortem bodies. We can call this notion the Patristic theory (it is also called the reassembly model). Only if God reassembles the very particles of which my body once consisted will the raised person be me. Otherwise, it will be a replica of me, where a "replica of me" is a person who is indistinguishable from me but, as a *de novo* creation, does not have my history and is not me.

Some contemporary thinkers have challenged this notion (we can call their idea the "modern theory").[7] They deny that sameness of matter is necessary to personal identity. Even if we allow that some of my bodily

---

[7] See John Hick, *Death and Eternal Life* (New York: Harper and Row, 1976), 186.

particles will endure until the time of the general resurrection, why insist that God must collect and reassemble them? As long as the particles of the raised person's body are configured in precisely the old way – so modern theorists hold – God can use entirely new matter. Moreover, even Aquinas assumed that my soul will be me and not a replica of me during the interim period between my death and my resurrection – that is, without any bodily particles at all. Thus, the soul alone – so he must have held – can guarantee personal identity. If that is true, why insist on the original bodily particles? It may be true that the soul is not the whole person and that the whole person, body plus soul, must (eventually) be raised. Still, doesn't my soul entail my existence?

This does not rule out the Patristic theory, however. It is possible to argue that when I die, my soul will be me during the interim period but that it will no longer be me if my soul in the eschaton animates a body consisting of entirely new matter, even if that body is qualitatively indistinguishable from the old one. (Perhaps an essential property of my soul is that it can only animate a body made of *these* particles.) Moreover, although it is true that the particles of our body are replaced during normal earthly life, perhaps gradual and causally regular replacement of particles is consistent with personal identity whereas sudden all-at-once replacement of them is not. Finally, a theological reason can be given in favor of the Patristic theory – it seems to be the most natural reading of Paul's argument in I Corinthians 15. He seems to suggest that the old body *becomes* or *changes into* the new body rather than being replaced by it, just as a seed (to use his simile) changes into a plant. Accordingly, just as there is material continuity between the seed and the plant, so there is material continuity between the old body and the new.

Still, it is not hard to see why the modern theory is attractive. Many contemporary Christians hold that the Patristic theory is scientifically outmoded and hard to accept; the idea that, in order to raise me, God must locate and collect the particles of which my earthly body once consisted seems to many to be absurd. In addition, as we have seen, personal identity does not seem to require the old particles.

Moreover, two serious objections have been raised against the Patristic theory, the first venerable and the other contemporary.

1. *The cannibal objection.* Suppose I die, a cannibal eats part of my corpse, and then he dies. Suppose further that God wants to resurrect both of us. It seems that God cannot do so. Some of the particles of which my body consisted at death are also particles of which the cannibal's body

existed at his death. Which resurrected person gets these shared particles, the cannibal or me? Because there is no principled way of deciding this question – so the objection goes – resurrection is impossible.

Surely this is a premature conclusion. What is required is merely that God follow some identity-preserving policy for what to do with the shared particles. Augustine, for example, made the interesting suggestion that the *first* person who possessed the shared particles will get them in the eschaton; God presumably will use new particles to fill in the empty spaces in the body of the one who got them later.[8] Because this and other potential policies seem quite possible, the cannibalism objection does not appear to be a serious threat to the Patristic theory.

2. *Van Inwagen's objection.* Peter van Inwagen objects to the Patristic theory in this way: What if God, here and now, in the presence of van Inwagen, the adult philosopher, brings into being a replica of van Inwagen's ten-year-old self, using only particles that were part of the ten-year-old's body but are not part of the adult philosopher's present body? Which person would be van Inwagen? Surely each could truthfully say, "I am van Inwagen."[9]

But in reply, there is a principled reason for holding that the adult philosopher is van Inwagen and that the ten-year-old is the imposter. The adult philosopher has a regular and predictable causal relationship with all previous temporal parts of van Inwagen whereas the child is, if we may put it this way, the result of a trick performed by God. Surely resurrection has always meant the continuation of the life of the person at the psychological stage that that person had reached at death. Theologians do not seriously claim that those who die at, say, age seventy, are resurrected with the personality, memories, beliefs, and levels of knowledge that they had at age ten, with sixty years of experience and memory simply wiped out. This same point can doubtless be made about the body. Perhaps damaged bodies will be repaired and they will certainly be glorified, but Jesus (the promise and model of the general resurrection) was not raised as a younger version of himself. So resurrection means the continuation of the bodily existence of the person who has died at the physiological state reached at death. Accordingly, van Inwagen's objection does not appear to refute the Patristic theory.

[8] Augustine, *The Enchiridion on Faith, Hope, and Love* (Chicago, IL: Henry Regnery, 1961), bk. 88. See also Augustine, *The City of God* (Garden City, NY: Doubleday, 1958), 22.20.

[9] Peter van Inwagen, "The Possibility of Resurrection," in *Immortality*, ed. Paul Edwards (New York: Macmillan, 1992), 242–46.

V. MATERIALIST THEORIES OF GENERAL RESURRECTION

Dualism versus materialism. The majority report of Christian theologians throughout history is a view of resurrection based on metaphysical dualism. In the contemporary scene, however, several Christian philosophers reject mind-body dualism and present theories of resurrection based on materialist notions of human persons. They claim either that human beings are identical to their bodies or are at least essentially constituted by their bodies.

In Christian thought, resurrection has had a complicated relationship with the theory known as the immortality of the soul. One common notion is based on mind-body dualism, which says: (1) human beings consist of physical bodies and immaterial souls; (2) the soul is the essence of the person; and (3) although united with a body in this life, the soul can exist apart from the body. Many Christian theologians from the second century onward combined resurrection and immortality in a view that we can call temporary disembodiment. The basic idea is this: When I die, my body decays but I continue to exist; for an interim time I exist in the presence of God as a disembodied soul; then at some time in the future, God will miraculously raise my body, reunite it with my soul, and reconstitute me as a whole and complete person.

This theory allows a neat way to harmonize Jesus' statement to the good thief on the cross, *"Today* you will be with me in paradise" (Luke 23:43) with the Pauline notion that the general resurrection only occurs in the last days (I Cor. 15:20–26).[10] The idea is that during the interim period when I exist as a disembodied soul, I can engage in purely mental activities such as thinking, believing, remembering, hoping, and so on, but cannot engage in bodily activities such as talking, eating, or walking. This is accordingly taken to be a highly attenuated type of existence. Full and complete human existence will only be possible when my soul and body are reunited in the general resurrection. Temporary disembodiment also avoids any temporal gap in the existence of persons – that is, a period when they do not exist.

Despite this point, resurrection and immortality are quite different notions. First, resurrection need not be based on dualism, although, as we have just seen, it often is. Second, immortality holds that survival of death is a natural property of souls, whereas resurrection entails that death would mean permanent annihilation except for the miraculous

---

[10] For a classic statement of temporary disembodiment, see Thomas Aquinas, *Summa Contra Gentiles* (Notre Dame, IN: Notre Dame University Press, 1975), 4.79.11.

intervention of God. Third, as noted, many theologians hold that classical mind-body dualism is not the biblical understanding of human beings.[11] Scripture, they say, understands human beings to be psychophysical entities – that is, as unities of body and soul. Perhaps the soul is, in some sense, separable from the body (II Cor. 5:6–8; 12:2–3; Phil. 1:21–23) but true and complete human existence is as a unity of body and soul.

Influenced by these points and others, several Christian philosophers have recently developed theories of resurrection based on physicalism. Of course, no Christian can embrace metaphysical materialism (the view that physical matter is all that exists), because God is a nonphysical being (John 4:24). However, the idea that human beings can exhaustively be described in materialistic terms is attractive to some Christian philosophers.[12] There are two main ways to understand the general resurrection in materialist terms.

We can call the first temporary nonexistence.[13] The theory holds that, at death, human beings simply cease existing; then later, at the general resurrection, God reassembles bodily particles, configures them in the right way, revives the reconstituted body, and thus raises the person from the dead. However, this theory has seldom been held in Christian history. Overall, the Bible does not support it (see Heb. 12:23 and Rev. 6:9–11, where "spirits" seem to be conscious after death). Moreover, some Christian philosophers hold that the temporal gap that is an essential aspect of the theory makes the problem of personal identity intractable.

We can call the second materialist theory of the general resurrection immediate resurrection. In this theory, people live and then die, but at the moment of death, God raises their bodies and reconstitutes them as persons. Because there is no temporal gap to contend with, the problem of personal identity is less intractable. However, the continuing presence of the corpse (in the grave or in the form of ashes) presents a new problem. If materialism is true, then I am identical to or essentially constituted by my body, but when I die it seems that I am simply my corpse. Accordingly, any new Stephen Davis-like body will not be me

---

[11] See, for example, Oscar Cullmann, "Immortality of the Soul or Resurrection of the Dead?" in *Immortality*, ed. Terence Penelhum (Belmont, CA: Wadsworth, 1973).

[12] See, for example, the essays collected in Part III of *Soul, Body, and Survival*, ed. Kevin Corcoran (Ithaca, NY: Cornell University Press, 2001).

[13] This theory is sometimes misleadingly called "soul sleep." The term is misleading because the soul as an immaterial essence plays no necessary role in the theory. Moreover, during the interim period the soul does not sleep – according to the theory, the person does not exist.

but a replica. Moreover, a biblical difficulty exists: Although there are a few texts that can be interpreted as supporting immediate resurrection (for example, Luke 23:43; II Cor. 5:1–10), the preponderance of New Testament testimony is that the general resurrection will occur at the eschaton.[14]

What then about the physics of immediate resurrection? There are at least three ways in which the envisioned event might occur. (1) At the point of death, God simply takes the particles of which one's body consists to the afterlife in the form of a resurrected heavenly body; simultaneously, God creates a simulacrum out of new atoms which then constitutes the corpse.[15] (2) At the point of death, God brings it about that the causal path traced by the particles of my body split into two qualitatively equal paths, one of which is then used by God to constitute my resurrection body and the other of which is used to constitute my corpse. (3) At the point of death, God reconstitutes me out of particles that were not parts of my body, and they exist as they do because they are immanently causally connected to the particles of my premortem body in a life-preserving way; they then constitute a continuation of my life.[16]

Such theories are ingenious and do, indeed, solve some of the philosophical problems incumbent on the idea of general resurrection. But if the Resurrection of Jesus is the model of the general resurrection, then perhaps these theories depart too far from that model. Of course, our resurrections will not be like Jesus' resurrection in all respects: He was raised soon after his death and we (or at least most of us) will not be; he was raised and reappeared for a time on earth and we will not; he was raised as the incarnate Son of God and we will not be. Still, as we read the Gospels, there was no simulacrum or body-splitting. This at least creates a presumption in favor of something like the Patristic theory: We will die, like Jesus, and some time later, like Jesus, God will raise our very bodies from the ground.

---

[14] These problems are dealt with in various ways by the friends of immediate resurrection. See Kevin Corcoran, "Physical Persons and Postmortem Survival without Temporal Gaps," in *Soul, Body, and Survival*, pp. 201–17. See also the essays in Part III of *Resurrection: Theological and Scientific Assessments*, ed. Ted Peters, Robert John Russell, and Michael Welker (Grand Rapids, MI: Eerdmans, 2002). See also Dean Zimmerman, "The Compatibility of Materialism and Survival: The 'Falling Elevator' Model," *Faith and Philosophy*, 16, no. 2 (April, 1999): 194–212.

[15] Van Inwagen, "The Possibility of Resurrection," 242–46.

[16] The second and third models are suggested by Kevin Corcoran in his "Physical Persons and Postmortem Survival without Temporal Gaps," in *Soul, Body, and Survival*, 201–17.

VI. THE DUPLICATION OBJECTION

However, a serious objection remains. It is a problem for all versions of resurrection. It is called *the duplication objection.*

Suppose there was a person X who died some time ago and suppose further that there is a Y in the afterlife who seems to be X raised from the dead. Now if it is possible for God to bring about a state of affairs in which X has survived death and is identical to Y, then, obviously, it is equally possible for God to bring about a state of affairs in which it seems that X is identical to two – or even two hundred – different Y-like people in the afterlife. That is, an all-powerful being could easily bring about the existence of two or two hundred virtually qualitatively indistinguishable candidates for X-hood in the resurrection world. But identity is a transitive and symmetric relation – if A is identical to B, and B is identical to C, then A is identical to C. So if X is identical to Y21 (one of the two hundred virtually qualitatively identical Ys in the resurrection world[17]), and if X is also identical to Y96 (another of them), then Y21 and Y96 (who exist simultaneously) are identical to each other, which is absurd. Because the survival thesis in this case would be absurd – so it is argued – it would be equally absurd in the first case, where there is only one candidate for X-hood.

Certainly the defender of resurrection can insist that God will allow no such scenario – if God wants to resurrect X, then, necessarily, God will allow there to exist only one plausible candidate for X-hood in the resurrection world, and that candidate will *be* X. That point seems correct, and does put to rest part of the problem. But the deeper issue concerns this claim (made originally by Bernard Williams[18]): The very logical possibility of the second sort of scenario makes any resurrection hypothesis untenable.

Perhaps this problem can be solved by considering the notion of the will of God. Christians believe that God is the creator of all contingent things. In fact, God not only created all contingent things but *sustains* or *upholds* them in being as long as they exist (Wis. 11:25; Acts 17:28; Col. 1:17; Heb. 1:3). Created things do not automatically or naturally endure in being. Apart from the constant preserving activity on God's part, contingent beings would lapse back into nonexistence. Contingent

---

[17] I say *virtually* qualitatively identical because their initial physical locations in the afterlife must surely be different. In addition, from that moment on, of course, they would have different experiences and thus different histories.

[18] Bernard Williams, "Personal Identity and Individuation," *Proceedings of the Aristotelian Society*, 76 (1956–1957): 332.

things continue to exist, and continue to exist as the things they are (with all their attributes and powers), only so long as God wills that they continue to exist. Everything is what it is because God wills it to be what it is. The world would be radically Heraclitean apart from the divine intention that it be stable and enduring. The will of God holds the world together and makes of it a cosmos rather than a churning chaos or even nothingness. This claim may be put in a metaphorical way: *The will of God is the glue of the world.*

Applied to resurrection, the claim is that Y is not X raised from the dead unless it is God's will that it be so.[19] This is a radical claim; theological concepts are rarely raised these days to help solve apparently purely philosophical problems. However, if the will of God is the glue of the world, then my continuing integrity through time as the person that I am is based not just on my own properties but also on the fact that God sustains and upholds me as the person I am. Both are necessary for my existence; neither is sufficient.

On this notion, perhaps the will of God is the "further fact" or "boundary line" that Derek Parfit says we need to resolve difficult cases of personal identity, but that he is unable to find.[20] The will of God makes human beings (contrary to Parfit's view) "separately existing entities"[21] and therefore renders personal identity (*pace* Parfit) a deep "further fact" that genuinely matters. It is quite true, as Parfit points out, that there are conceivable test cases in which personal identity seems indeterminate, in which the question, "Is Y the same person as X?" seems to have no principled answer. However, it cannot be the case that personal identity does not matter and that (as Parfit argues) what really matters is "psychological connectedness and/or continuity with the right kind of cause," where "the right kind of cause could be any cause."[22] What if there turns out to be psychological connectedness between me today and, some time after my death, a bar of soap? That is, suppose the future bar of soap will have my memories, will believe itself to be me, and will think and feel and opine the way I do. (Don't ask how this scenario could possibly occur: Parfit is the one who says that *any* sort of causation will do.) Would the future existence of this bar of soap be "nearly as good" to me as my survival? It hardly seems so.

[19] See R. T. Herbert, *Paradox and Identity in Theology* (Ithaca, NY: Cornell University Press, 1979), 150–55.

[20] *Reasons and Persons*, 210, 239, 242, 277–79.

[21] *Reasons and Persons*, 240.

[22] *Reasons and Persons*, 215.

Three possible misunderstandings must be cleared up. First, this thesis is not that in difficult personal identity cases, God investigates matters thoroughly, sees what the truth is (say, that Y is indeed a continuation of the life of X), and then wills accordingly. Rather, the claim is that the will of God is a constitutive factor in determining what the truth, in fact, is. To put the point baldly, what makes an apparent replica of X to be X is God's will that the apparent replica be X.

Second, this thesis does not entail any sort of pantheism or divine idealism. The doctrine of divine preservation of all contingent things does not deny the real existence of those things. They do exist – and exist as things separate from God. They are not illusions (as in the *maya* of Advaita Vedanta Hinduism) or parts of God (as in pantheism) or mere ideas in the mind of God (as in the philosophy of Berkeley). They have a reality of their own for as long as they exist.

Third, this thesis does not imply that God is the cause of everything that happens in the sense that whatever occurs – including that last sin that I committed – occurs because God causes it to occur. The idea is that God has chosen to create human beings with libertarian freedom and follows the policy of sustaining or preserving us even in our evil deeds, despite the fact that they are contrary to God's will.

VII. RESURRECTION AND THE ESCHATON

In recent years, a few theologians have begun to look at Christian eschatological claims in the light of what current science says about the universe's long-term future.[23] Some worry that Christian eschatological hopes for a supremely good future seem inconsistent with current cosmological theories about how the world will end. Perhaps the cosmos will "freeze" in eternal expansion or "fry" in a re-collapse into heat death. Both possibilities seem gloomy, hardly suggesting a limitlessly good end-state.

The first possibility is raised by Big Bang cosmology plus entropy. If the universe is a closed system, and if energy always flows from heat to cold, and if the Big Bang was the hottest moment in the history of the universe, then its future involves only further and further expansion and cooling. Entropy will increase to a point where the temperature of the cosmos asymptotically approaches absolute zero. The second possibility is raised by the specter of the total amount of matter in the universe, including dark matter, being great enough to overcome the initial

---

[23] See again *Resurrection: Theological and Scientific Assessments.*

explosive force of the Big Bang. Gravity will eventually cause the cosmos to stop expanding and start to collapse; its fate is the death of an incredibly high density and temperature (the "big crunch"). In either case, then, the cosmos and all life in it will come to an end. As theologian Ted Peters puts it, "The freeze or fry scenarios for the far future do not fit with the Easter promise of a coming new creation."[24]

However, this profound worry is puzzling. The concern would be entirely appropriate if atheism or deism were correct, but resurrection points the way for us here. Christians do not hold that the Resurrection of Jesus occurred, or that the general resurrection will occur, as natural consequences of the laws of physics. Rather, the idea is that, at a certain point, God will miraculously intervene and bring about an event that, absent divine intervention, would not have occurred. The universe is not a closed system.

So Christians should not envision the end of all things as the natural and predictable result of the operations of the laws of nature. They should see the eschaton as the result of a mighty act of God. At a decisive point in history, God will seize the initiative, raise the dead, and give those who love and obey him a new "heart of flesh." At that point, "they shall be my people and I will be their God" (Ezek. 11:19–20). In that act, God will "make all things new" (Rev. 21:5).

[24] *Resurrection: Theological and Scientific Assessments*, p. xiii.

9 Atonement

GORDON GRAHAM

The word *atonement* is unusual in being a term with English origins that has entered the standard vocabulary of Christian theology. Broken into its component parts – at-one-ment – it naturally suggests a state of affairs in which two parties are united or reconciled, but in both its theological and nontheological uses, it more usually refers to the act or process by which this has come about. Just as we speak of atoning for our mistakes and wrongdoings, the traditional Christian belief in the Atonement refers primarily to the spiritual significance of the life and work of Jesus Christ. It is a central affirmation of Christianity that Christ atoned for the sins of the world and thus reconciled a fallen humanity to God. Though this affirmation is not expressly included in any of the three principal creeds – Apostles', Athanasian, and Nicene – few Christians, if any, would dispute it. Intellectual problems and theological disagreements only arise when we attempt to expand on this simple affirmation.

Just what was our condition before Christ's work of reconciliation? Was it estrangement in the way members of a family become estranged when the natural affection and sympathy they ought to have for each have dried up, or been hurtfully transferred to nonfamily members? Or is it rather the alienation of law-breakers from the society whose laws they break, manifested in their being shut away in prisons, and in extreme cases, being put to death because they are no longer "fit for society"? Both models have scriptural warrant – the first strikingly so in the parable of the prodigal son, and the second emphasized again and again in St Paul's writings on sin and the law. And was it the life or the death of Christ that was crucial to the Atonement – his Incarnation or his Crucifixion? Again there is scriptural warrant for both, though Christian theology, especially in the Protestant tradition, has tended to make his death on the cross the key component.

Both these issues are obviously important, but across the centuries it is principally a third question that has occupied theologians and

Christian philosophers – namely, how exactly did the Atonement accomplish its effect? Christian thought on this question has revolved around four principal ideas. One is that Christ "redeemed" or "ransomed" a fallen humanity by paying the "price" of sin. A second is that he was the perfect sacrifice or "propitiation" that true worship requires, the sacrificial "Lamb of God" who effectually replaced the ineffectual slaughter of ordinary lambs in the temple at Jerusalem. A third concept – "justification" – is perhaps the most prominent in the history of theology. This is the idea that by bearing, on behalf of us, all the punishment that sinful human beings justly deserve, Christ "blotted out" our transgressions in much the way that (on a retributive model) criminals are restored to their normal status as citizens once they have undergone just punishment. In contrast to all three of these suggestions, which lend special importance to the Crucifixion, a fourth recurring suggestion gives a greater emphasis to the life of Christ by focusing on his conduct as a spiritual exemplar; Jesus was the first fully human being who showed how to be wholly obedient to God, even unto death.

All these suggestions can find scriptural warrant, but none of it is sufficient to declare authoritatively for one view over the rest. This ambivalence is what opens the door to theological and philosophical investigation, an investigation to which some of the greatest Christian philosophers have contributed, notably Origen, Anselm, Abelard, and Aquinas, as well as the great Reformed theologian John Calvin. In this chapter, we will not be concerned to determine the scriptural basis or to trace the theological history of these various suggestions, but to explore the philosophical problems to which they give rise and consider how they might be overcome.

RANSOM AND REDEMPTION

Matthew's Gospel (20:28) declares Jesus to be "a ransom" for many. If so, to whom is this ransom paid? In the normal case, ransoms are demanded by and paid to kidnappers. When construing the Atonement in this way, early Christians had a ready answer – human beings are held captive by Satan, a fallen angel whose immense power and cunning human beings, left to their own devices, are unable to foil or to escape. For modern minds, the first obstacle to accepting such a view may appear to be its necessary postulation of satanic powers. Yet, despite modernity's self-image in this regard, belief in demonic possession, and even in Satan, is by no means dead in the twenty-first century. It is still a powerful element within Christianity, especially in the non-Western world, and so it would be a mistake to dismiss the ransom theory of Atonement on this ground alone. To concede (or suspend) the question of satanic powers, however, simply means we must tackle the difficulties premodern Christians, notably St. Anselm, found with the idea of Christ's death as the payment of ransom. Two problems are of special importance.

First, kidnappers' demands are acceded to by governments and individuals only when they lack the necessary means to free their victims by other means. Because no one thinks the kidnappers' demands are legitimate, it is necessity, not justice, that obliges us to pay them. Unlike human beings, singly or collectively, God cannot be subject to such necessity. Being omnipotent, he has whatever power it takes, even over superhuman agents like Satan, to thwart evil designs. Indeed, we can say more than this. Just as any government that had the means to free kidnap victims, but chose instead to pay the ransom demand, would be acting unjustly, so it is incompatible with the justice of God to suppose that he would pay the ransom Satan demands.

There is an interesting thought in Origen that might provide an answer to this first objection. We have to remember that God loves his creation, and that Satan, however rebellious, is part of that creation. This places limits on the means God can willingly use to defeat him. He cannot return evil for evil. Accordingly, the means by which Satan is finally defeated must fall short of his destruction and secure instead his transformation. Thus, Satan unjustly demands a ransom which he thinks he wants, but the one that is paid to him is one that he "cannot bear the torment of holding" (Origen, quoted in Porter 2001: 597). In other words, though Satan believes his rebellion against God will have been successful when he has compelled God to pay the ransom he demands, once this actually happens he finds his satisfaction has turned to ashes of shame and mortification as he looks on the beautiful innocence of the self-sacrificing victim on the cross.

There is something deeply attractive in this suggestion, and it may be that it can be used successfully to make the idea of ransom compatible with God's justice. The second difficulty that the ransom theory encounters, however, is not so readily resolved. In ordinary cases, kidnap victims are not prisoners of war. That is to say, they are not enemy combatants, but bystanders, and this is what makes them *innocent* victims. Normally, when government forces (say) attempt to free them, the captives play no significant part in securing their own release and are unable to ensure that the attempt is a sensible one, any more than they can prevent a disastrous failure. So too, with the idea of *Christus Victor* (the Latin expression often used to convey Christ's role as humanity's liberator). If the ransom story has the same logical structure in the divine as in the human case, then it is a power struggle between superhuman forces in which human beings just happen to be caught up. This means that human beings are innocent from start to finish. What then of the "fall," and how is it our *salvation*, as opposed to our *release*, that Christ's victory secures? There appears to be a serious omission here. Atonement is required only if there has been estrangement, and it is deeply written into the Christian religion (as in many others) that estrangement from the divine is the outcome of human sin, folly, or self-centeredness. The insurmountable problem with the ransom conception, if we follow its conceptual structure in other contexts, is that it can give no account of this.

SACRIFICE AND SATISFACTION

A more obviously religious alternative to the idea of ransom conceives of the Crucifixion as an atoning sacrifice or "propitiation" for the sins of the world. The archaic nature of this second term, which has no common currency today, is an indication that some considerable work is needed if this second account of the Atonement is to make any sense to a modern audience. Indeed, in this context, even the term *sacrifice* needs special explanation because, in contemporary English, its religious dimension is either muted or absent altogether. Etymologically, and originally, "sacrifice" means "making sacred." Nowadays, it simply means giving up something in a good (though not necessarily specially important) cause – sacrificing leisure time for charity work, for instance, or sacrificing a career in order to have a family.

One way of bringing out this contrast between older and newer uses is to consider the now largely extinct practice of animal sacrifice. The Old Testament is full of occasions on which "burnt offerings" of cattle or sheep or birds were made in ritual sacrifice in order to thank, honor, satisfy, or placate (propitiate) Yahweh. These sacrifices have little in common with the modern concept and in most places today would be thought both pointless and repugnant. Yet they provide the context in which Christ's atoning work has sometimes been interpreted, an interpretation built into many Christian liturgies, prayers, and hymns. Even in the ancient world, however, we can find serious doubts being raised about such practices. In the dialogue *Euthyphro*, for instance, Plato observes that we cannot bestow benefits on the gods, because the gods can secure for themselves anything that mere mortals might offer. In the Old Testament itself, the prophet Isaiah is scathing about the spiritual value of burnt offerings, in contrast to genuine contrition on the part of sinners.

Both kinds of objection – that the idea of humans benefiting God is absurd and the offering of fine food and drink especially inept – might be thought to be met in the contention that the death of Jesus on the cross is "the full, final sacrifice." That is to say, it is a once-and-for-all replacement of these lesser and ultimately ineffectual sacrifices, a replacement, moreover, that results from a divine initiative. God sees the necessary futility of the all-too-human attempts that are made to please him, and by becoming Incarnate in Jesus, he provides a "Lamb of God" that accomplishes what no mundane sacrifice could ever do – a reconciliation between God and an alienated humanity.

There is still something inherently difficult for modern ways of thinking about this account of the Atonement, however. It may well be that the divinely provided sacrifice of Christ on the cross is infinitely better than the killing and burning of animals, but why is *any* sacrifice of this kind needed? The God of the Old Testament is, in many places, like the gods of Greece and Rome – vengeful and capricious – and perhaps the only way to deal with such an unpredictably wrathful being, as in the case of a political tyrant, is to try to find out what he likes and give it to him. However, if so, it is hard to see how we could square such a conception with the one that is supposed to replace it – namely, the death of Jesus as a divinely initiated alternative. It seems obvious to say, as most Christians have said, that the motivation for such an initiative is God's love for his creation, his longing for reconciliation, and his willingness to undergo suffering unto death to bring it about. How can he, at the same time, be a fearsome God whose anger must be propitiated? In short, the idea of an atoning sacrifice has its origins in a perception of divine wrath that is at odds with the loving God who makes it.

We might effect something of a bridge between the wrath and the love of God by saying that, unlike the capricious tyrant, God's anger is *righteous* anger, and is thus essentially connected with his justice. Because God hates nothing that he has made, his love extends not just to the lovable, but to tyrants, torturers, serial killers, and child sex abusers. At the same time, his love for their victims means he is outraged (in the fullest sense) by the offenses perpetrated on them. It is this that grounds his anger in justice, and saves it from being simply an expression of temporarily thwarted power and authority, as it was, for example, in the case of Stalin's anger against the Ukrainians. This means, importantly, that however much God loves his creatures, he cannot simply disregard their wrongdoings. Without some consequence for sin, the moral order of the world collapses, to be replaced by a regime of indiscriminate "love" that is indistinguishable from indifference.

It is worth noting that even in those episodes from the Old Testament in which Yahweh seems at his most capricious, there is almost always some suggestion of righteous anger in the background. God is not simply angry, but justifiably so. This element of justification makes the picture rather more acceptable, but it also moves it on, conceptually speaking, from propitiation to punishment. The sacrifices that are due to God are no longer things merely "pleasing in his sight," but penalties justly demanded.

If this is true, though, it seems that the concept of sacrifice is incidental to atonement. This is for two reasons. First, even understood in more modern terms, religious sacrifice is appropriate for reasons other than sinfulness. If "sacrifice" means "making sacred," then it has a clear modern sense. People still speak quite easily of "sacred space," for example, and they make space sacred by setting it aside for exclusively religious use. They might do this, and often have done, out of gratitude rather than guilt. Thus, in thankfulness for the life of a much-loved family member (say), money that might have been spent on houses or holidays is given for the construction of a church or chapel dedicated exclusively to the worship of God – a sacred space in which no other use is fitting. This is sacrifice in a plain sense, but not for sin. Similarly, when Hannah relinquishes the infant Samuel to God, leaving him to be brought up by Eli in the temple, this tremendous sacrifice on her part is not an act of propitiation, but the fulfilling of a promise she has made.

Second, sacrifices require a willingness that punishment and penalty do not. When criminals are given, and serve, punishments the severity of which justly reflects the gravity of their crimes, they are said to have paid their debt to society, whether they did so willingly or not. There may be a sense (as Hegel held) in which criminals necessarily will just punishment, but it is not the same as that in which they willingly accept release from prison when it comes. Retributive justice is served so long as the guilty are punished and the innocent are thereby vindicated. It does not matter whether the guilty accept their punishment, or indeed, whether the angry feelings of the innocent are assuaged.

Both these points seem to bear out the following contention. If atonement is about sinners setting things right with God, sacrifice is neither necessary nor sufficient as a means of accomplishing this. The relevant concept is punishment. God is rightly angry with a sinful humanity he loves, and his anger is only to be placated by the punishment their sinfulness deserves. This leads to a third, and historically very important, understanding of the Atonement – the penal model.

PUNISHMENT AND PENAL SUBSTITUTION

If, taking our cue from the story of Adam's fall in the Garden of Eden, we suppose it is sin that has caused our estrangement from God, and we think of sin as a quasi-legal concept – namely, violation of the laws that God has laid down for humanity – then it seems to follow that the only way to set things right is for people to be punished in the way they deserve. However, the cumulative penalty for the sins of millions upon millions of wayward human beings is immense – too great for them to bear, in fact – so that if the matter remains in the hands of human beings, reconciliation through just punishment will forever remain impossible. Against this background, Christ's atoning work is readily interpreted as his taking upon himself the punishment the world deserves, something he is uniquely able to do (this model usually adds) because of his perfect innocence.

Prominent though this account of the Atonement has been, it pretty evidently encounters some major objections. First, why is punishment essential to reconciliation? Why can the same effect not be brought about by forgiveness? It often is in nontheological contexts, after all, given that people can and do forgive each other insults and injuries, and thereby heal relationships that were ruptured. Why should we not expect God to be willing and able to do the same? This objection has generally been regarded as a singularly important one, because the claim that God is a forgiving God is a recurrent theme in Scripture and in Christian teaching, and one that sits rather uneasily with the idea that he needs to see people punished.

One response repeats an earlier point. If God is just, he cannot be indifferent to wrongdoing. For instance, if God were to say in the face of wickedness on the scale of the Holocaust, "It's all right, I forgive you" and thereby put Nazi and Jew on the same level, divine "love" would be indistinguishable from indifference. That is why, this response alleges, forgiveness is not enough. The point is a good one, but it does not follow that *punishment* is required; guilt and innocence can be marked by requiring *penitence* on the part of the guilty. In point of fact, this is more in accord with Christian teaching, which, by proclaiming that God forgives the sins of those who are truly penitent, makes penitence rather than punishment the key to reconciliation. Of course, true penitence is not cost free. To acknowledge that we have wronged someone and to make express apology for having done so can be psychologically and emotionally difficult. Nevertheless, any cost of this kind does not amount to punishment.

A further response is to say that, though forgiveness and penitence may be enough for the purposes of reconciliation, punishment can secure a number of other valuable ends. To punish the penitent as well as the impenitent is a way of vindicating the innocent – all those other people who have not stolen, tortured, killed, and so on – and it makes a forceful public expression of the commitment to good over evil. It is these further purposes that make most sense of another familiar phenomenon in nontheological contexts – an acceptance on the part of people who are truly sorry for what they have done that still they deserve punishment. Furthermore, their being willing to accept it serves as both proof of repentance and a means to make restoration in a way that penitence alone cannot. Pursuing this line of thought, we can argue that God does forgive wrongdoers and that he could forgive them without exacting any punishment. But he also wants to secure the other valuable ends that punishment can accomplish, including making his justice known, and it is this that warrants the imposition of punishment by a nonetheless forgiving God.

Let us suppose that this response to the first objection brought against the penal model of atonement is a good one. It still leaves untouched an objection that has widely been regarded as insurmountable – namely, the impropriety of transferring punishments to anyone other than the people who have performed the acts that merit them. Here, we encounter the important concept of penal substitution and the question of its possibility. How can justice be done unless punishment is meted out to wrongdoers? When, in the wake of a terrorist act, military forces punish whole villages because they have been unable to identify the actual perpetrators of the outrage, this is not a retributive act of justice, but an indefensible act of injustice. And just so far as its victims include individuals who could not even be accused of complicity – infants and the very aged, for example – its injustice is compounded. Now, if, as Christians hold, Jesus is uniquely innocent, this implies that he is precisely the one person in the whole of history who should *not* be punished for the sins of the world.

Does it alter the position if the substitute is willing? People sometimes voluntarily pay the fines that courts have imposed upon others. In such cases, the person who committed the act that warranted the fine does not pay it, yet the law has still taken its course, and the appropriate fine has, in fact, been paid. Why should it not be the case here also?

Recently some philosophers have argued that if Jesus takes the place of sinners voluntarily, this is still in conformity with God's law, and because punishment exacted from imperfect human beings may actually result in their further alienation (in just the way that just punishment can further alienate criminals from society), this may be a much better way for God to secure the other valuable ends that just punishment can serve. However, the problem is that this "solution" to the impropriety of penal substitution appears to beg the question. One of the important ends that punishment serves, which forgiveness alone cannot, is the affirmation of right over wrong, good over evil. If penal substitution is unjust, it cannot have this result. Accordingly, the argument we have just considered must assume that penal substitution is just – an illicit assumption since that is precisely what is at issue.

It might strengthen the objection to penal substitution to observe that the logic of punishment and reward are the same here. It seems no more fitting to punish those who have committed no crime, than to give the prize to someone who did not win the race. Giving prizes is not like making gifts. We make gifts as and where we will, and usually with the hope of benefitting other people; on occasion, this might rightly justify us in giving gifts to the poor and refusing them to the rich. However, though prizes often (though not always) take the form of valuable benefits, in determining who ought to get them, what is called for is a strict observance of the rules, irrespective of the benefit we can expect the winners and losers to get from them.

A similar argument can be made with respect to punishment. One of the benefits that is meant to flow from an act of punishment is the deterrence of other potential criminals. Critics of the deterrence theory of punishment have often observed, however, that punishment of the innocent can have deterrent effects, and judges regularly hand out "exemplary" sentences for deterrent purposes, which is to say punishments more severe than the offense committed actually deserves. In both cases (let us assume) valuable social benefits are forthcoming. It nevertheless remains the case that an injustice is done.

It seems, then, that penal substitution cannot be just. It is possible to achieve good effects by punishing innocent people, and perhaps these are enhanced when the victims voluntarily undertake to pay undeserved penalties. However, such punishments remain unjust. Just as the winner and the recipient of a prize must be one in the same person, so the identity of the perpetrator and the identity of the person punished must be one and the same. This means that God's punishment of the innocent Jesus on the cross, even if it brought highly beneficial results, would remain unjust, and thus an action unworthy of, and hence impossible for, God.

There is more to be said on this point, but it will be best to wait until we have considered the fourth most common account of the Atonement – namely, moral exemplification.

OBEDIENCE AND IMITATION

Some Christian thinkers, notably Peter Abelard, have had reservations about all three of the accounts of atonement so far considered. This is because, in their different ways, they invoke a deeply unattractive image of a God who is willing to have intense suffering inflicted on an innocent and supposedly beloved Son in order to assuage his own wrath and sense of righteousness. Moreover, by putting so much emphasis on the Crucifixion, these theories of atonement appear to render the life, example, and teaching of Jesus largely superfluous.

It seems that we can obviate both these objections if we cease to focus exclusively on the Crucifixion and give due weight to the whole of Jesus' life, including his death on the cross, certainly, but also the ministry that preceded it. Taken as a whole, the birth, life, and death of Jesus constitutes a unique example of how the estrangement between God and humanity can be overcome through perfect obedience. Given the intense hostility of those who opposed Jesus, in the end this meant obedience unto death, but his death is neither more nor less significant than any other event in his life. To believe in Christ and his atoning power on this account of the matter is to live in imitation of his example and to follow faithfully the teaching that illuminates it.

The signal strength of this fourth account of the Atonement is what has been called its subjective element. "Objective" theories such as those that employ the concepts of ransom and sacrifice seem to secure reconciliation with God quite independently of any action or even wish on the part of the sinners. The ransom is paid or the sacrifice made regardless of any activity on our part. In sharp contrast, making reconciliation dependent on the believer's faithful imitation of Christ satisfactorily explains how the practices of prayer, worship, and almsgiving have a key role in the story of our redemption.

By the very same token, however, the imitation theory also seems one-sided, though in the other direction. Jesus is no more than a guide or a template. He is no longer the saviour of the world, but one more prophet or teacher who points the way. His life and death contain valuable lessons for us but, in themselves, they accomplished nothing. It is we who must do the essential work. From an orthodox point of view this drastically diminishes his status as the Christ. A "many paths to one God" view of world religions might welcome this, but there is the further objection that it seems to constitute some variation on the Pelagian heresy – the heresy that we can be the means of our own salvation. The problem with Pelagianism is not just that it has been declared heretical, but that it constitutes a counsel of despair. The longing for salvation precisely arises from a perception of the depth of human weakness and sinfulness. How can there be any hope in a doctrine of the Atonement that makes human efforts to follow in the footsteps of Jesus so central? Don't we know that, left to our own devices, we are bound to fail?

Objective and subjective

The foregoing considerations might be summarized as follows. The most promising of the objective theories is the penal model – Christ died so that the estrangement from God that results from human sinfulness may be overcome in a way that does nothing to discount its seriousness. However, the concept of penal substitution that the model necessarily employs is problematic. How can human beings, without any cost to themselves, be absolved of their guilt by the death of an innocent Christ? Coming at the issue from the other direction, the "imitation" theory does lend a central role to human action given that it requires those who seek reconciliation with the divine to follow the teaching and unique example of Jesus, the only fully human being whose will was perfectly obedient to God. On the other hand, by thus placing the emphasis on the efforts of the faithful, it diminishes the role of Jesus, and thus relegates him from the position of Savior to that of teacher. What is needed, therefore, is a way in which the strengths of these two conceptions can be combined and their difficulties circumvented.

Some progress in this direction can be made if we consider again the concept of penal substitution. Suppose I justly incur a financial penalty that I am unable to pay, and so you pay it for me, thereby expunging my criminal status. Justice will have been done if I pay you back eventually. It is not necessary that the perpetrator of the crime is the person who first pays it back; it is only necessary that I *become* the person who pays the fine, which I do when I have taken over the loss that temporarily you bore on my behalf. In such a case, it is your action that restores my civil status, but my later action that makes this restoration just.

We might apply this idea to the doctrine of the Atonement. The historical Jesus was able to pay the price of sin in a way that ordinary human beings are not. Unlike the case of a simple fine, there is no obvious way in which we can pay him back, but there is, nonetheless, a way in which we can *become* the person who has paid the price of sin – namely by self-sacrifice in the strict sense; that is to say, submerging our "selves" in the person of Christ. The Bible as well as Christian teaching and practice consistently make reference to this idea. St. Paul speaks of "putting on Christ," for example; the theology of the Church describes its members collectively as "the body of Christ"; and prayers are almost always offered "*through* our Lord Jesus Christ." Whereas the devout Jew tries to live by the Law, and the devout Muslim strives to follow the teachings of the Prophet, the disciple of Christ aims at something more – mystical unity or being one with him. This implies a willingness to sacrifice "self" for life in Christ, and by doing so, to become the person who pays the price of sin. Moreover, because unity with Christ is unity with the Second Person of the Trinity, Atonement and Incarnation thus work together to secure a perfect reconciliation between God and humanity.

PAUL K. MOSER

In philosophical theology, any discussion of sin and salvation involves a notion of God, particularly if sin is regarded as at least sin against God and salvation is regarded as at least salvation by God. A central use of the term God in traditional monotheism offers the term as a maximally honorific title that entails worthiness of worship in a titleholder. Worthiness of worship requires, among other things, moral perfection, including a perfectly loving character altogether free of hate toward other agents. As such, an agent who hates some people will not be a genuine candidate for the titleholder of God. As a result, many alleged Gods fail to qualify as the true God, and emerge instead as imposters. Sin and salvation take on distinctive traits against the background of a God worthy of worship. We shall identify some of these traits in order to illuminate the topic of divine–human redemption in Christian philosophical theology.

SIN

It is arguable that we humans are experts regarding sin, even if we don't know it and even if we don't like to talk about it. It doesn't follow, of course, that we can immediately offer an adequate portrayal of sin. One can be an expert regarding deception, for instance, even if one can't offer an adequate portrayal of deception. The relevant distinction concerns an expert in the *realization* of sin in contrast with an expert in the *characterization* of sin. Realization expertise doesn't entail characterization expertise. One's *assessing* a claim to realization expertise in sin, however, will require one's having a characterization of sin, but such assessing would go beyond mere realization expertise. Given our current interest in assessing, we need to begin with a characterization of sin.

Reinhold Niebuhr (1941, 1949) suggested that the Christian view of sin is empirically verifiable. One relevant consideration, however, is that Christians have held many different views of sin, and thus any talk of the Christian view of sin is questionable from the start. Augustine, for instance, suggested a view of "original sin," implying that one's being in a state of sin is somehow inherited from one's original ancestors, Adam and Eve. He writes:

> Properly speaking, human nature means the blameless nature with which man was originally created. But we also use it in speaking of the nature with which we are born mortal, ignorant, and subject to the flesh, which is really the penalty of sin. In this sense the apostle says: "We also were by nature children of wrath even as others" (Eph. 2:3). As we are born from the first pair [namely, Adam and Eve] to a mortal life of ignorance and toil because they sinned and fell into a state of error, misery, and death, so it most justly pleased the most high God... to manifest from the beginning, from man's origin, his [God's] justice in exacting punishment, and in human history his mercy in remitting punishment (Augustine 395, Book III, xix, 54 – xx, 55).

Augustine thus regards human sin after the fall of Adam and Eve as, at least in part, an inherited defective state that is part of the divine penalty for the sin of Adam and Eve. According to Augustine, we human successors to Adam and Eve inherit our state of sin without initially choosing or willing it (see Mann 2001, Cherbonnier 1955; Chapters 8–9).

Niebuhr has offered a view of original sin contrary to Augustine's. He holds, with Augustine, that "... the corruption of evil is at the heart of the human personality," but, against Augustine, that original sin "... is a corruption which has a universal dominion over all men, though it is not by nature but in freedom that men sin..." (1949, p. 122). This view denies Augustine's position that original sin in the wake of Adam and Eve is an inherited defective state prior to one's free decisions. Niebuhr's view evidently finds support in the following statement of the apostle Paul: "... sin came into the world through one man and death through sin, and so death spread to all men *because all men sinned*" (Rom. 5:12, RSV, italics added). Paul does not say that sin and death spread *just because* Adam and Eve sinned; instead, he points to the significant fact that all men sinned. Paul's view is more attentive to individual human accountability than Augustine's, and it thus accommodates the moral truism that a child should not be held accountable or punished (especially by a perfectly loving God) for the sins of his or her parents. One morally important consideration is that the child lacks the ability to prevent the parents from committing their sins.

We should avoid any simplistic view that characterizes sin as just morally wayward actions that violate rules or regulations. This simplistic view depersonalizes the objects of sin as rules or regulations. In contrast, according to some important strands of Jewish and Christian theism, sin is inherently *personal* in its subject and its object. As Emil Brunner notes, "...sin is a change in man's relation to God: it is the break in communion with God, [owing] to distrust and defiance.... Man wants to be on a level with God, and in so doing to become independent of [God]" (1952, p. 92; compare Brunner 1939, pp. 129–32). Abraham Heschel, likewise, offers an inherently personal characterization of sin: "To the [Jewish] prophets, sin is not an ultimate, irreducible, or independent condition, but rather a disturbance in the relationship between God and man; it is...a condition that can be surmounted by man's return and God's forgiveness" (1962, p. 229). Similarly, the apostle Paul identifies human sin with one's resisting the honoring of God as God, including one's preferring to exclude God from one's knowledge (see Rom. 1:21, 28). The irreducibly personalist view of Paul, Brunner, and Heschel captures a central theme of many of the biblical writers: Human sin is ultimately sin *against God*, even if in virtue of human sin against God's commands.

Human sin against God involves more than human actions as external behavior against God. It includes human psychological attitudes against God as well as human habits against God. In particular, human sin is evidently anchored not in external behavior against rules but, rather, in a morally responsible human *will* against God – specifically, a human will against God's perfectly loving will. As a result, any genuine solution to human sin (as offered by a program of divine–human salvation) must be corrective somehow of not just external human behavior but human wills as well. More specifically, if human sin includes resistance to human communion or fellowship with God, then divine–human salvation must somehow supply or empower human fellowship with God.

Perhaps, at its core, divine–human salvation is divine–human fellowship. Such a view is suggested by the following remark attributed to Jesus in John 17:3: "This is everlasting life: that they know you, the only true God, and the one whom you sent, Jesus Christ." (Translations from the Greek New Testament are my own unless otherwise noted.) The relevant "knowing" of God is not mere propositional knowledge that God exists (which even resolute enemies of God can have); instead, it includes volitional agreement and even fellowship with God (as explained in Moser 2008). Let's turn to the nature of this solution to human sin.

FROM SIN TO SALVATION

The fellowship central to salvation evidently would have to be lasting fellowship, and not just a temporary fix. This consideration agrees with the aforementioned talk of everlasting life in John 17:3. However, some people will doubt that divine perfect love, as a salvific antidote to human sin, would actually yield everlasting life for willing recipients of such love. For instance, Timothy Jackson has raised this doubt on the ground that "to have love is not to have all good things [including everlasting life], but it is to have the *best* thing" (1999, p. 170). Evidently, Jackson assumes that having love is, even if temporary, the best thing.

Consider, by way of reply, that the best thing would be for willing humans to have divine love *everlastingly*, and not just for the short term. If God is perfectly loving, and thus wants the best for humans, God would give us the opportunity to have divine love everlastingly. Jackson fails to give this view due consideration, and claims that "love can endure even without faith in one's own resurrection" (p. 168). The immediate issue, however, is whether a perfectly loving God's wanting the best for humans would include God's giving us the opportunity to have a life of divine love everlastingly, rather than just for the short term. The answer, I submit, is definitely yes. Indeed, Jackson himself unknowingly offers the needed support as follows: "Love is concerned with preserving and enhancing *all* good things, *to the greatest extent possible....*" (p. 218, italics added). Accordingly, a perfectly loving God would offer willing humans the opportunity to receive a life of divine love everlastingly, in lasting fellowship with God. Divine–human salvation would follow suit.

Divine salvation from human sin would rest on divine authority, anchored in divine perfect love, rather than on morally questionable human preferences. We see intimations of such authority in the earliest reports about Jesus, who stood in contrast with his Jewish contemporaries who dared to speak for God (Matt. 7:28–29). This was a kind of authority very different from that of secular authorities who, according to Jesus, "lord it over" others (Mark 10:42–45). The apostle Paul referred to this authority from Jesus as "the authority in the gospel" (1 Cor. 9:18), and he understood "the gospel" as "*the power* of God for salvation" (Rom. 1:16, italics added). Let's identify this power-authority and see how it contributes to divine salvation of humans from sin.

Strikingly, Jesus manifested an authority that led to his being worshipped as the divine personal means of human salvation by his earliest followers, including even such an educated Jewish monotheist as the apostle Paul (Phil. 2:5–11, 1 Cor. 1:2, Gal. 4:4–5, 1 Thess. 5:8,

Rom. 3:24). Jesus began his ministry as the preacher of the Good News about *God's* arriving kingdom, under clear influence from the book of Isaiah (compare Mark 1:1–15), but he became, soon after his death, *an object of focus* in the preaching of the Good News by his earliest, Jewish disciples. In short, the *preacher* became part of the *preached*; the *proclaimer* became part of the *proclaimed*, as Bultmann (1955, vol. 1, p. 33) and many other New Testament scholars have noted.

In the tradition of C. H. Dodd (1936), Eugene Lemcio has identified a common *kerygma*, or proclamation, regarding the Good News of salvation in nineteen of the twenty-seven books of the New Testament. He has isolated this *kerygma* in all of the main representatives and traditions of the New Testament, and he sums up the unifying *kerygma* thus: "It declares the Good News of God's sending [Jesus] or raising Jesus from the dead. By responding obediently to God, one receives the benefits stemming from this salvific event" (1991, p. 127). We thus may speak of *the* Good News *kerygma* of salvation, beyond any multiplicity of *kerygmas* (compare Hunter 1943).

In one of the earliest statements of the Good News in the New Testament, Paul writes:

> For I delivered to you of first importance what I have received: that Christ died for our sins according to the Scriptures, that he was buried, that he was raised on the third day according to the Scriptures, and that he appeared to Peter, and then to the twelve. After that, he appeared to more than five hundred brothers at the same time, most of whom remain until now, but some have fallen asleep. Then he appeared to James, then to all the apostles, and last of all he appeared also to me, as to one untimely born.... If Christ has not been raised, our preaching is futile and your faith is futile too. We are also then found to be false witnesses about God, because we have testified about God that he raised Christ from the dead.... If Christ has not been raised, your faith is futile; you are still in your sins.... If we have hope in Christ only for this life, we are to be pitied more than all men. But Christ has been raised from the dead, the firstfruits of those who have fallen asleep (1 Cor. 15:3–8, 14–15, 17, 19–20).

The Good News of salvation, according to Paul, includes that Christ died for our sins and was raised from the dead. Indeed, Paul regards the Good News as false and futile in the absence of the Resurrection of Jesus, because he links the Resurrection of Jesus to divine forgiveness of human sins in such a way that if there is no divine Resurrection of Jesus, "you are still in your sins."

A central theme of the Pauline Good News of salvation is that human sins are forgiven or pardoned by God, and humans are thereby offered reconciliation with God, in connection with the life, death, and Resurrection of Jesus. If atonement is divine–human reconciliation that effectively deals with human sin as resistance to divine unselfish love and fellowship, then the heart of the controversy about the life, death, and Resurrection of Jesus is a debate about atonement. Exactly how do the life, the death, and the Resurrection of Jesus figure in (intended) divine–human atonement? Furthermore, how is such atonement to be appropriated by humans for salvation from sin?

According to Matthew's Gospel (26:28), Jesus announced at the Last Supper that he will die "for the forgiveness of sins." The atoning sacrifice of Jesus as God's sinless offering for sinful humans is, according to Matthew's Jesus, at the center of God's work toward human salvation. John's Gospel (John 1:36) and Paul's undisputed letters (1 Cor. 5:7, 2 Cor. 5:21, Rom. 3:24–26) agree with this lesson about salvation. The unique role assigned to Jesus in divine–human salvation sets him apart from every other known key religious leader, including Moses, Confucius, Krishna, Gautama the Buddha, and Muhammad. As portrayed by Matthew, John, and Paul, Jesus uniquely offered himself as God's atoning sacrifice to God for human salvation from sin. Only Jesus, therefore, emerged at the center of the Good News proclamation of God's intended salvation of humans.

The Crucifixion of Jesus may seem to leave him as ultimately a failure, even as one "cursed" before God (see Gal. 3:13, Deut. 21:23). In contrast, at least Paul, Matthew, and John proclaim the crucified and risen Jesus as the central mediating figure in God's ironic atoning sacrifice and turnaround victory for human salvation. Out of the fatal apparent defeat of Jesus, according to the Good News, God brought a unique manifestation and offering of divine love and forgiveness toward humans, including toward God's enemies. The Crucifixion of Jesus is thus proclaimed as a central part of God's intended grand reversal of the dark human tragedy of alienation from God for the sake of human salvation.

The salvific divine reversal aims at divine–human reconciliation by means of a powerful manifestation of God's character as exemplified in Jesus, God's innocent victim (of human sin) who offers forgiveness and fellowship instead of condemnation to guilty humans. Let's call this *the divine manifest–offering* approach to atonement or salvation (in keeping with Rom. 3:21–26, which repeatedly uses talk of manifestation). What is being made *manifest* is God's character of righteous and forgiving love, and what is being *offered*, in keeping with that character, for the sake of salvation is lasting divine–human fellowship as a gracious divine gift. This divine gift for humans is anchored in both (a) the forgiveness offered and manifested via God's atoning sacrifice in Jesus, the innocent victim of humans, and (b) God's Resurrection of Jesus as Lord and as Giver of God's Spirit.

The manifestation of God's self-giving character in Jesus reveals the kind of God who is thereby offering forgiveness and lasting fellowship to humans for the sake of salvation. The death of Jesus does not bring about divine–human reconciliation by itself, but it aims to provide God's distinctive means of implementing salvation via divine manifestation and offering. For the sake of actual divine–human reconciliation, humans must still *receive* the manifest–offering of forgiveness and fellowship via grounded trust or faith in the God extending the offer. (For a brief outline of some prominent alternatives to the manifest–offering approach to atonement, see Berkhof 1986, pp. 304–12; compare O'Collins 1995, pp. 197–201.)

Jesus, as divinely appointed Lord and as Giver of God's Spirit (1 Thess. 5:10), came from God to identify with humans in our weakness and trouble, while he represented his divine Father in righteous and merciful love. He thus aims as God's salvific mediator to represent, and to serve as a personal bridge between, God *and* humans by seeking to reconcile humans to his Father with the divine gift of fellowship anchored in merciful, forgiving love as the power of God's own intervening Spirit. Jesus' obedient death on the cross, commanded of him by God (Rom. 3:25, 1 Cor. 5:7, Phil. 2:8; compare Mark 14:23–24, John 18:11), aims to manifest how far he and his Father will go – even to gruesome death – to offer salvation, including divine forgiveness and fellowship, to wayward humans. By divine assignment, Jesus gives humans all he has, from his Father's self-giving love, to manifest that God mercifully and righteously loves humans to the fullest extent and offers humans salvation as the gracious gift of unearned forgiveness, fellowship, and membership in God's everlasting family via reception of God's own Spirit (compare Rom. 5:8, John 3:16–17). This is the heart of the Good News of salvation that emerges from Jesus and surpasses anything on offer elsewhere.

The Good News of salvation proclaims the cross of the obedient Jesus as the place where selfish human rebellion against God is mercifully judged and forgiven by God. This does *not* mean that God punished Jesus, a reportedly innocent man. No New Testament writer teaches that

God punished Jesus, although some later, less careful theologians have suggested a contrary view. According to the Good News, God sent Jesus into our rebellious world to undergo, willingly and obediently, gruesome suffering and death at human hands that God would deem adequate for dealing justly, under divine righteousness, with our selfish rebellion against God and God's unselfish love. Jesus thus pays the price on behalf of humans for righteous divine reconciliation of sinners, and thereby, in manifesting and offering divine forgiveness, removes any need for self-ish fear, condemnation, anxiety, shame, guilt, and punishment among humans in relation to God (Rom. 8:1).

A central lesson of Paul's Epistle to the Romans, in keeping with Jesus' parables in Matthew 20:1–15 and Luke 18:9–14, is that divine righteous grace trumps "justice as ordinarily understood." It is thus a mistake to treat God's salvific atonement via Jesus as an episode in which "justice as ordinarily understood" is satisfied. On this ordinary understanding of justice, Jesus would have to undergo punishment (by God) for every sin ever committed, because justice is retaliatory, an eye for an eye. Divine righteous grace, according to Paul and Jesus, cannot be understood by the standard of such justice, despite the demands of some people to the contrary. Instead, God's righteousness, or justice, must be understood in terms of divine grace that manifests and offers mercy, even to enemies of God.

The Pauline Good News identifies the ultimate motive for the Crucifixion of Jesus as (the manifestation of) his Father's *righteous love* for humans. Unlike many later theologians, Paul definitively links God's aforementioned righteousness, or justice, with God's love: "God manifests his own love (*agape*) for us in that while we were yet sinners, Christ died for us. . . . Since we have now been justified by his blood, how much more shall we be saved by him from the wrath [of God]. . . . [W]hile we were enemies [of God], we were reconciled to God through the death of his Son. . . ." (Rom. 5:8–10). God, according to Paul, takes the initiative and the crucial means through Jesus in offering a gracious gift of divine–human reconciliation for the sake of human salvation. This offer, as suggested, manifests God's forgiving love as well as God's righteous-ness. Accordingly, Paul takes the sacrificial death of Jesus to manifest divine forgiving love and righteousness. He seems to have thought of divine gracious love as *righteous love*.

Mere forgiveness of humans by God would fail to counter adequately the wrongdoing that called for divine forgiveness – namely, human neglect of divine gracious authority (on the latter topic, see Rom. 1:21, 28). In exposing and judging the basis of human wrongdoing, God upholds perfect moral integrity in divine salvation of humans, without condoning evil. According to the Good News, through the loving self-sacrifice of Jesus, *God* meets the standard of morally perfect love *for us* humans, when we couldn't, wouldn't, and didn't, and then God offers this gracious gift of divinely provided righteousness to us, as God's Passover lamb for us (1 Cor. 5:7), to be received by trust in Jesus and God as salvific gift givers. Otherwise, our prospects for meeting the standard of divine perfect love and thus for salvation would be bleak indeed. (On gift righteousness from God, in contrast to human righteousness via the law, as central to Paul's thought, see Phil. 3:9, Rom. 3:21–26, 10:3–4, Gal. 3:11–12; compare Westerholm 2004.)

The main motivation of the cross *for Jesus* was his perfectly loving obedience to his Father on our behalf for the sake of divine–human reconciliation via divine forgiveness. Jesus expressed the crucial role of obedience to his Father in Gethsemane: "Not what I will, but what You will" (Mark 14:35–36; compare Mark 14:22–25). Likewise, Paul vividly identified the central role of Jesus' obedience: "Christ Jesus, who, being in the form of God, did not consider equality with God something to be grasped, but he emptied himself, taking the form of a servant, being made in human likeness. Being found in appearance as a man, he humbled himself and became *obedient* to death, even death on a cross" (Phil. 2: 6–8, italics added; compare Rom. 5:18–19). The acknowledged obedience of Jesus in his death is obedience to the redemptive mission of his divine Father, who gave Jesus his salvific cup of suffering and death for the sake of reconciling humans to God (Rom. 8:3–4; compare John 18:11). Jesus thus obeyed in Gethsemane in order to be able to manifest and to offer divine merciful reconciliation to humans. Jesus emerges, then, as God's salvific Passover lamb on our behalf (1 Cor. 5:7; compare John 1:29), that is, God's atoning sacrifice to God for us (Rom. 3:25), because he was perfectly obedient and thus fully righteous in the eyes of his perfectly righteous Father.

SALVATION IN NEW CREATION

The Good News redemptive mission of Jesus included not only his death but also his Resurrection by God. The aforementioned divine manifest–offering approach to salvation captures this fact by acknowledging the divine gracious offering of *lasting* divine–human fellowship under Jesus as Lord. Such divinely offered fellowship and salvation requires that Jesus *be alive* to be Lord *lastingly* on behalf of humans. This illuminates Paul's comments that Jesus "was raised for our justification" and that "we shall be saved by his life" (Rom 4:25, 5:10), once we acknowledge that justification and salvation (from human alienation and final death) are, like forgiveness, divine gifts for the sake of lasting divine–human fellowship under Jesus as Lord (compare 1 Thess. 5:10).

The Resurrection of Jesus from death is part of God's approval and even exaltation of God's obedient, crucified Son, the atoning sacrifice from God for humans (Phil. 2:9–11). The Resurrection of Jesus thus gets some of its significance from the cross, where Jesus gave full obedience to his Father in order to supply a manifest–offering of divine–human reconciliation, including divine forgiveness, to humans. In his life-surrendering obedience, Jesus manifested his authoritative Father's worthiness of complete trust and obedience, even when death ensues. Jesus confirmed through his full obedience the preeminent authority of his Father for the sake of forgiving and redeeming humans, and his Father, in turn, vindicated and exalted Jesus, likewise for the sake of forgiving and redeeming humans. Both Jesus and his Father, then, play a crucial role in the divine manifest–offering aimed at the atoning salvation of humans.

The Good News calls humans to receive the gracious gift of salvation via trust or faith in God and Jesus, on the basis of what God has done for humans. The Good News call to faith in Jesus (compare Gal. 2:16) stems from his being God's perfect human atoning representative (Rom. 5:8–11, 15–19), who offers what mere humans themselves cannot supply. The offered gift cannot be earned or merited by human works that obligate God to redeem humans (Rom. 4:4), because humans have fallen short of the divine standard of perfect unselfish love (Rom. 3:10–12, 23). Nonetheless, obedience as internal volitional submission to God's authoritative call in the Good News to human repentance and divine–human fellowship is central to appropriating the offered gift (compare Rom. 1:5, 6:16, 16:26, 2 Thess. 1:8). Such appropriating via "the obedience of faith" does not entail the earning or meriting of a reward. The divine gift of righteousness to humans comes not by human earning at all but rather by divine gracious reckoning via human trust, which includes volitional yielding, toward the gift giver (see Rom. 4:5–11, 10:8–10). As a result, human prideful boasting or taking of *self-credit* for personal achievement in salvation before God is altogether misplaced (Rom. 3:27, 1 Cor. 1:28–31).

We do well to clarify human *appropriation* of the salvific gift on offer. At the heart of the Good News of divine salvation of humans, we find an important (but philosophically neglected) theme that exceeds divine forgiveness for human sin. It involves, on the basis of Old Testament prophecies from Jeremiah, Ezekiel, and Joel, *one's being made new in spirit by God's Spirit* as one dies to one's selfish life and participates in God's Jesus-manifested life of self-giving righteous love. According to the Good News, God's Spirit intervenes in a willing person's spirit (or motivational center) to empower that person to love as God loves, in fellowship with God. Salvation is thus Spirit-oriented and spirit-oriented. Accordingly, one must die to selfish ways, including selfish autonomy, in order to live to God by God's Spirit.

In Paul's thinking, we humans must be "crucified with Christ" (Gal. 2:19–20; compare Col. 3:1–4), in dying to the anti-God selfish ways of the world and of ourselves. Only then can we be free to love as God loves, unselfishly and with forgiveness toward enemies. Only God's Spirit working within us can motivate the sea change from selfishness to unselfish love, even toward enemies. This change resembles a heart transplant, but at the level of one's spirit or motivational center. It alters the core of our nagging problem of sinful selfishness, even if some residue persists, and it offers an opportunity for a lasting life of divine–human fellowship and salvation in place of alienation and final death. We thus should expect a perfectly loving God to advance "kardiatheology" – that is, a theology aimed at the human heart, deeper than mere thoughts or feelings. (For discussion of the relevant notion of spirit, see Moser 1999 and Wiebe 2004; on the pertinent notion of heart, see Meadors 2006.)

According to the Pauline Good News, the gift of divine perfect love manifested in Jesus includes an offer of *dual* resurrection, despite this being overlooked by many theologians. The duality includes willing humans' being raised *spiritually* to new life *now* with God and their being raised *bodily* later after the model of Jesus' bodily resurrection. Paul has spiritual, but not bodily, resurrection in mind when he writes: "We were buried therefore with [Christ] by baptism into death, so that as Christ was raised from the dead by the glory of the Father, we too might walk in newness of life.... So you also must consider yourselves dead to sin but alive to God in Christ Jesus.... [Y]ield yourselves to God as [people] who have been brought from death to life" (Rom. 6:4, 11, 13, RSV; compare Col. 2:12). Paul thus supposes that followers of Jesus will "walk in newness of life" *now* to God, "as Christ was raised from the dead" (compare 2 Cor. 5:17). He assumes that they are already "alive from the dead," as a literal translation of Rom. 6:13 says. Paul holds that *bodily* resurrection for humans awaits a future time (1 Cor. 15:22–24); so, he must have *spiritual* resurrection in mind.

Paul credits the source of spiritual resurrection to the Spirit of the crucified Jesus sent by God to receptive humans, "into [their] hearts, crying 'Abba! Father!'" (Gal. 4:6; compare Rom. 8:9, 1 Cor. 15:45). Similarly, in John's Gospel, Jesus as God's atoning sacrifice is identified directly with the one who gives God's Spirit to receptive people *now* (John 1:29–33, 20:21–23; compare Mark 1:8). The divine manifest–offering atonement in Jesus thus includes the *empowering means of realizing* this salvation in receptive humans: the sending of God's Spirit through Jesus to empower receptive people to live anew *now* in fellowship with God and with each other in lasting unselfish love. Paul thus proclaims: "If anyone is in Christ, [that person is a] new creation" (2 Cor. 5:17; compare Gal. 6:15). Here, alone, we find, in such new creation, the divinely offered salvific antidote to human sin.

Paul's Good News "new creation" proclamation echoes the remarkable prophecy of Ezekiel 36:26–27: "A new heart I will give you and a new spirit I will put within you; and I will take out of your flesh the heart of stone and give you a heart of flesh. And I will put my spirit within you and cause you to walk in my statutes and be careful to observe my ordinances" (RSV; compare Ezek. 37:14, Jer. 32:39–40). In keeping with this promise, Paul proclaims the cross and the Resurrection of Jesus as the manifest–offering salvific avenue for God to impart God's Spirit to all receptive people, including Gentiles as well as Jews (see Rom. 10:11–21). This fits with the aforementioned kardiatheology aimed at the human heart, beyond mere thoughts or feelings.

A new human volitional center depends on the direct, firsthand reception and ongoing availability of God's empowering Spirit by a receptive human agent. Such a new volitional center is at the heart of spiritual resurrection as understood by Paul and John (compare John 3:1–12). Such spiritual resurrection has straightforward cognitive as well as salvific importance: It yields experiential acquaintance with powerful evidence of God's intervening Spirit at work in one's motivational center, leading one away from selfishness and toward unselfish love, in fellowship with God. Such experiential evidence indicates what Paul calls a "new creation" in a person and what John calls "a person's being born from above." (On the topic of new creation in Paul, see Hubbard 2002.)

Paul writes: "...hope [in God] does not disappoint, because the love of God has been poured out in our hearts through the Holy Spirit given to us" (Rom. 5:5; compare 2 Cor. 1:22, 5:5). Through God's Spirit given to us as we willingly yield to God's authoritative call in conscience to volitional fellowship, our innermost personal center (that is, our "heart") would welcome God's powerful self-revelation of perfect love and thereby begin to be changed from being selfish to manifesting God's imparted unselfish love. This would be an agent-to-agent salvific power transaction that moves us noncoercively from human selfish fear (the root of sin) to shared divine unselfish love (the root of salvation), and from death to life. It would occur at the innermost personal center of a human life, where the problem of sinful selfishness arises and endures, but it would not automatically remove all human selfishness at once. The power transaction would yield, nonetheless, a new default motivational center in a manner that no merely intellectual or similarly surface work could.

Paul's Spirit-focused soteriology bears directly on purposively available *evidence* of divine reality. Human hope in God (to fulfill divine promises, including the promise of salvation) can find a conclusive *cognitive* anchor in our evident experience of willingly receiving God's Spirit, whereby God's love begins to change our hearts toward the distinctive character of divine unselfish love. Paul expresses a related theme in referring to the God who "has put his seal upon us and given us his Spirit in our hearts as a guarantee" (2 Cor. 1:22, RSV; see also 2 Cor. 5:5; compare Eph. 1:13). According to Paul, the Spirit given to receptive human hearts guarantees, as an evidential, cognitive down payment, that God will complete the salvific work of transformation begun in those hearts. Such human volitional transformation toward divine love is salient evidence of God's reality and intervention in a receptive human life. We can benefit now from attention to that distinctive evidence in human transformation. (For additional detail on this epistemological topic, see Moser 2008.)

According to Paul, the Spirit of God is also the Spirit of Jesus, who gave his life as God's obedient Son to manifest his Father's powerful unselfish love for humans and thereby to offer divine–human reconciliation, in fellowship with God. Furthermore, the Spirit of God is the Spirit of *adoption* of humans into God's family of obedient children, who thereby acknowledge God as "Abba, Father" (see Rom. 8:9, 15), and this adoption includes one's being led by the power of God's Spirit (Rom. 8:14). This approach to God's Spirit fits with the importance of *filial* knowledge of divine reality (on which, see Moser 2008, Chapter 3). Worldly powers of selfishness go in the opposite direction of one's being led by the unselfish power of a perfectly loving God's Spirit. In expecting evidence of God's reality to fit with worldly powers, including worldly religious powers incompatible with unselfish love, people blind themselves from apprehending God's reality.

According to Paul, God's intervening Spirit reveals God's reality and our relationship with God: "... we have received ... the Spirit from God, *in order that* we may know the things freely given to us by God" (1 Cor. 2:12, italics added; compare 1 Cor. 12:7–8, in which Paul speaks of the manifestation of God's Spirit). The Spirit of God, as God's own divine agent of salvific intervention and communication, would automatically know the things of God, including divine intentions and other attitudes, so, ultimately, the Spirit of God could authoritatively reveal God's reality and God's ways to humans. Paul thus concludes that we are given the Spirit of God *in order that* we may know God's reality and God's ways of self-giving love. He arguably has a kind of *volitional* and *filial* knowledge in mind, because human reception of God's Spirit requires human willingness to be adopted into God's family of obedient children, in cooperative fellowship with God.

By giving God's own Spirit to receptive humans, as a resident default but noncoercive guide and motivator, God extends volitional and filial knowledge of God's reality to humans. More specifically, God's intervening Spirit confirms to a receptive individual's spirit, via conscience, that he or she is a child of God, called into filial fellowship, including volitional cooperation, with God as perfectly authoritative and loving Father (see Rom. 8:15–16, Gal. 4:6–7, 1 Cor. 1:9; compare 1 John 4:13). The role of conscience is crucial because it involves the spiritual heart of a person; in addition, God can use various means, including other people, to prompt a response in one's conscience.

Filial fellowship with God involves noncoercive perfectly authoritative and loving *ownership* of a child on God's part and willingly *being owned* by God on the child's part. Paul states, accordingly, that followers of Jesus under God as Father are not their own but "have been bought with a price" and thus belong to God (1 Cor. 6:19–20; compare Rom. 14:7–9). Paul would say, accordingly, that the urgent question for a human is not so much "Who am I?" as "*Whose* am I?" John's Gospel follows suit: "The one who is of [that is, belongs to] God hears the words of God; on account of this, you do not hear them, because you are not of [that is, do not belong to] God" (8:47). A key motivational question thus arises: *By whose power* am I living? By the lasting power of God's Spirit of authoritative unselfish love, or by my own short-lived, largely selfish power? The presence of one's selfishness is a litmus test for one's being motivated by dying human power antithetical to the lasting unselfish power of a perfectly loving God.

Obedient human reception of God's Spirit is not a merely subjective matter. It yields one's becoming unselfishly loving to some discernible degree as God is unselfishly loving, even toward enemies. It bears discernible fruits of the intervening Spirit of a perfectly loving God, such as love, joy, peace, patience, kindness, goodness, faithfulness, humility, and self-control (compare Gal. 5:22–23). These fruits are not merely subjective phenomena, but are, instead, discernible by anyone suitably attentive to them. As the powerful overflow of divine love in a receptive human life, they emerge in human lives in ways that are identifiable and testable, even though one needs willing "eyes to see and ears to hear" them. The fruits of God's Spirit arise and function in a larger context of a willing life under transformation by this Spirit as a salvific gift from God to be received via experientially grounded trust (Gal. 3:2, 14).

Jesus announced the human need to test competing people and their positions: "Beware of false prophets, who come to you in sheep's clothing but inwardly are ravenous wolves. You will know them by their fruits.... Every sound tree bears good fruit, but the bad tree bears evil fruit. A sound tree cannot bear evil fruit, nor can a bad tree bear good fruit" (Matt. 7:15–18). Similarly, one can know the authenticity of God's intervening Spirit by means of the fruits demanded and yielded by the Spirit in one's own life. This Spirit noncoercively demands and empowers one, in fellowship with God, to become loving to some degree as God is unselfishly loving, even toward enemies. This is, in keeping with God's perfectly loving character, the primary fruit of God's intervening Spirit in a receptive person (1 Cor. 13:1–13; compare Eph. 3:17–19, Col. 2:2, 3:14), and it is identifiable and testable in a willing person's life. God's intervening Spirit thus comes with salient evidence observable by any suitably attentive person, and such evidence enables one to exclude imposters. We can say the same for divine salvation from sin and the many dangerous counterfeits in circulation.

References

Augustine. [395] *On Free Will (De Libero Arbitrio)*. In *Augustine: Earlier Writings*, ed. and trans. J. H. S. Burleigh. (Philadelphia: Westminster, 1953), 102–217.

Berkhof, Hendrikus. *Christian Faith*, 2nd ed., trans. S. Woudstra (Grand Rapids, MI: Eerdmans, 1986).

Brunner, Emil. *Man in Revolt*, trans. Olive Wyon (London: Lutterworth, 1939).

———. *The Christian Doctrine of Creation and Redemption*, trans. Olive Wyon (London: Lutterworth, 1952).

Bultmann, Rudolf. *Theology of the New Testament*, trans. Kendrick Grobel (New York: Scribner, 1955).

Cherbonnier, Edmond La B. *Hardness of Heart* (Garden City, NY: Doubleday, 1955).

Dodd, C. H. *The Apostolic Preaching and its Developments* (London: Hodder and Stoughton, 1936).

Heschel, Abraham. *The Prophets* (New York: Jewish Publication Society, 1962).

Hubbard, Moyer. *New Creation in Paul's Letters and Thought* (Cambridge: Cambridge University Press, 2002).

Hunter, A. M. *The Unity of the New Testament* (London: SCM, 1943).

Jackson, Timothy. *Love Disconsoled* (Cambridge: Cambridge University Press, 1999).

Lemcio, Eugene. "The Unifying Kerygma of the New Testament," in Lemcio, *The Past of Jesus in the Gospels* (Cambridge: Cambridge University Press, 1991), 115–31.

Mann, William E. "Augustine on Evil and Original Sin," in ed. Eleonore Stump and Norman Kretzmann, *The Cambridge Companion to Augustine* (Cambridge: Cambridge University Press, 2001), 40–48.

Meadors, Edward. *Idolatry and the Hardening of the Heart* (London: T & T Clark, 2006).

Moser, Paul K. "Jesus on Knowledge of God," *Christian Scholars Review* 28 (1999): 586–604.

———. *The Elusive God: Reorienting Religious Epistemology.* (Cambridge: Cambridge University Press, 2008).

Niebuhr, Reinhold. *The Nature and Destiny of Man*, vol. 1: Human Nature (New York: Scribner, 1941).

———. *Faith and History* (New York: Scribner, 1949).

O'Collins, Gerald. *Christology* (Oxford: Oxford University Press, 1995).

Westerholm, Stephen. *Perspectives Old and New on Paul* (Grand Rapids, MI: Eerdmans, 2006).

Wiebe, Phillip. *God and Other Spirit* (New York: Oxford University Press, 2004).

11 The problem of evil

CHAD MEISTER

Most Christians, indeed most theists generally, believe there exists a God who is a perfect moral being and who has unlimited power and knowledge. However, given the imperfect world in which we live, believing in this God poses a vexing problem with which philosophers and theologians have been grappling for millennia. The roots of the problem go back as far as the ancient Greek philosopher Epicurus (341–270 BCE), whose paradox of evil is succinctly paraphrased by David Hume:

> Is [God] willing to prevent evil, but not able? Then he is impotent. Is he able, but not willing? Then he is malevolent. Is he both able and willing? Whence then is evil?[1]

Does it make sense to believe in God given the evil that exists in the world? Does it make sense to believe in God when, in the midst of terrible suffering and pain, it seems that God does nothing about it?

In Shusaku Endo's novel, *Silence*, a young Jesuit priest from Portugal named Sebastian Rodrigues is sent to Japan to comfort Christian converts and to investigate claims that his spiritual mentor – a Jesuit missionary also sent to the country – has committed apostasy. Out of suspicion and concern about the rapid growth of the Christian faith in Japan, feudal lords, under the auspices of the shogun (the military governor ruling Japan), attempted to drive Christianity out of the country and Christian men, women, and children were rounded up and required to recant or face some of the most gruesome persecutions imaginable. Reflecting on these horrors, Rodrigues finds that he "cannot bear the monotonous sound of the dark sea gnawing at the shore. Behind the depressing silence of this sea, the silence of God... the feeling that while men raise their voices in anguish God remains with folded arms, silent."[2] Sadly, while *Silence*

---

[1] As quoted by David Hume in his *Dialogue Concerning Natural Religion* (Indianapolis, IN: Hackett, 1988), 63.

[2] Shusaku Endo, *Silence*, trans. William Johnston (New York: Taplinger, 1969), 61. For an interesting and abbreviated version of the story of *Silence*, see Philip L. Quinn,

is a work of fiction, it is *historical* fiction – one based on the actual oral histories of several Japanese communities in the sixteenth century. Amidst the tortures, the issue that continually arises in Sebastian's mind is *the silence of God*. Why does God seem to be absent? Why does God allow such pain and suffering? If God really exists, why does God not respond to the prayers of the saints?

The kinds of evils depicted in the novel are dubbed *moral evils* because they are, in some sense, the result of a moral agent. Some moral evils are great, as are these horrors of torture and murder. Other examples include genocide, child abuse, and rape. There are also less severe types of moral evils, such as lying, stealing, or betraying someone's trust. Another category of evil has to do not with moral agents, but with naturally occurring events or disasters. Examples of *natural evils* include disease, floods, hurricanes, tornadoes, famine, and other terrible events that do harm to humans and other living creatures.

The moral and natural evils that exist seem, *prima facie*, to be incompatible with the existence of an omnipotent, omniscient, and omnibenevolent God, or at least to count as evidence against such a God. This is the problem of evil. The problem has taken many forms throughout the centuries, and so it may be better to speak of *problems of evil*, as there are a host of them for the theist. In this chapter, I limit the discussion to intellectual problems, first addressing them as they are discussed in philosophy of religion and then focusing on Christian philosophical theology.[3]

THE LOGICAL ARGUMENT

One of the intellectual problems of evil is the alleged logical incompatibility between the following two claims:

G. God (an omnipotent, omniscient, and omnibenevolent being) exists.

and

E. Evil exists.

Essays in the Philosophy of Religion, ed. Christian B. Miller (Oxford: Clarendon Press, 2006), 94–106.

[3] Besides intellectual problems of evil, there are other categories as well, including what is sometimes called the existential problem of evil (other titles include the "religious problem," "moral problem," "pastoral problem," "psychological problem," or "emotional problem"). Simply put, it concerns the existential disgust or dislike one has of a God who would allow evil to exist.

Because contradictory claims are necessarily false, if G. and E. are, in fact, contradictions, one of the claims must be false. Because we know that E. is true, G. must be false.[4] God must not exist.

However, it is not immediately clear that these two claims are logically incompatible. In attempting to show how they are, J. L. Mackie developed an argument that can be structured this way:

1. A wholly good being always eliminates evil as far as it can.
2. There are no limits to what an omnipotent and omniscient being can do.
3. Therefore, based on 1 and 2, if a wholly good, omnipotent, and omniscient being exists, it eliminates evil completely.
4. Evil has not been eliminated completely.
5. Thus, following from 3 and 4, a wholly good, omnipotent, and omniscient being does not exist.[5]

If Mackie's argument is sound, it provides deductive proof that God's existence (God understood as a wholly good, omnipotent, and omniscient being) is logically impossible. God cannot exist.

Despite its apparent logical force, it has been widely agreed in recent days that arguments of this kind are unsuccessful. The problem with the argument is that it presupposes an incorrect view of omnipotence – incorrect at least in the way omnipotence typically has been understood by theists historically. Most Christian theists long have recognized that there are some things an omnipotent being cannot do. An omnipotent being cannot make logical impossibilities, for example, such as making a square circle or creating a being more powerful than itself.

Furthermore, an omnipotent being cannot make an agent with a certain kind of free will do only what is good. According to *libertarian free will*, a free action is one in which the agent has the power to do otherwise than what she or he does. An agent's free choices are truly up to the individual, not someone else (even God). Therefore, if it is possible there are such agents, then even God could not make them freely do only what is good. Now, it is also possible that free will of this libertarian kind – free will that is incompatible with any sort of determinism – is a very great good. It may be, for example, that creatures

---

4 Most theists and atheists agree that evil exists, but some belief systems deny this claim.
5 See J. L. Mackie, "Evil and Omnipotence," *Mind* (1955), collected in *The Problem of Evil*, ed. Robert M. Adams and Marilyn McCord Adams (Oxford: Oxford University Press, 1990), 25–26.

capable of producing moral good and of reflecting true love and other virtues must have libertarian free will. However, creatures with this kind of autonomous free will can choose to do evil as well. Not even God could cause them to freely do only what is good, for this would entail a contradiction, which is impossible. In addition, a world containing creatures with libertarian free will may be more valuable than a world without such creatures. Think of a world with no free agents – one that has only preprogrammed robots, say. It does seem that the former world is more valuable, all else being equal, than the latter. Thus God may have a morally sufficient reason for not preventing evil completely; evil may be an unavoidable consequence of a very good world with free creatures.

Such a view of things does appear to be logically possible. If it is possible, then claims G. and E. are not necessarily logically incompatible. And if they are not incompatible, the argument fails. Theists and atheists alike now generally agree that the logical argument is unsuccessful.[6]

This rebuttal of the logical argument – what is often referred to as the *free will defense*[7] – does not end the discussion of evil, however, nor does it solve all of the problems related to God and evil. In recent times, challenges to the existence and goodness of God given evil have shifted from the strong claim that theism is necessarily false to the more reserved claim that theism (as traditionally understood) is probably false. This kind of challenge, what is often called the evidential argument, attempts to demonstrate not that claims G. and E. are logically incompatible, but rather that it is not plausible to affirm G. given E.

THE EVIDENTIAL ARGUMENT

One form of evidential argument from evil is based on the assumption – typically agreed on by theists and atheists alike – that an

---

[6] Atheist philosopher William Rowe states the following with respect to the logical argument: "Some philosophers have contended that the existence of evil is *logically inconsistent* with the existence of the theistic God. No one, I think, has succeeded in establishing such an extravagant claim. Indeed, granted incompatibilism, there is a fairly compelling argument for the view that the existence of evil is logically consistent with the existence of the theistic God." In "The Problem of Evil and Some Varieties of Atheism," *American Philosophical Quarterly* 16 (1979); reprinted in Chad Meister, *The Philosophy of Religion Reader* (London: Routledge, 2008), 523–35. Citation on page 534, note 1.

[7] Alvin Plantinga offered the first detailed presentation of his free will defense in his *God, Freedom, and Evil* (New York: Harper and Row, 1974).

omnipotent, omniscient, omnibenevolent being would prevent gratuitous or meaningless evil. William Rowe formulates the argument this
way:

(i) There exist instances of intense suffering which an omnipotent,
omniscient being could have prevented without thereby losing some
greater good or permitting some evil equally bad or worse.

(ii) An omnipotent, wholly good being would prevent the occurrence
of any intense suffering it could, unless it could not do so without
thereby losing some greater good or permitting some evil equally
bad or worse.

(iii) There does not exist an omnipotent, omniscient, wholly good
being.[8]

Rowe maintains that this is an evidential or probabilistic argument
because premise (i) is probably true (he believes), though not decisive.
If the first premise is probably true, because premise (ii) is true (most
theists and atheists concur on this one), it follows deductively that conclusion (iii) is probably true.

At first glance, it appears that theists would agree with both
premises. But because this argument is valid in form, if one agrees with
the premises, the conclusion follows: an omnipotent, omniscient, and
omnibenevolent being does not exist. What is the theist to do? Several
prominent theists have challenged premise (ii), but most grant it,[9] so the
debate typically centers on premise (i). Rowe offers a particular example
of natural evil to support this premise. The example includes a fawn,
affectionately called Bambi, which apparently experiences pointless and
terrible suffering. The fawn is in a forest when lightning strikes and
starts a forest fire. Trapped, the fawn is terribly burned and lies in misery for days until it finally dies. Rowe then asks, "Could an omnipotent,
omniscient being have prevented the fawn's apparently pointless suffering? The answer is obvious, as even the theist will insist. An omnipotent, omniscient being could have easily prevented the fawn from being
horribly burned, or, given the burning, could have spared the fawn the
intense suffering by quickly ending its life, rather than allowing the fawn
to lie in terrible agony for several days."[10] Here is a case, Rowe argues
– a case that represents countless examples of animal suffering that
actually occur in the world – that gives reason to believe that premise

---

[8] William Rowe, *op. cit.*, 527.

[9] William Hasker offers a challenge to it in "The Necessity of Gratuitous Evil," *Faith and Philosophy* 9 (1992), 23–44.

[10] Rowe, *op. cit.*, 529.

(i) is probably true; the poor fawn's painful death does not seem to be a necessary condition for some greater good.

Theists have gone in different directions in responding to this argument. Some argue that there are good reasons to believe that premise (i) is false, whereas others argue that we are not in an appropriate epistemic position to know that premise (i) is true. The first approach involves *theodicy* – the attempt to justify God and the ways of God given the evil and suffering in the world. We will explore two theodicies in this chapter. The second approach involves questioning the reasons one might affirm premise (i). Rowe asks if it is "reasonable to believe that there is some greater good so intimately connected to that [fawn's] suffering that even an omnipotent, omniscient being could not have obtained that good without permitting that suffering or some evil at least as bad?" His conclusion is: "It certainly does not appear reasonable to believe this."[11] Because there "does not appear" to be any good or any sufficient reason for affirming so, there probably is not one. But is this a good inference to make? Stephen Wykstra has called arguments such as this noseeum arguments; namely, if you do not see X, that is a good reason for thinking not-X. In this case, it is alleged that after carefully looking for a greater good that might come about from some gratuitous evil none can be found, so it is a good inference to conclude that there is none.[12]

Noseeum arguments can be strong or weak, good or bad. Suppose a friend told you that, after careful astrological reflection, he believes that you are going to be killed in an automobile accident in the next few days. After examining his materials on the subject (horoscopes and Tarot cards), it doesn't seem to you that this claim is true or reasonable to believe. You don't see any evidence in what he has presented to you, and you have reason to believe that astrology is suspect. In this case, your noseeum inference that his claim is false is a good one. But consider another example. Suppose that you go to the dentist with a terrible toothache. The dentist takes a quick look at your teeth and says that she doesn't see anything amiss. You inquire about X-rays, but the dentist says that since she doesn't see anything, X-rays are not necessary; you don't have any cavities and your teeth are quite healthy. In this case, the noseeum inference is a bad one.

What about the atheist's inference from evil? Is it more like the first example or the second? Some theists, such as those affirming *skeptical*

---

[11] *Ibid.*, 529–30.
[12] See, for example, Stephen J. Wykstra, "The Human Obstacle to Evidential Arguments from Suffering: On Avoiding the Evils of 'Appearance,'" *International Journal for Philosophy of Religion* (1984) 16: 73–93.

theism, claim that the atheist's inference is like the second. Skeptical theists argue that because many of God's ways are inscrutable, we are in no position to judge as improbable the claim that there are great goods secured by God through the various evils that exist. There may well be many great goods brought about by evil acts that we cannot comprehend, given our cognitive (and other) limitations. Because God's ways are so far beyond the ability of finite minds to grasp, we are simply not justified in affirming there are evils that have no point, even though they may appear to us this way. An analogy may help. I was recently playing chess with my ten-year-old son. He's a novice at the game (I must admit that I'm a novice myself, yet several years advanced beyond him), and he failed to understand why I made a certain move in the game. Given his limited understanding of chess, he is not justified in affirming that the move was pointless. He is simply not able to recognize its point.[13]

Something like this point emerges in the Old Testament in the book of Job where, after suffering great personal harm and loss, Job demands a response from God. "Then the LORD answered Job... 'Who is this that darkens counsel by words without knowledge?.... Where were you when I laid the foundation of the earth? Tell me if you have understanding. Who determined its measurements...?'" (38:1–4) As the questioning continues, Job is brought to silence before his Maker. He has no answers. Finally Job realizes the depths of his own cognitive limitations with respect to God and the created order and responds: "I know that you can do all things.... Therefore, I have uttered what I did not understand, things too wonderful for me, which I did not know" (42:2–3).

Rowe has offered several responses to skeptical theism, including that, on this view, there could never be *any* reason for doubting God's existence given evil, no matter how horrific and extensive it may be.[14] The skeptical theist, he argues, has made the divide between God's knowledge and human knowledge too wide – wider than what theism (as described in the argument as the claim that an omniscient, omnipotent, omnibenevolent creator exists) affirms. Therefore, although a modified view of God that widens the human/divine cognitive chasm may suffice

---

[13] I owe this insightful analogy to William Alston, "Some (Temporarily) Final thoughts," in *The Evidential Argument from Evil*, ed. Daniel Howard-Snyder (Bloomington, IN: Indiana University Press, 1996), 316–17. However, the chess match between my son and I actually occurred as described.

[14] See Daniel Howard-Snyder, Michael Bergmann, and William Rowe, "An Exchange on the Problem of Evil," in *God and the Problem of Evil*, ed. William Rowe (Oxford: Blackwell, 2001), 124–28, 156–57.

as a response to premise (i) of the evidential argument from evil, *theism* does not. In other words, Rowe maintains, Wykstra has unjustifiably imported the further notions of God's mysterious and incomprehensible purposes and human cognitive limitations into the argument, which renders it invalid. The Christian skeptical theist need not see this as a liability, however, but rather as an asset. The human limitations and inscrutability of God propounded by Wykstra are, in fact, broadly the traditional Christian views of the matter.

Another recent move by Paul Draper has advanced the discussion. He argues that what we know about the world, with its distribution of pains and pleasures, is more likely on a "hypothesis of indifference" (whereby "neither the nature nor the condition of sentient beings on earth is the result of benevolent or malevolent actions performed by nonhuman persons") than it is on theism.[15] If theism is true, because God is morally perfect, there must be morally good reasons for allowing biologically useless pain, and morally good reasons for producing pleasures even if such pleasures are not biologically useful. However, given our observations of the pains and pleasures experienced by sentient creatures, including their biologically gratuitous experiences, the hypothesis of indifference provides a more plausible account than theism.

However, as Peter van Inwagen has demonstrated, this argument can be countered by contending that, for all we know, in every possible world that exhibits a high degree of complexity (such as ours, with sentient, intelligent life), the laws of nature are the same or have the same general features as the actual laws.[16] Therefore, we cannot assume that the distribution of pain and pleasure (including the pains and pleasures reflected in biological evolution, say) in a world with a high degree of complexity such as ours would be any different given theism. We are simply not in an epistemic position to assign a probability either way, so we cannot make the judgment that theism is less likely than the hypothesis of indifference.

So far, it has been assumed that the burden of proof is on the theist, but perhaps where the burden of proof should lie is another point to consider in this discussion. Perhaps this is a case where issues of world view are brought into sharp relief. If one has *prima facie* reasons for affirming atheism prior to attending to cases of apparently gratuitous

[15] Paul Draper, "Pain and Pleasure: An Evidential Problem for Theists," *Noûs* 23 (1989): 331–50.

[16] Peter van Inwagen, "The Problem of Evil, the Problem of Air, and the Problem of Silence," in *Philosophical Perspectives*, ed. James Tomberlin, Philosophy of Religion (Atascaderg, CA: Ridgeview, 1991), 5: 135–65.

evil, then perhaps the burden lies with the theist to demonstrate how such cases of evil can be justified given theism. On the other hand, if one has *prima facie* reasons for affirming theism prior to attending to cases of apparently gratuitous evil, perhaps the burden of proof lies with the atheist to demonstrate how such cases of evil cannot be justified given theism.[17] We will return to atheism toward the end of this chapter.

Theodicy involves theism taking on this burden and attempting to offer a justification of God's allowing the evil that exists in the world.

THEODICY

Throughout the centuries, a number of theists have believed there are no pointless evils – that there are greater goods that justify the evil in the world. Attempts to vindicate God by providing an explanation for evil come in a variety of forms, and two of the best known are Augustine's free will theodicy and John Hick's soul-making theodicy.

Augustine's free will theodicy

One important theodicy was formulated by St. Augustine (354–430), and it has probably been the most prominent response to evil in the history of Christian thought. Fundamental to the position is Augustine's view that the universe God created is good; everything in the universe is good and has a good purpose, some things to a greater extent, some to a lesser one. Evil, then, is not something God created. Evil is a *privatio boni* – a privation of the good. Augustine uses the example of being blind. Blindness is not a thing in itself, let alone a good thing. It is a privation of seeing. Evil, he argues, is like blindness; it is a privation of good.

Then, if God created a very good world, what brought about the privations? How did evil arise? It came about, he maintains, through free will. The story is familiar. Some of God's good creation – namely persons, including angels and humans – were given the good gift of freedom of the will, a gift that reflected God's image of being morally culpable and creative. However, some of God's free creatures turned their will from God, the supreme Good, to lesser goods. This act of turning from God was, in essence, the Fall. It happened first with the angels and then, after being tempted by Satan (one of the fallen angels), with humans. This is how moral evil entered the universe and this moral fall, or *sin*, also brought with it tragic cosmic consequences, for it ushered in natural

---

[17] Jane Mary Trau raises burden of proof issues in "Fallacies in the Argument from Gratuitous Suffering," *The New Scholasticism* 60 (1986): 485–89.

evil as well. The Fall was no insignificant event; it was a disaster of cataclysmic proportions in the universe that accounts for all the moral and natural evils throughout history. Augustine's theodicy does not end without resolution, however, for in the eschaton God will rectify evil when he judges the world in righteousness, ushering into his eternal kingdom those persons who have been saved through Christ and sending to eternal perdition those persons who are wicked and disobedient and have rejected his good offer of salvation.

Although this free will theodicy does exonerate God from evil by placing full responsibility for it upon free creatures, and although it has been extensively advocated by Christians since its development in the fifth century, it has been highly criticized in recent times.[18] One problem with this type of theodicy is that, even granting a robust libertarian view of free will, could God not have prevented the consequences of the evil decisions made by free creatures – consequences having to do with both moral and natural evils? For example, could God not have prevented the Asian tsunami in 2004 that swept through eleven countries, killing more than 200,000 innocent people? Could he not have stopped the Black Plague in the fourteenth century, which wiped out well over thirty percent of Europe's population? And although perhaps God was not able to avert members of the Khmer Rouge from *deciding* to torture and execute hundreds of thousands of Cambodian people, could he not have orchestrated events such that the totalitarian leaders failed in their attempts – thus preventing the killing fields?

Richard Swinburne, a contemporary defender of the free will theodicy, responds by arguing that not only do free will choices have great value, but their successful implementation also has great value – value great enough that God is perfectly justified in not thwarting the consequences of such choices, even if they are evil.[19] Furthermore (and this brings up the issue addressed earlier regarding skeptical theism), how do we know that there are not greater goods that result from these evil actions that would not have arisen without them? It seems likely that we are simply not in an epistemic situation to make such an assessment. As has been discovered by those working in the field of chaos theory, the slightest perturbations of the early conditions of a dynamic system can have significant effects on larger systems that would have been impossible to predict given empirical observations. The death of

---

[18] For a recent and impressive defense of the free will theodicy, see Richard Swinburne, *Providence and the Problem of Evil* (Oxford: Clarendon Press, 1998).

[19] Also see Richard Swinburne's *Providence and the Problem of Evil* (Oxford: Oxford University Press, 1998), 82–107, for his engagement with this problem.

one European peasant centuries ago could have had incredible effects on others at later times and places that would provide God with a morally sufficient reason for allowing it to happen.[20]

Another problem that has been raised with Augustine's theodicy is that, given modern scientific understandings of the biological and social development of *homo sapiens*, it no longer seems plausible to maintain that human beings began in a state of moral and spiritual maturity and perfection and then fell into a state of moral depravity as depicted in the early chapters of the book of Genesis. Rather than biological, social, and moral devolution, the story of human history is now generally seen as one of evolutionary development and progress. Furthermore, geology has demonstrated that natural evils existed long before the emergence of human life, and thus could not have been the consequence of a human fall.

However, perhaps the Augustinian theodicy can survive intact despite these developments. First, it is at least possible that natural evils are the result of the choices of free agents in the spirit world prior to the emergence of humans. Perhaps an angelic fall could account for "nature red in tooth and claw," to quote Tennyson. Although this will seem farfetched to many modern ears, it is within the general purview of the Christian story, as C. S. Lewis intimated in his space trilogy.[21] Furthermore, as Michael Murray has recently argued, it is possible to explain at least some natural evil as an unavoidable byproduct of a nomically regular, natural, good world.[22] With respect to the evolutionary account of human beings, it can be argued that there is no irreconcilable conflict between the standard neo-Darwinian account of human evolution and the view that there was an early pair of morally culpable hominids in whom God granted moral and spiritual awareness not unlike those depicted in the garden story of Genesis. Nevertheless, another attempt at theodicy developed by John Hick provides an overall better fit with the current scientific story of human development.

John Hick's soul-making theodicy
Based on the work of Irenaeus (c.130–c.202 CE), John Hick developed a theodicy that is, in some ways, in stark contrast to the Augustinian

---

[20] William Lane Craig brought this chaos analogy to my attention in private conversation. For a fascinating introduction to the developing field of chaos theory, see James Gleick, *Chaos: Making a New Science* (New York: Penguin, 1998).

[21] See C. S. Lewis, *Perelandra* (New York: Macmillan, 1944).

[22] See Michael Murray, *Nature Red in Tooth and Claw: Theism and the Problem of Animal Suffering* (Oxford: Oxford University Press, 2008).

approach. He maintains that his soul-making theodicy has the benefit of God's having a close, developing relationship with his creation over time, whereas the Augustinian type presupposes an impersonal or sub-personal relationship between God and creation.[23] Instead of God creating a paradise with perfect human beings who then freely fell into sin, on this account God created the world as a good place (but no paradise) for developing a race of beings from an early state of animal selfishness and self-centeredness to an advanced state of moral and spiritual maturity.

> God's purpose was not to construct a paradise whose inhabitants would experience a maximum of pleasure and a minimum of pain. The world is seen, instead, as a place of "soul making" or person making in which free beings, grappling with the tasks and challenges of their existence in a common environment, may become "children of God" and "heirs of eternal life." Our world, with all its rough edges, is the sphere in which this second and harder stage of the creative process is taking place.[24]

God created good but undeveloped persons and moral, spiritual, and intellectual maturity requires experiencing trials and hardships in life. Evil, then, is not the result of perfect persons choosing to sin but, rather, is an inevitable part of an environment necessary for developing mature character. Thus, by placing evolving beings in this challenging environment, through their free will to choose what is right and good, they can gradually grow into the mature persons that God desires them to be, exhibiting the virtues of patience, courage, and generosity, for example. Furthermore, as the theodicy goes, God will continue to work with human persons, even in the afterlife if necessary, by allowing them noncoercive opportunities to love and choose the good so that eventually everyone will be brought into a right and full relationship with God; everyone will finally experience redemption.[25] In this view, God allows moral and natural evils in the world to nurture virtues within individuals in order to make morally and spiritually mature souls or persons.

---

[23] Hick spells out this criticism of the Augustinian theodicy in his *Evil and the God of Love* (London: Palgrave Macmillan, 2007), 193–98.

[24] John Hick, *Philosophy of Religion*, 4th ed. (Englewood Cliffs, NJ: Prentice Hall, 1990), 45–46.

[25] Eleonore Stump develops a version of the soul-making theodicy that centers on a particular theological good. See her "The Problem of Evil," *Faith and Philosophy* 2 (1985): 392–418.

One objection that can be raised is that although it may be true that a soul-making environment cannot be a paradise, the degree and extent of pain and suffering that exist in the world surely are not justified. Why need there be an Auschwitz, for example? Could not mature characters be developed without this kind of horror? In addition, some evils seem to be character destroying rather than character building. Not all people improve through the hardships they endure; often, the difficulties in one's life cause it to end in tragedy. Think of a child with a debilitating disease who is made fun of or who is always the recipient of charity, and then dies at an early age; or a woman who is brutally raped, held captive, and then murdered days later. Do such examples of gratuitous evil not count against soul-making type theodicies?

Hick responds by claiming that apparently pointless evils are not, in fact, without purpose and merit. The kinds of sympathy and compassion, for example, that are evoked by such seemingly indiscriminate and unfair miseries are very great goods in and of themselves – goods that would not arise without the miseries appearing as unfair and indiscriminate.[26] Although God did not intend or need any particular evils (such as Auschwitz) for his soul-making purposes, he did need to create an environment where such evils were a possibility. Thus, although each individual instance of evil may not be justified by a particular greater good (purpose or merit), the existence of a world where evil is possible is necessary for a world where soul-making takes place. Furthermore, as noted earlier, on this theodicy a positive doctrine of life after death is crucial, for there are cases in which difficulties in an individual's life breed bitterness, anger, fear, and a lessening of virtuous character. So in these instances, at least, the soul-making process would need to continue on into the afterlife if it is to be successful. In addition, as will be argued subsequently, on a Christian account of resurrection, an afterlife could also perhaps provide future goods that are great enough to justify even the worst horrors experienced in this life.

The free will and soul-making theodicies share a common supposition that God would not permit evil that is not necessary for a greater good. But a number of theists affirm that some evils are not justified, that some horrors are so damaging there are no goods that outweigh them. If there are such evils, why would God allow them? It may be that "restricted standard theism" – the view that there exists an omniscient, omnipotent, omnigood being who created the world, accompanied by

---

[26] See Hick, *Evil and the God of Love*, Chapter 15.

other religious claims – is inadequate to provide a response. Perhaps an adequate reply requires "expanded theism" – the view that there exists an omniscient, omnipotent, omnigood being who created the world, accompanied by other religious claims, such as those provided by orthodox Christian theism.[27]

CHRIST, EVIL, AND INFINITE GOODS

It is surprising that much of the work done on the problem of evil by Christian philosophers over the centuries has had little, if anything, to say about Jesus Christ. Recently, there have been some important exceptions, though, and it seems to me that the trajectory of discussion on evil, at least within the Christian tradition, would greatly benefit from utilizing the rich resources of its own tradition. One important example of this approach is the recent work of Marilyn McCord Adams, who pushes theodicy beyond restricted standard theism to an expanded Christian theism utilizing a Christocentric theological framework.[28] Adams focuses on the worst sorts of evils – what she calls "horrendous evils" (evils which, when experienced by a particular person, give that person reason to doubt whether her or his life could, considered in totality, be taken to be a great good to her or him) – and argues that the Christian theodicist should abandon the widely held assumption that responses to evil can only include those goods which both theists and atheists acknowledge. She maintains that goods of this sort are finite and temporal, whereas the Christian has infinite and eternal goods at her or his disposal. An intimate, loving, eternal relationship with God, for example, may well be a good that is infinite and incomparable with any other kind of good. "If Divine Goodness is infinite, if infinite relation to It is thus incommensurately good for created persons, then we have identified a good big enough to defeat horrors in every case."[29]

She further argues that taking a "general reasons why" approach, whereby some general reason is offered to cover all forms of evil (for example, God's desire to make a world exhibiting a perfect balance of retributive justice constitutes a reason why a perfectly good God would

[27] The terms "restricted standard theism" and "expanded theism" were coined by William Rowe in his "Evil and the Theistic Hypothesis: A Reply to Wykstra," *International Journal for Philosophy of Religion* 16 (1984): 95–100.

[28] Marilyn McCord Adams, *Horrendous Evils and the Goodness of God* (Ithaca, NY: Cornell University Press, 1999).

[29] *Ibid.*, 82–83.

make a world with the kinds and amounts of evil we have in this world),
doesn't seem to be the kind of help we need.[30] For example, is the following really an acceptable reply to the horror of a mother discovering
that her young son was killed by a drunk driver: "This was the price
God was willing to pay for the world in which we live – one which has
the best balance of moral good over evil"? Adams doesn't believe so.
As a *Christian* philosopher, she believes a more adequate response can
be provided, which involves the compossibility of God and the evils in
the world. Rather than focusing on the possible reasons *why* God might
allow evils of this sort, she maintains that it is enough to show *how*
God can be good and yet permit their existence. She claims there is
good reason for the Christian to believe that all evils will ultimately be
defeated in one's life and that God will, in the end, engulf all personal
horrors through integrating participation in the evils into one's relationship with God. Such integration is possible, she suggests, through first
identifying with the sufferings of Christ. Through the Incarnation, God
the Son participated in horrendous evil through his passion and death,
and the human experiences of pain and suffering can be a way of identifying with the suffering Christ. This is precisely what some of the
Christian saints and mystics prayed for.[31]

A second possible integration includes experiencing divine gratitude, as expressed in the work of Julian of Norwich. In her sixth vision,
Julian describes a heavenly welcome in which God thanks those who
experienced evil in their earthly lives: "I thank you for your suffering,
especially in your youth."[32] This experience of divine gratitude, she
notes, will be so glorious that it will fill one's soul far beyond any merit
of such suffering.

Yet a third possible integration is identifying temporal suffering with
a vision into the inner life of God. It could be, for example, that God is
passible (*pace* medieval theology) – that God is not a detached observer,
an unmoved cosmic gazer, but rather grieves over evil and is incensed
over injustice. Perhaps our deepest sufferings are, in some sense, visions
of God's inner life and experience. If so, and if a vision of God is a very
great good, then suffering (even horrendous suffering) could have a good
aspect to it. In the opening section of this chapter I made mention of the

---

[30] See Marilyn McCord Adams, "Horrendous Evils and the Goodness of God," in *The
Problem of Evil*, ed. Marilyn McCord Adams and Robert Merrihew Adams (Oxford:
Oxford University Press, 1990), 209–21.

[31] See, for example, Julian of Norwich, *Revelations of Divine Love*, trans. Elizabeth
Spearing (New York: Penguin Books, 1998), Chapter 17.

[32] *Ibid.*, chapter 14, 62.

apparent silence of God in the view of Japanese Christians experiencing
the pain and suffering of persecution as depicted in Endo's novel. Toward
the end of the book, after Rodrigues the priest has undergone terrible
persecution, the silence of God is broken through an encounter he has
with Christ when, in prayer, he says, "Lord, I resented your silence."
Christ's reply: "I was not silent. I suffered beside you."

Given integrations such as these, all human beings (even those who
have experienced the most horrific evils on earth) will, in the eschaton,
be redeemed and thus be able to find ultimate meaning and goodness
in their lives. This approach is parochial (and Adams acknowledges as
much), for atheists, nontheists, and non-Christian theists would not
agree with at least some of the premises of the argument. Nevertheless,
this more expanded theism is certainly better able to explain how God
can defeat horrors than is generic theism.

John Stackhouse also affirms the fundamental role of the resources
of the Christian tradition in responding to evil:

> In Jesus we see what we desperately need to see: God close to
> us, God active among us, God loving us, God forgiving our sin,
> God opening up a way to a new life of everlasting love. If Jesus
> is the human face of God, Christians affirm, then human beings
> have a God who cares, a God who acts on their behalf (even to
> the point of self-sacrifice), and a God who is now engaged in the
> complete conquest of evil and the reestablishment of universal
> shalom for all time. If Jesus is truly God revealed, then we can
> trust God in spite of the evil all around us and in us.[33]

Indeed, if, as Christians believe, Jesus Christ is the incarnate son of God,
then the ultimate resolution of evil is rooted in him – the one who has
triumphed over evil. After all, it was only because of the victory of Christ
that the Apostle Paul had the hope that even though he, himself, had
experienced a variety of evils, they were only "slight momentary afflic-
tions" as compared to the "eternal weight of glory beyond all measure"
awaiting in the consummation of all things (2 Cor. 4:17–18). Thus, on the
traditional Christian account, the belief in an afterlife is not an ad hoc
addition to generic theism; the idea that God overcomes sin and death
through the Resurrection of Christ is foundational and central, without
which there would be no Christianity, and it provides opportunity for
future goods beyond human imagination.

[33] John G. Stackhouse, Jr., *Can God Be Trusted? Faith and the Challenge of Evil*
(Oxford: Oxford University Press, 1998), 103–04.

THE PROBLEM OF EVIL AND BELIEF IN GOD

Evil is ubiquitous. In a world riddled with the kinds of horrors we find in it, this fact alone seems to reduce the likelihood of the existence of a perfectly good, all-powerful, omniscient God. But it is inappropriate to consider the problem of evil alone, because whether it is reasonable to believe that God exists is relative to one's entire set of beliefs and experiences, not just to the existence of evil. As Alvin Plantinga has argued, even if a certain claim p is improbable on a certain claim q, it does not follow that one who accepts both p and q is irrational or guilty of epistemic impropriety (even granting that she or he believes that p is improbable given q), because p may be probable with respect to other things she or he knows or believes.[34] For the Christian, other factors come into play when considering the likelihood of God's existence given evil, including, perhaps, arguments from natural theology, the testimony of the Holy Spirit, and John Calvin's *sensus divinitatus*. For the Christian who affirms the traditional doctrines of the Incarnation and Resurrection, these further beliefs also include Christ, himself, experiencing pain and suffering of the worst kind and his final victory over evil.

A few further points are worth mentioning. First, while the theist, rather than the atheist or the pantheist or the Taoist, and so on, is usually the one attempting to respond to evil (as the theist should, for the problem is, indeed, a very grave one), it is also important to note that the atheologian and nontheist are not off the hook in providing an account of the evil in the world. Whether it is karma and reincarnation, or evolutionary misfirings, or overattachment to ego, every worldview offers its account of what evil is, why it exists, and how to respond to it. Christian theism is in no worse (and I suggest it is in a much better) position than atheism in providing an account of evil. One reason is this. If evil truly exists – what we could call objective evil – then objective moral values exist. (By objective moral values, I imply mean moral values that are binding on all people, whether they acknowledge them as such or not.) If rape, racism, torture, murder, government-sanctioned genocide, and so forth are objectively evil – evil in all times and places – then the following question arises: What makes them so? What makes them truly evil, rather than simply vices we dislike? What made the Japanese atrocities noted earlier evil, even though the shogun

---

[34] For more on this point, see Alvin Plantinga, "Epistemic Probability and Evil," in *The Evidential Argument from Evil*, ed. Daniel Howard-Snyder, 69–96.

and his henchmen maintained otherwise? The problem here is that one cannot consistently affirm both that there are no objective moral values, on the one hand, and that rape, torture, and so on are objectively morally evil on the other. If there are objective moral values, then there must be some basis – some metaphysical foundation – for their being so. It does not seem to me that atheism has any such foundation, because on atheism the cosmos is not morally good, nor is there any morally good being who might bring goodness out of evil.

Furthermore, on Christian theism, evil is an *aberration*, something abhorrent to the nature and purpose of the cosmos. Evil should not be occurring, is not willed by God, and is against the very purpose of creation. In an atheistic framework, what we call evil is built into the very fabric of reality. This is not to suggest that an atheist has no ground for fighting evil; she or he need not accommodate evil in the sense of welcoming it as merely one among other necessary aspects of what is. But there remains a philosophical accommodation of evil that does not occur in classical Christian theism, which not only recognizes our need and calling to overturn evil, but sees that evil as contrary to how things ought to be. Consider a Christian theist who remains faithful to the apparent silence of God (who believes God opposes all such cruel persecution and horror) amidst evil and an atheist facing the absolute silence of the universe. As Endo notes at the end of the novel, when Christians are engaged in the struggle of evil and place themselves at God's service in the battle for good, they have a strength with which to gravitate; they have a God who suffers with them who is working toward ultimate victory over evil. For the atheist, there is only cosmic silence. Clearly, much more work is needed by philosophers of religion in the comparative analysis of the various religious and secular accounts of evil.[35]

No doubt, evil will continue to be a problem worthy of careful scholarship and of earnest, diligent personal reflection on values.[36]

---

[35] I have engaged in this type of comparative analysis in my *Evil: A Guide for the Perplexed* (London: Continuum, forthcoming). Charles Taliaferro addresses the problem of evil from various religious perspectives in his *Philosophy of Religion: A Beginner's Guide* (Oxford: OneWorld Press, 2009).

[36] I am extremely grateful to Charles Taliaferro, James Stump, and David Cramer for their insightful comments and suggestions on an earlier draft of this chapter.

12 Church

WILLIAM J. ABRAHAM

Theologians are relatively secure on what counts as relevant topics in ecclesiology; they pursue questions relative to the identity, nature, structures, ministry, sacraments, and mission of the church. It is much less clear what role philosophers should have in this domain.[1] This may arise because the kind of intellectual tools and skills deployed by philosophers simply do not have traction when applied to issues in ecclesiology; the questions that show up in ecclesiology are such that they are not susceptible to philosophical analysis. There is, however, a more likely explanation. Modern philosophy of religion has focused on generic theism. There has not as yet been a systematic exploration of the philosophical dimensions of the whole range of topics that exercises the Christian theologian. This omission may be well and good in philosophy of religion, but it cannot be allowed to stand as the default position in philosophical theology. In the latter instance, the preliminary starting point surely must be that no topic in Christian theology should be off limits to philosophical investigation. Only time can tell whether philosophical reflection on the church can yield the kind of insight that is common, say, on the Trinity or atonement. In this chapter, I focus on conceptual and epistemological dimensions of ecclesiology. I end by sketching the kind of tasks that are likely to detain the philosopher.

CONCEPTUAL ISSUES

One way into this work as a whole is to take up conceptual issues. The initial question to be addressed is obvious: What is the meaning of the word church? We can look immediately to two arenas for an

---

[1] Little has been written. For exceptions see Philip L. Quinn, "Kantian Philosophical Ecclesiology," in Philip L. Quinn and Christian Miller, Essays in Philosophy of Religion (Oxford: Oxford University Press, 2006), 255–78; Bruce H. Kirmmse, "The Thunderstorm: Kierkegaard's Ecclesiology," Faith and Philosophy 17, no. 1 (2000): 87–102.

answer – the earliest traditions of Christianity in the biblical traditions and ordinary usage. The Greek word for church is *Ekklēsia*. *Ekklēsia*, derived from the Greek *ek* (out) and *kaleo* (called), etymologically suggests that the church is "the called out people of God." However, this can be misleading because etymology is only of marginal help in understanding a concept. We also have to look at usage. There is general agreement that in the first century *ekklēsia* simply meant a gathering or an assembly. This dovetails with the use of *ekklēsia* to translate the Hebrew word *qahal* in the Septuagint, where it also means assembly. The suggestion here is that the word initially indicates an activity (a gathering together, assembling), but then began to stand for an entity – that is, the people gathered or assembled. In this regard, it could be used of both a local body of Christians and a wider body scattered over a region.

However, this was but one term used to describe Christian communities in the first century. They also were picked out by the term *sunagōgē*, a term that was also used as a synonym for *qahal*. This dropped out as the division between Christians and Jews developed. The Christian usage mirrored the developments of *sunagōgē* within Judaism, when *ekklēsia* eventually shifted from "assembly" to "community" to "buildings." The use of the term is uneven in the New Testament. It shows up in Matthew and Acts but not in Mark, Luke, or John; in Paul but not in 1 and 2 Peter. The danger is that we read this material anachronistically, projecting current usage into a time when the term church did not have the range of meaning we associate with it today. Regrettably, modern usage does not offer any additional help. The range of sense and reference for "church" is bewildering. The term can refer to a building, a local Christian community, a modern Christian denomination, and the whole body of Christians worldwide. Even then, this common usage is deeply contested by various groups of Christians. The Roman Catholic Church will not apply the term church to Protestant communities; these are ecclesial bodies, not churches. To make matters even worse, the term Roman Catholic Church is not agreed upon; it is the term used by those outsiders who reject the exclusive claims of the Bishop of Rome; insiders insist on referring to themselves as the Catholic Church.

There is no neutral conceptual analysis of the term church. The word is theologically loaded – that is, it is governed by background theological convictions. Over the years, the term church has acquired additional meanings that radically change the criteria determining its application. Once these theological considerations are factored into the discussion, it looks as if we have reached a conceptual impasse. To draw this conclusion is not just premature; it makes two false assumptions about the nature of our concepts. First, it assumes that our concepts are simple in nature – that is, that they must be governed by agreed upon and unchanging criteria of application. Second, it assumes that intellectual progress can only be made when we deploy such simple concepts. Consider now the following thought experiment.

Imagine a situation in which there has been religious conflict that has spilled over into persistent violence. The civil authorities call in all the leaders of the Christian communities and invite them to participate in a forum. The government gives each group a budget of $500,000. A relevant portion of the budget is to be used for accommodation at the Stormont Hotel in Belfast, where the experts are to be quarantined until they submit a written report identifying what is nonnegotiable for their church or group. All agree to this. Another portion of the budget is to be spent on hiring biblical scholars, theologians, and historians. Philosophers are permitted as silent observers. All also agree to this. However, the most substantial part of the budget is to be spent on experts chosen by their own groups to name and articulate the issues that are most significant to their self-identities.

Consider the relevant experts chosen by the warring parties. The Roman Catholic experts focused on apostolic succession, papal infallibility, and sacramental theology; the Orthodox, on liturgy, hierarchy, and theosis; the Anglicans, on the Lambeth Quadrilateral (Scripture, creeds, historic episcopate, and the sacraments of baptism and Eucharist); the United Methodists, on the "Methodist" Quadrilateral (Scripture, tradition, reason, and experience); the Presbyterians, on the glory of God and proper order as constituted by scriptural presbyters; Lutherans, on justification by grace through faith in Christ alone; Pentecostals, on supernatural gifts of the Spirit; Baptists, on believer's baptism and evangelism; Evangelicals, on Scripture, conversion, and evangelism; Pietists, on holiness; and Quakers, on pacifism. When the reports are submitted, the government calls on the philosophers to analyze their content.

The philosophers draw attention to the following features of the reports. Virtually all the groups have a set of doctrines; and within this there is ready agreement that almost all of them share a common faith on the identity of God (the doctrine of the Trinity) and the identity of Jesus Christ (the incarnate son of God). They all also agree on the indispensability of the activity of God in their communities (the work of the Holy Spirit). Virtually all are committed to certain pivotal practices (baptism, Eucharist, weekly worship, and the like). They also agree on the indispensability of various written materials as essential to their welfare (Scripture, varied tradition, and the writings of formative leaders).

Virtually all the groups also agree that they are committed to diverse structures or institutional organization (episcopacy, hierarchy, priests, presbyters, elders, and the like).

Not surprisingly, they also deeply disagree on a host of issues: on the place of certain doctrines in the overall coherence of Christian beliefs (for instance, justification by grace through faith and speaking in tongues), on the number and meaning of sacraments, on the interpretation of Scripture, on the internal ordering of their institutional life, on spirituality, on moral teaching, and on mission. Most important of all, they do not agree on whether all the groups have a right to self-identify themselves as "church" as opposed to fellowships of Christians or ecclesial bodies. They do not agree on the identity of the one, holy, catholic, and apostolic church – that is, what constitutes the true church of Jesus Christ. The philosophers also note that despite these differences, the delegates make concerted efforts to persuade those present that their own take on the issue in hand is the correct one.

The philosophers are engaged in a characteristically philosophical exercise. To use the language of John Passmore, they are engaged in the "critical discussion of critical discussion."[2] If we construe the discussion as circling around the idea of the church, we can note the following. First, theologians use the concept of the church in an appraisive manner. The "church" is a community that embodies some kind of valued achievement. Thus Roman Catholics stress the pivotal significance of communion with the Bishop of Rome. Presbyterians make much of the importance of elders in church polity. Second, the desired achievement is internally complex even though it is attributed to the church as a whole. Hence, explanation of the valued achievement usually involves reference to various aspects of the church, with a single feature often singled out as more important than others. Thus Pentecostals may focus on speaking in tongues but this is integrated into a complex doctrine of the Christian life. Third, prior to the discussion, there is nothing absurd in considering varied ways of describing the valued achievement. Otherwise, the complexity of the discussion is short-circuited and critical questions begged. Fourth, the accredited achievement is open in that it allows for development and modification over time; moreover, it is not possible to predict such modification in advance. Fifth, each party to the discussion recognizes that its use of the term church as related to its valued achievement is contested by other parties to the discussion. On

[2] John Passmore, "Philosophy," in *The Encyclopedia of Philosophy*, ed. Paul Edwards (New York: Macmillan, 1967), 6, 221.

the one hand, they know that the criteria they use to pick out "church" are not agreed; they can recognize that others have different criteria and can provide a rationale for them. On the other hand, they continue to deploy their own criteria without apology; they do not abandon their usage even though they know that critics may find it offensive and can marshal relevant evidence in favor of their opposition.

If this description is allowed, we have a paradigm case of what W. B. Gallie identified as "an essentially contested concept."[3] This is a concept "the proper use of which inevitably involves endless disputes about their proper use on the part of their users."[4] Similar to such concepts as religion, democracy, Christian doctrine, and morality, we are not dealing with a straight description of an entity that can be picked out by common agreement.[5] Hence, diversity, dispute, and disagreement are not necessarily signs of linguistic malfunction; they signal the need for intellectual sensitivity and dexterity. In these circumstances, we cannot simply dogmatically assert that this or that constitutes the essence of the church; we have to grapple with disputes about what constitutes the essence of the church. This is exactly what we find in ecclesiology and in ecumenical work, in which Christians find themselves staying at the theological table even as they disagree in seemingly incompatible ways about matters they cannot surrender without serious loss.

Outsiders often dismiss the whole debate as empty of cognitive content; after all, there is no universal or stable agreement on the criteria of appraisal in play. This disposition betrays a narrowness of conceptual sensibility. What is, in fact, at issue is how best to capture the complexity and beauty of the life of the church. Speaking theologically, the challenge is to do full justice to the work of the Holy Spirit in the church. Similar insensitivity shows up on the part of insiders who fall into triumphalism and party spirit, looking for the quick and decisive move that will secure victory for their side to the debate. Those aware of the essentially contested nature of the issues at stake will take a different view. As Gallie notes:

> Those who love the truth in any field will be happy to advance towards it – or in some cases simply succeed in not retreating

---

[3] See W. B. Gallie, "Essentially Contested Concepts," Chapter 8 in *Philosophy and the Historical Understanding* (London: Chatto and Windus, 1964), 157–91.

[4] *Ibid*, 158.

[5] There are interesting metaphysical questions about the ontological referent for "church" that parallel metaphysical queries about the status of corporate entities generally.

from it – no matter how long and wearing the effort involved must be. The true religious devotee, like the true democrat or man of genuine goodwill, can never be a believer in "quick results." Each, on the contrary, is willing to wait and work till the last day to effect a genuine conversion to his point of view. Each knows that there is no error so fatal as that which insinuates that the only good opponent is a liquidated one.[6]

NATURE, IDENTITY, AND AUTHORITY OF THE CHURCH

We are now beginning to understand in a deeper way why Christians are so tenacious in disputes about the nature and identity of the church. The seemingly insuperable challenges in ecumenical discussion are not just a matter of bigotry or misunderstanding; they represent the effort to gain greater self-understanding and to develop more helpful reconfigurations of old disputes. We can also understand why it is that disputes in ecclesiology take the shape they do. Thus the questions cluster around doctrine (the creeds and justification by grace through faith), the activity of the Trinity (how is the church related to divine action in redemption in the Son and through the Spirit), indispensable attributes (oneness, holiness, catholicity, and apostolicity), core practices (worship and sacraments), essential structures (authority and ministry), and mission (the purpose of the church). Most importantly, there has been extensive attention to questions of authority (Scripture, hermeneutics, and papal infallibility). All of these clusters of issues signify elements that Christians take to be of great value in their respective communities. Let's explore this last issue more carefully, for it highlights the way in which conceptual and epistemological considerations can intersect in philosophical ecclesiology.

We can readily understand why ecclesial disputes have readily gravitated to disputes about authority. In part this is so because theologians have hoped that once they settle the problem of authority in the church then all the other issues can, in principle, be resolved. The assumption is this: if we have in hand a right method, or a right set of criteria, then once we apply these correctly we have good reason to think we can reach agreement on topics such as doctrine, divine action in the church, valid sacraments, and so on. At this level, it is crucial to note initially that the dispute on authority is an epistemic dispute. This is

[6] *Ibid*, 189.

often missed because "authority" can also refer to the exercise of executive authority.[7] This is clearly an important issue as it relates to the nature of ministry and oversight. Thus, different churches have different ways of delegating the right to make various decisions, say, about ordination, or legitimate councils. However, this kind of authority is conceptually distinct from epistemic authority – that is, considerations that lead to securing truth and right belief. The latter is often seen as logically and psychologically more basic because, it is thought, once we establish proper authority in the epistemic sense we can then resolve disputes about executive authority.

It is very natural in these circumstances for philosophers to locate the debate about the identity and nature of the church firmly within an epistemic context. Epistemology is one terrain where they feel at home. The drift toward epistemology is nicely illustrated in the work of Richard Swinburne. The doctrine of the church, in his case, becomes an extension of his doctrine of divine revelation. Thus, the church is first and foremost that community instituted by Christ to ensure the plausible interpretation of divine revelation. "Catholic, Orthodox, and Protestant alike have always maintained that the most that the Christian Church can do is to interpret the original revelation."[8] Of course, the church has many aims, such as converting unbelievers, baptizing, comforting the faithful, and worship of God.

> But among its aims, and necessary for pursuit of other aims,
> is to interpret the original revelation to later generations with
> their presuppositions and their interests. For to convert people
> to some belief, you have to be able to expound that belief in
> terms which they understand; and to teach people to follow the
> Christian way, you have to be able to explain how to do that in
> different circumstances.[9]

This, in turn, requires that we distinguish clearly between original revelation and the interpretation of that original revelation. Once this is in place, then the critical question becomes that of determining the criteria for identifying which one or more ecclesial bodies is the whole or part of the Church Jesus founded. This question, in turn, is answered primarily

---

[7] For a fine discussion, see Richard T. de George, *The Nature and Limits of Authority* (Lawrence, KS: University Press of Kansas, 1985).

[8] *Idem.*

[9] Richard Swinburne, *Revelation, from Metaphor to Analogy*, 2nd ed. (Oxford: Oxford University Press, 2007), 172.

by exploring the twin criteria of connectedness and continuity of aim with the apostolic church.[10]

Classical Protestants would naturally turn to Scripture for a resolution of this second-order question about the criteria for identifying the true Church. This, for Swinburne, is a dead end. Protestants disagree on the interpretation of Scripture and consequently split into a host of diverse bodies. Moreover, the identity of the Scriptures is not self-evident; the identity of Scripture is furnished by the church, for it was the church that canonized the books of Scripture. Most importantly, to appeal to Scripture is to appeal to divine revelation because Scripture really operates as the record of divine revelation, the core deposit of faith. So we have not addressed the primary issue before us – namely, how we properly interpret the original divine revelation given in Scripture.

We have circled back to the problem of identifying the body that best satisfies the criteria of continuity of aim and continuity of organization with the apostolic church. On the first of these, should we look to finding that body that can display proper derivation of its doctrine from Scripture, or that can establish its teaching in the work of ecumenical councils, or can show that it has an appropriate teaching *magisterium* centering in the pope, or some combination of these? In the end, there is no clear answer to this question. As a result, establishing continuity of aim turns out to leave us at an impasse on rival claims to represent the church established by Jesus. This means that the issue of continuity of organization becomes utterly critical. Regrettably, we are saddled immediately with a network of weak speculation. We have no secure account of the organization of the church in the period after Christ; we have no agreed account of organizational procedures for securing continuity of leadership; and we have differences on how to identify what counts as an ecumenical council. Things clear up considerably once we get to the fifth century, but prior to that we have no best candidate. When we add the period of intense division after the Reformation, we face even more options on best candidate. In the end, the results are bleak indeed: perhaps there is one body that satisfies the relevant criteria; perhaps two or more bodies may do so; perhaps two bodies are equally best. Swinburne fails to mention another obvious possibility: There is no body that satisfies the criteria of continuity in aim and organization with the apostolic church.

---

[10] Swinburne also mentions the criteria of holiness and the presence of miracles, but these are marginal for him.

One way around this is to challenge this pessimism and argue that Swinburne's conclusions on the best candidate are much too bleak. There is, in fact, one body, it might be said, that can establish continuity of aim and organization better than any other – namely, the Roman Catholic Church. John Henry Newman is often quoted for his felicitous articulation of the relevant line of argument.

> In proportion to the probability of true developments of doctrine and practice in the Divine Scheme, so is the probability also to the appointment in that scheme of an external authority to decide upon them, thereby separating them from the mass of mere human speculation, extravagance, corruption, and error, in and out of which they grow. This is the doctrine of the infallibility of the Church.[11]

John Haldane, building on this, expresses the matter concisely.

> If something like the Christian revelation were true, then one would expect that God would have provided the means for its inerrant transmission across space and time. The Church of Rome proclaims itself to be possessed of such a gift that thus fulfills that expectation. Such reasoning is defeasible in as much as its premises may be contested and its mode of inference is not deductive. But my task has not been to prove the doctrine of infallibility...To quote Newman again, but from another context, "one step enough for me." In a religious context, infallibility and authority are only important if they support and are supported by a faith rooted in Scripture and in the teaching traditions of the Church.[12]

Before evaluating this whole way of thinking, it is important to dispose briefly of a more recent attempt to find a way forward in ecclesial disputes. Thus, George Lindbeck has proposed that we should see divisions in the church as intimately related to a proper account of the grammar of religious discourse.[13] The Nicene Creed, for example, should be seen not as a propositional exposition of divine revelation, nor as an expression of common religious experience, but as a cultural–linguistic phenomenon akin to a grammar. To be a Christian is to learn the

---

[11] Quoted in John Haldane, "Infallibility, Authority, and Faith," in his *Faithful Reason, Essays Catholic and Philosophical* (London: Routledge, 2004), 72.

[12] *Idem.*

[13] See George A. Lindbeck, *The Nature of Doctrine* (Philadelphia, PA: Westminster Press, 1984).

grammar of faith; it is to be initiated into a complex form of life with its own particular discourse that cannot be reduced to propositions or to descriptions of experience. The real continuity should be located in continuity of grammar. Christians eventually differ on the nature of the church because they disagree on how to extend their language in new situations; the resolution of deep ecclesial differences will then come about through careful attention to the grammar of the very language that secures their identity. Thus, Swinburne and Haldane can be sidestepped by way of a very different account of the nature of Christian discourse.

Unhappily, Lindbeck's alternative way out will not work. To express the conclusion abruptly, his account of religious language is simply mistaken, in that it is clear that, say, the Nicene Creed is best construed not as a grammar but as a network of ontological and theological assertions about God, Christ, the church, the life to come, and the like. Moreover, this interpretation of what is at stake does not begin to take seriously the epistemic context in which Swinburne and Haldane have lodged the doctrine of the church. It is this deeper issue that has to be ferreted out and analyzed.

EPISTEMIC AUTHORITY

As a way into this terrain, it is interesting that Swinburne's approach to the doctrine of the church makes an epistemological assumption that has been central to much modern epistemology: Find the right criteria for settling disputes that lead to unresolved impasses, and the resolution of that logically prior question in all likelihood will move us beyond the unresolved impasses. Applied to disputes in ecclesiology, the first task is to tackle the problem of authority; the problem of authority in turn resolves into the problem of finding the right divine revelation; once we have found the right divine revelation we then must look for the location of the right interpreter of that divine revelation to provide an infallible interpretation of the divine revelation, and this is secured by the twin criteria of continuity in aim and organization with the apostolic church. The whole debate about the church has become a debate about the proper interpretation of divine revelation; it has become a problem in the epistemology of theology. This problem, in turn, is governed by the quest for universally agreed criteria that will settle particular ecclesial disputes.[14]

---

[14] This is an important insight if we are to develop more accurate accounts of the origins of the modern quest for right criteria or the right method in epistemology. See my *Canon and Criterion in Christian Theology* (Oxford: Clarendon Press, 1998).

The very same quest for universal criteria inhibited the identification of essentially contested concepts. Thus, philosophers were quick to dismiss disputes in politics, religion, morality, art, and the like, as lacking in cognitive merit because there were no agreed criteria by means of which they might be resolved. Topics in these domains were then banished from the realm of reason and treated as expressions of emotion, disguised imperatives, or, worse still, as forms of bigotry and superstition. What we saw earlier, however, is that essentially contested concepts alert us to the fact that progress on deeply contested issues is not necessarily tied to finding universal criteria. On the contrary, that quest may blind us to the kind of reflection that is vital if we are to make progress. Applied to ecclesiology, wise rational agents recognize that tenacious commitments to one's own best initial judgments yoked to continuing engagement with opponents is precisely the way to make progress. The effort to frame the primary issue as the issue of epistemic authority, and then cast that debate in terms of the quest for an agreed account of epistemic authority and all that goes with it, is a philosophical cul-de-sac. Critical discussion of this discussion should lead us out of this cul-de-sac and back onto the main road of new insight and discovery.

The captivity to epistemology runs so deep that it is very difficult to see what is at issue. Thus, treating Scripture as a record of divine revelation and canon as a criterion for settling disputes are so endemic in theology that alternatives are simply dismissed out of hand. Consequently, it is virtually impossible to consider other ways of thinking about the church and its doctrines, structures, practices, and the like. For example, it is historically false to say that the church identified its canon of Scripture and then had the foundation and criterion from which it could then develop its doctrines. On the contrary, doctrinal commitments enshrined in the rule of faith in part determined which books made it into the New Testament canon.[15] There was an agreed canon of doctrine long before there was any agreed canon of Scripture. Furthermore, the term canon was often applied not just to books of the Bible but also to doctrines, bishops, saints, councils, and other phenomena. Thus "canon" is much more plausibly seen as a list rather than as a criterion, much less a criterion of truth, right belief, knowledge, and the like. The crucial insight that has to be recovered here is that the church of the early centuries was well able to reach agreement on its doctrines without at all reaching agreement on the reasons for those doctrines, much

---

[15] See Paul L. Gavrilyuk, "Scripture and the *Regula Fidei*: Two Interlocking Components of the Canonical Heritage," in *Canonical Theism*, ed. William J. Abraham, Jason E. Vickers, and Natalie B. Van Kirk (Grand Rapids, MI: Eerdmans, 2008), 27–42.

less agreeing on an underlying epistemology of theology. There was no agreed account of the relation between faith and reason; the church was well able to live with radical diversity at this level.

Reorientation in this domain requires a rethinking of the place of epistemology in the life of the church. This is not to say that work in epistemology does not matter. What is at issue is the status of epistemic claims in the life of the church in its formative period and thereafter. It is bad enough that epistemic claims dressed up as debates on authority are made constitutive of the identity of the church; it is much worse when epistemic claims are built into the meaning of discourse related to the church. The climax of this way of thinking emerges when the church is to be identified as the body that is the best interpreter of divine revelation. We can be sure that philosophical moves like this will engender the fragmentation of the church. Agreement in epistemology is no guarantee generally of agreement in particular judgments; it is even less so in disputes about the nature of the church. To express the matter theologically, initiation into the church does not mean initiation into an epistemology of theology; it is initiation into the life of God mediated by baptism and faith, and sustained through the manifold canonical heritage of the church. Once we make this reorientation, it is clear what the next step in ecclesiology should be. We need to pursue the possibility that progress in ecclesiology will begin with the work of Holy Spirit in Christian communities across the world.

At this point, we have fully passed over into the terrain of the theologian. For the moment, this is as far as the philosopher need journey. What I have done is to ferret out two interrelated blind spots in the work of ecclesiology that have ended in a theological cul-de-sac. We have missed the fact that "church" is an essentially contested concept and we have lodged the concept of church on the terrain of epistemology. Against this, I have proposed that we look more carefully at the nature of our concepts and that we need to relativize epistemic considerations, concentrating on the activity of the Holy Spirit as a point of entry into disputes about ecclesiology. Mapping philosophical assumptions in play is clearly one kind of task that belongs in the philosopher's brief as it related to the doctrine of the church.

SOME FURTHER CONSIDERATIONS

Philosophers traditionally have been interested in at least five other tasks in their reflection on religion. First, they have been interested in conceptual considerations and in wider questions about the nature of religious language. In the case of ecclesiology, this can begin with the term church and then extend into wider issues – say, the role of images and metaphors in our descriptions of the church. Second, they have been extremely interested in identifying and assessing the kind of arguments that show up in religion. In ecclesiology, there are few, if any, deductive or inductive proofs; reflection beyond this leads us into the epistemology of theology. Third, they have sought to assess the internal consistency and coherence of religious belief. Fourth, they have been helpful in identifying and exploring metaphysical issues that crop up in the articulation of a religious tradition. In ecclesiology, one thinks immediately of how best to construe the communion of saints. Fifth, they have been interested in mapping the relation between religion and other areas of life. In ecclesiology, one place to begin would be to look at the relationship between doctrines of the mission of the church and, say, politics.

The first three tasks suggest that we should expect philosophers to attend to conceptual and epistemological issues that emerge in debates in ecclesiology. The other four tasks intimate that philosophers can help hermeneutically – that is, in understanding more deeply the kind of claims being advanced. As we proceed, we can be open to revision of these expectations evoked by the material content of ecclesiology.

13 Religious rites

CHARLES TALIAFERRO

What are religious rites in general, and Christian rites in particular? A definition of religious rites needs to cover a wide range of acts that I simply list at the outset in order to record the breadth of practices that need to be covered. Religious rites include prayers involving praise (worship or adoration), petition and confession, vows, commissions such as ordination, rites of passage such as baptism, confirmation, marriage ceremonies, funeral rites and burials, communion or the Eucharist (also called mass, the Lord's supper), feasts, fasts, alms giving, vigils, lamentations, blessings, thanksgiving, grace before meals, and contemplative or meditative prayer. By way of a general definition of religious rites, I suggest the following: *religious rites are repeatable symbolic action involving the sacred*. There may be times when it is not obvious whether one is participating in a religious rite. For example, one may pray to God without engaging in a rite, but once that prayer forms a pattern that can be repeated and employs symbolic action such as bowing the head, folding hands, and so on, one is at least in the early stages of engaging in a rite. While some religious acts may not be clear cases of ritual, I take it that the current definition would cover all or most of the formal acts of prayer, praise, and so on, carried out in mosques, temples, ashrams, cathedrals, churches, and Christian communities today. A definition of Christian religious rites may be refined as *repeatable symbolic action involving God*. In a Christian context, prayer, praise, vows, lamentations, feasts, fasts, and so on, all involve some reference to the God of Christianity.

I believe this definition is sound enough for us to get started in this chapter, and the concept and nature of repetition and symbolic acts can be clarified as we proceed. After a brief survey of why the topic of religious rites has been largely neglected in some mid–twentieth-century philosophy of religion, I offer some reasons why religious rites are a current, promising area for philosophical investigation. Four sections follow after such preliminary observations: The Virtues of Christian Rites,

The Liability of Christian Rites, The Nature of Worship and Petitions, and Sacramental Realism. The chapter concludes with some suggestions regarding further inquiry.

THE NEGLECT AND RE-DISCOVERY OF RITUAL

There are at least three reasons why modern philosophers have not given substantial attention to religious rites.

First, from the mid–twentieth-century to the 1970s, philosophers focused on the analysis and critique of religious beliefs that seem to be presupposed by religious rites. If there are good reasons to think that our language and concept of God are incoherent or we have compelling reasons to think there is no God, then there seems little to be gained in the philosophical exploration of ritual involving God. Such a philosophical inquiry would, at best, help elucidate the causes or reasons behind why persons would come to mistakenly think and act as though there is a God.

Second, some philosophers who did attend to religious practices reached the conclusion that religious practices, themselves, seemed to rule out as irrelevant the philosophy of God and the traditional domain of philosophy of religion (arguments about whether it is reasonable to believe there is a God or the soul or an afterlife). D. Z. Phillips argued tirelessly that Christian religious beliefs and practices involving prayer or talk of an afterlife and the soul did not at all reveal an implicit commitment to believing there actually is a God who hears prayers or there actually is an afterlife for the soul. If Phillips was right, then attention to Christian practices should not stimulate and enhance philosophical investigations into the nature and power of God, the possibility of surviving death, and so on. Phillips's goal was to critique and shut down any of the theistic metaphysics, epistemology, or values that might be suggested by prayer, worship, and other rites.

Finally, the great liturgical renewal that took place in Christian traditions after World War II took the focus off the traditional topics that Christian philosophers addressed when it came to ritual. In the medieval and early modern European era, philosophers developed accounts of the elements involved in the Eucharist: Is the consecrated bread and wine the actual presence of Jesus Christ's body and blood? This was largely a disputed question among theologians who focused on Scripture, but it also called on philosophical treatments of substance and accidents, form and matter, strict identity, mereology (the relationship between parts and wholes), realism versus nominalism (the status of universals), the concept of participation (in which the elements may be said to participate in the glorified body of Christ), and the like. The liturgical movement focused more on the role of the religious community, individual and collective experiences, and not on the status of the sacraments as objects of supernatural significance. This movement actually can do (and has done) more to stimulate further philosophical inquiry than to stifle it; however, at the outset, the movement did little or nothing to revive the heritage of past philosophical work on the sacraments.

Today, the state of play in philosophy of religion has changed radically. With respect to the three points just made, we are no longer in an age of anxiety during which religious belief seems to face a monumental, unanswerable critique. The heyday of logical positivism and forms of scientism has given way to a more pluralistic philosophical era. There are still efforts to dispense with anything that goes beyond contemporary science, such as the appropriately titled recent book, *Every Thing Must Go: Metaphysics Naturalized*, but the more common position might be better put in the claim *Every Thing Must Be Examined*, and this includes Christian rites.[1] The work of the late D. Z. Phillips has been unsuccessful in swaying philosophers that Christians who pray for aid or who worship God or who claim to long for redemption beyond this life are not addressing a God whom they believe powerfully loves the world and works to bring good out of evil. Phillips's appeal to religious practice in order to critique traditional and contemporary philosophy of religion has failed to carry the day in the field of philosophy of religion.[2]

Moreover, Phillips's work has been increasingly seen as not at all a disinterested examination of religious ritual and the limitations of philosophy of religion, but as an account of ritual and religion that shares most of the conclusions of secular naturalism. The only difference between Phillips claiming it is nonsense to ask about what the soul's life with God is like after death and a naturalist claiming it is simply false to think the soul has an afterlife seems to be a matter of style, for both deny any Christian claim that there is an opportunity for persons to find redemption and union with God after death.[3] As for the liturgical

---

[1] *Every Thing Must Go: Metaphysics Naturalized* by J. Ladyman, D. Ross, D. Spurrett, and J. Coller (Oxford: Oxford University Press, 2007).

[2] For an overview, see the final three chapters of my *Evidence and Faith; Philosophy and religion since the seventeenth century* (Cambridge: Cambridge University Press, 2005).

[3] For a critique on naturalism, see *Naturalism* by Stewart Goetz and Charles Taliaferro (Grand Rapids, MI: Eerdmanns, 2008).

movement, it has opened the gates for more philosophy of ritual rather than less, as I hope to show subsequently.

Three other reasons that favor the development of the philosophy of religious ritual in general, and Christian rites in particular, involve history, the apparent inescapability of ritual, and ecology.

Historically, it seems that ritual has played an enormous role in sustaining and shaping Christianity. William Abraham has argued persuasively that a philosophical evaluation of Christianity must do more than take seriously natural theology and Scripture. This wider inquiry should include assessing how the Christian community practices its faith and has articulated this practice. Indeed, there is an old dictum to the effect that the rule of faith is a reflection of the rule of prayer (*lex orandi legen statuat credendi*).[4]

A philosophy of ritual also can be motivated by the fact that ritual seems inescapable in religious or secular societies. Of great interest to contemporary philosophers are rites involving confession, guilt, punishment, and mercy. Although such rites can have purely secular forms, they also run parallel with religious rites.[5]

One other motive behind developing a philosophy of Christian rites worthy of note involves ecology. Christianity has been accused of promoting a dominion environmental philosophy that sees the material world as a mere tool for human fulfillment. In his famous critique of Christianity, "The Historical Roots of Our Ecological Crisis," Lynn White writes: "By destroying pagan animism, Christianity made it possible to exploit nature in a mood of indifference to the feelings of natural objects. . . . To a Christian a tree can be no more than a physical fact."[6] Anyone with any understanding of Christian rites should know this is not true. Sacred Christian rites celebrate elements of the created order such as bread and wine, water and oil, and even take trees seriously;

---

4 See Georges Florovsky, "The Function of Tradition in the Ancient Church," in *Bible, Church, Traditions: An Eastern Orthodox View* (Belmont, MA: Nordland Publishing Co., 1972), Paul Bavrilyuk's "Canonical Liturgies" in *Canonical Theism*, ed. W. Abraham, J. Vickers, and N. VanKirk (Grand Rapids, MI: Eerdmans, 2008), and the following three books by William Abraham: *Crossing the Threshold of Divine Revelation* (Grand Rapids, MI: Eerdmans, 2006), *Divine Revelation and the Limits of Historical Criticism* (Oxford: Oxford University Press, 1982), and *The Divine Inspiration of Scripture* (Oxford: Oxford University Press, 1981).

5 See, for example. Christopher Bennett, *The Apology Ritual: A Philosophical Theory of Punishment* (Cambridge: Cambridge University Press, 2008).

6 Lynn White, "The Historical Roots of Our Ecological Crisis," in *Earth Ethics*, ed. James Sterba (Upper Saddle River, NJ: Prentice Hall, 2000), 24–25. This essay was first published in 1967.

one cannot think of trees in a Christian context without thinking of the Tree in the Garden, the Tree of Life, and the wood of the cross. Abundant natural images form part of Scripture and are woven into liturgical readings (in the Gospel of John, 15:1–6, Jesus is the vine, those called to him are to be branches). This is not to say that historically Christians have not exploited the natural world and treated it irresponsibly, but it is to claim that Christian rites see the natural world as not mere physical facts, but an avenue for celebrating God as Creator and imaging Jesus as Redeemer (note the liturgical use of "A Song of Creation" in the Book of Common Prayer, *Benedicite, omni opera Domini*).[7]

THE VIRTUES OF CHRISTIAN RITES

As we approach a more focused look at Christian rites, let us consider three virtues involved in their symbolic nature, and then examine the value of repetition. I then propose a portrait of Christian rites that involves a host of interwoven goods.

The virtues I delimit involving symbols build on a tradition that goes back to Plato and Aristotle, and are defended in the twentieth century by Franz Brentano and Roderick Chisholm. These philosophers took note of how values can be magnified by being imitated or loved; they held that if something is good, then loving it or imitating it counts as a further good.[8]

The Virtues of Symbolic Reference: I propose as a general thesis about values, that if something is good (friendship, justice, beauty), then it is a *prima facie* good to refer to it. Conceiving and referring to the good allows for other goods such as the love of the good. Imagine you have a friendship with someone, but this is never referred to or acknowledged. It may be just as vital for both friends without such a reference, but other things being equal, there is an additional good when one can have the opportunity to focus on the fact that the friendship exists. Let's call this *the virtue of reference*. Recognition of the power of reference has been noted in early philosophy (the Socratic and Confucian projects of

---

[7] The song begins: "O all ye works of the Lord, bless the Lord...." and goes on to reference water, heat, seasons, snow, beasts, and so on as part of a praise of God's creation. Water and the like are no mere physical facts. For an interesting argument that Christian liturgy can inform ecology, see "Liturgy and ethics: The liturgical asceticism of energy conservation," by M. R. Pfeil, *Journal of the Society of Christian Ethics* 27, no. 2 (2007): 127–49.

[8] See Roderick Chisholm's *Brentano and Intrinsic Value* (Cambridge: Cambridge University Press, 1986).

developing clear references to the virtues) and is even widely acknowledged in popular culture (for example, Harry Potter fans know the danger
of referring to He-Who-Must-Not-Be-Named). I submit that there is an
additional good we may call *the virtue of expression* when it is the case
that the good in question is expressed through gesture or action. Imagine,
again, a friendship that is referenced but never expressed through physical gestures. The friendship may be deeply valuable, but other things
being equal, a friendship that one may express through word and action
has an added good. There is a further good we may call *the virtue of
embodiment* in which the good is so referenced and expressed that the
persons involved may be said to embody or display the good even more
fully. Imagine a friendship in which the relationship is celebrated by an
embrace or kiss or dance or ceremony.

These three stages whereby a good may be symbolically referenced,
expressed, or embodied refer to three stages in which a good may be
magnified. The plausibility of this thesis may be bolstered by considering the opposite case of when an evil is magnified. Imagine you hate
another person, and the feeling is mutual, but this is never expressed.
It may or may not be good that it not be referenced, but by referencing
the enmity there is a sense in which the evil is magnified or given a
foothold in one's consciousness or self-consciousness. The enmity is no
longer an unspoken resentment, but one that is named. Once expressed
(imagine you routinely inform your enemy that you hate him, and he
returns a similar report) and then embodied (imagine you make ugly,
physical gestures displaying your hatred), the enmity is magnified or
increased.

Christian rites involve the goods of reference, expression, and
embodiment insofar as prayer, praise, and the acknowledgment of a
relationship with God are, themselves, a good, even a supreme good.
Compare two Christian communities that are otherwise identical except
that in one there is no symbolic reference, expression, and embodiment
involving God; perhaps the rites in such a community involve only silent
prayer and meditation. I suggest that such a community would lack a
good that would be enjoyed in a community that (in addition to silent
prayer and meditation) practiced worship and prayer involving embodied
reference and expression in relation to God.

The Virtue of Repetition: There can be (as I note later) dangers to
bare repetition. One can drain the meaning of almost any word simply
by engaging in a mind-numbing repetition of it. I have had one student
who claimed to be so opposed to repetition that he only tells a person
once that he loves them. He claimed that once you tell a person you

love them, you are only repeating yourself if you report that you love them at some future time. For most of us, I assume, matters differ: repeating (from time to time) that you love your beloved can be a way of renewing the reference, expression, and embodiment of your love. We might even think of love as something that is indexed to time. While love is not time's fool (as Shakespeare points out), to say you love someone on Monday is a different event than if, on Tuesday, you say you love him or her. Whatever your philosophy of personal relations, Christian rites are explicitly aimed at renewing one's relationship with God. This is why, in many Christian communities, persons renew their faith through reciting one of the creeds (typically, the Nicene Creed) and, in the Eucharist, there is a repeated re-enactment of what Christians believe are the essential stages in salvation. These stages consist of the confession of sins, offering a sign of repentance by renouncing evil, and receiving God's restorative forgiveness through embracing God's grace through Jesus Christ. Christian rites thereby involve drama (in the sense of dynamic change) and the romantic (in the sense of inward, affective change). Repeated, ritual or liturgical meditation on Christ's life and word, the suffering, passion, death, and Resurrection are used in and by Christian communities to build up solidarity within the community, a passion for outreach, and a commitment to social justice, and to foster education in the word of God.

Rather than delineate a list of separate goods that may be at work in such repeated, symbolic Christian rites, I offer the following general portrait. At best, Christian rites such as the Eucharist involve fostering religious virtues (faith, hope, love). Philosophers as diverse as Aristotle and Pascal have observed how acting in certain ways (or developing certain habits) can cultivate virtues, and this is no less true in Christian rites. Such rites can involve the good of mediation; some goods can be enhanced by mediation, such as when someone gives you a gift that you might have otherwise acquired on your own. The exchange of gifts in liturgy thus can have a similar enhancing dimension. Christian rites can involve a host of aesthetic goods (good music, icons, churches); they can involve cross-generational relations (old and young worship together), and can even enhance mind–body coordination.[9] Christian rites can enhance an experiential encounter with God as creator, redeemer, and sanctifier, involving instruction, correction, edification, or consolation.

---

[9] On the latter point, see Gareth Matthews' "Ritual and the Religious Feelings" in *Explaining Emotions*, ed. Amelie Oksenberg Rorty (Los Angeles: University of California Press, 1980), 339–53.

One may also have the great good that is available in sacramental realism, a topic we will consider after briefly noting how Christian rites can go wrong.

THE LIABILITY OF CHRISTIAN RITES

There are abundant ways in which Christian rites can go horribly wrong. They can eclipse the religious goods that they were fashioned to cultivate when ceremonies become more important than interior transformation. They can become virtually void of meaning due to failures of attention, intentionality, or moral and religious hypocrisy. Repetition and symbolism can become mere repetition and symbolism. Rites can serve to fan unjustified beliefs about God and cruelty (anti-Semitism, racism, sexism), they can be a motive for unwarranted schisms, and they can be carried out contrary to their intended purpose (for example, a Eucharist can be held not out of thanksgiving – the literal meaning of Eucharist – but to curse one's enemies). Another abuse of Christian rites can occur when they are imposed involuntarily (coerced baptism). Finally, neither last nor least, Christian rites can go badly when they break the eleventh commandment (Thou Shalt Not Be Boring) – when they are simply tedious and vapid.

Probably the two most sustained critiques of Christian rites are the ways in which they can eclipse moral virtue and the danger of treating God as a familiar, controllable reality.

The moral critique of rites runs through the Old and New Testaments. Perhaps the best known is from Amos 5:21–24: "I hate, I despise your festivals, and I take no delight in your solemn assemblies. Even though you offer me your burnt offerings, I will not accept them.... But let justice roll down like waters, and righteousness like an ever-flowing stream." The critique of rites as promoting a too-familiar concept of God is complex, but stems from the tension in Christianity between apophatic theology (which stresses the inability to form any positive concepts of God) and catophatic theology (which stresses the positive images and concepts of God from Scripture and tradition). In support of the apophatic path, consider Isaiah 55:8: "For my thoughts are not your thoughts, nor are your ways my ways, says the Lord. For as the heavens are higher than the earth, so are my ways higher than your ways and my thoughts than your thoughts."

There is no way to easily address such challenges in this chapter. I suggest that all these reasons are good reasons to beware how the corruption of Christian rites can lead to disaster. I believe this is partly because (as the old saying goes) the corruption of the best is the worst. It is possible to see the aforementioned problems as genuine corruptions or ways in which Christian rites can be tainted when not carried out with reverence, intentionality, balance, and wisdom.

As for the moral critique, it is noteworthy that many Christian communities have liturgies in which the book of Amos is read, along with the admonishes of Jesus against empty ceremonies (Matt. 23). Christian rites have built into them warnings about the profane subordination of justice to ritual.

As for the challenge of the apophatic, some liturgies emphasize the radical otherness of God. This seems especially true in Orthodox and so-called high liturgies in the West that employ incense, prostrations, vigils, and long periods of silence. The liturgies might seem to some to play into the objection that Christian rites treat God as too immanent (or too human, even) but they often also explicitly promote the otherness and numinous nature of God.[10] Christianity has long held in creative tension the thesis that God is utterly different from the creature and yet God encounters us in images and words we can understand. Isaiah 55:8 needs to be paired with Isaiah 1:18: "Come let us reason together, says the Lord, though your sins are like scarlet, they shall be like snow...."

THE NATURE OF WORSHIP AND PETITIONS

Before turning to the topic of sacramental realism, let us consider briefly two philosophical puzzles that emerge from Christian rites themselves. The first involves what has been called the Vanity of God. Some Christian worship is based on what seems to involve offering to God an endless series of compliments. Why would God, a supremely perfect, good Creator, desire or require worship? Biblical language about the ills of idolatry even suggests God is jealous when creatures find solace in objects or events other than God. The second involves the nature of petitionary prayer. In Christian rites, there are often prayers for world peace, for the healing of the sick, for blessings on relationships, and so on. If God is all good and all powerful, why would God's action depend upon petition? If it is good for someone to be healed from an illness, why wouldn't God simply heal the person, irrespective of whether there was any such petition? This topic is covered excellently in the chapter "Prayer" by Harriet Harris, but it is worth brief attention here.

---

[10] D. Liderbach brings out the numinous dimension of the Lord's Supper in "The Community as Sacrament," *Philosophy and Theology* 5, no. 3 (1991): 221–36.

A full response to both objections would be too ambitious here, but there is space to begin a reply. As for the first objection, one of the most promising replies is to stress the deep Anselmian insight that God is unsurpassably good or excellent. According to Anselm and many philosophical theologians from Boethius and Augustine to Aquinas to contemporary Anselmians such as T. V. Morris, to worship or praise God involves taking pleasure and awe in that which is supremely excellent. Worship is not so much focused on an omnipotent ego as it is on the essential goodness that comprises God's superabundant nature.[11] As for divine jealousy and the worry about idolatry, there have been times in Christian theology when it has been thought that any love of the world must be strictly subordinate to the love of God so that the creation is only to be loved because God loves the creation. However, there is a greater theological testimony to the effect that one can and should love the creation both for its own sake as well as for its being a creation, and that one can love God through loving the creation, and love the creation through loving God. In this broader framework, how might jealousy function? Imagine God is essentially good and that awe of and pleasure in (that is, worship of) God's nature and action is good in itself as well as good for the creature. But imagine further that the creature delights, instead, in the pursuit of personal glory and reputation so that the creature becomes wrapped up in what seems like an idolatrous love of pre-eminence. Why would it not be fitting for an essentially good God to be described as jealous insofar as God is believed to lovingly desire the good of the creature in a fulfilled relationship with goodness and the Creator?

Part of the plausibility of this reply depends on whether you think jealousy is always a vice. I suggest it is not. Imagine you have a son whom you love and with whom you have had, until he goes to college, a fulfilled relationship. In college, however, he meets an alcoholic, sexist, racist, filthy philosophy professor whom the son idolizes and calls "Daddy." Jealousy might not be one's first emotion, but wouldn't there be some sort of role for feeling that the son has misplaced his affection and is engaged in a damaging, bizarre surrogate father–son relationship? The sense of loss, the desire for re-union in a healthy relationship would (I suggest) be a case of healthy jealousy.[12]

---

[11] See my "The Vanity of God" in *Faith and Philosophy* 6 (1989): 140–55); P. Copan's "Divine Narcissism: A Further Defense of Divine Humility" in *Philosophia Christi* Series 8 (Winter 2006): 313–25.

[12] See my "The Jealousy of God," *New Oxford Review* (Jan-Feb. 1990), 12–15.

The objection about petitionary prayer raises issues that are deep in terms of the overall problem of evil. Why is not God more active in righting world evils? I have addressed the problem of evil in several places, but focus now on the question of whether it would be wrong or evil or somehow unfitting for an all good God's actions in the creation to depend, in part, on the petitions of creatures.[13] If so, this is far from obvious. Given that it is permissible for an all good God to create a world in which the goods and welfare of a creature depend on the responsible, free assistance of other creatures (that is, for there to be a creation of free, interdependent beings), why would it be wrong for the responsible free assistance of creatures to consist in prayers to which God responds? Arguably, such involvement of the creature in the Creator's action offers a richer, deeper understanding of the responsibility of creatures for one another. If you object that it would be simply wrong in the first place for any creature of an all good God to have responsibility for others, then you will not find this response satisfactory. If you, at least in principle, believe that human freedom is good, and that a good God would create a cosmos of free creatures, then it is hard to see why it would be unfitting for God to care for the creation in response to human petitions.

Consider an objection: Doesn't this create a problem of fairness? Would an all good God only act on behalf of those prayed for? Imagine hospitalized twins who share much of the same history and values. Only one twin is prayed for and (let us imagine) God heals that twin but not the one who is not prayed for.

Two replies are in order: First, Christian rites give us reason to believe that everyone, everywhere is prayed for. In *The Book of Common Prayer*, there are abundant prayers for all people. That means the thought experiment is built on a false premise. Second, imagine there are disparities among those specifically prayed for versus those who are not, and discrepancies between prayers for healing that are answered and those that are not. It seems this is no more problematic than the general distribution of goods and ills across creation. Some children are born into poverty, some are not. The overall Christian teaching on this matter is that the cosmos is not now the way it was and is meant to be by God, and that evil is contrary to the nature and will of God. Unlike secular determinists who believe that cosmic ills, by necessity, had to happen given the laws of nature and cosmic conditions, Christians hold that cosmic ills must and should be overcome through compassionate aid, seeking justice, and so on. It is further believed (traditionally) that

[13] See my *Dialogues about God* (Lanham, Maryland: Rowman & Littlefield, 2008).

God enters into this movement to overcome evil through prophets, the incarnate Jesus, and even through some (but not constant and not predictable) miracles, including the great miracle of life after death. In short, the fact (if it is a fact) that some rather than all healing takes place by God in this life in response to prayer has to be seen in light of the great comprehensive vision that God will (in this life and the next) draw all persons into the opportunity of a redeemed life.[14]

As noted earlier, to complete this line of response would take us deep into the problem of evil literature (a literature I have sought to address elsewhere).[15] Let us now turn to a central Christian rite: the Eucharist.

SACRAMENTAL REALISM

Much medieval and early modern philosophical theology included reflection on the sacraments that are involved in Christian rites. In fact, schism in the West between Roman Catholicism and emerging Protestant movements were often as focused on the sacraments as on the interpretation of Scripture, the nature of works and grace, jurisdiction in matters of politics and the soul, and the perceived corruption of the Roman Magisterium (the indulgence controversy). Historically, Christians have resisted any literal identity between the consecrated bread and wine with the corporeal body and blood of Christ (notwithstanding the accusation in the first century that Christians practiced cannibalism). There are, however, strident claims in the New Testament that seem to involve a genuine communion or partaking of the body and blood of Jesus. "Jesus said to them, 'Very truly, I tell you, unless you eat the flesh of the Son of Man and drink his blood, you have no life in you...'" (John 6:53; see 54–58). Roman Catholic teaching evolved to affirm that the consecrated elements retain all the appearances (accidents) of bread and wine and yet in substance become the body and blood of Christ.

The Orthodox have been more reluctant (as have Anglicans) to define the mode of Christ's presence but they affirm "the real presence of Christ." Sometimes this is described as the elements participating in the

---

[14] See my "Prayer" in *The Routledge Companion to Philosophy of Religion*, ed. Chad Meister and Paul Copan (London: Routledge, 2007), 617–25; M. Murray's "God Responds to Prayer" in *Contemporary Debates in the Philosophy of Religion*, ed. M. Peterson and R. Van Arragon (Maldon, MA: Blackwell, 2004), 242–54, and E. Stump's "Petitionary Prayer" in *American Philosophical Quarterly* 16 (1979): 81–91.

[15] See my *Philosophy of Religion: A Beginner's Guide* (Oxford: OneWorld Press, 2009).

risen and glorified Body of Christ or as being efficacious signs that mediate the presence of Christ or as outward and visible signs of an invisible and inner reality. Some Christians treat the Eucharist as entirely symbolic of Christ without invoking any presence other than the presence of Christ within the life of the believers through the power of the Holy Spirit. Communion or Eucharist, on this view, may be a memorial or a sign of the second coming, but not a special mediation of divine grace in which Christ is sacramentally (and yet really) made present through the liturgy.

Rather than canvas and compare these different models, I propose a general account of Christian sacramental realism according to which the participation in the Eucharist involves a genuine experience or encounter with the risen Christ. It may be called modal sacramental realism, as it concerns the modes in which Christ may be made evident and encountered sacramentally. The modal account is intended to be neutral with respect to Roman Catholic, Protestant, Orthodox, or Anglican doctrinal commitments. It could, in principle, be the case that both the modal account and the Roman Catholic account of the Eucharist are true. In developing modal sacramental realism, I refer to the experiential encounter with Christ in terms of seeing, but I do not want the account to be limited to the visual seeing or perceiving of Christ. Liturgy can involve all the senses as well as the faculties of memory, reason, reflection, passions, and the like, but it will be easiest in presenting the account simply in reference to seeing, and then indicate how Christian rites can offer an expanded sensory and cognitive arena for an encounter with Christ. I should add that although the term *modal sacramental realism* may be new, I make no claim to originality. Quite the opposite; I hope this framework effectively captures the belief of many or most Christians who engage in the Eucharist.

Consider four types of seeing, which may be called representative seeing, seeing through incorporation, seeing through interpretation, and seeing as disclosure or revelation. I shall develop these with some analogies.

Representative seeing: In an extended sense, you can see someone (a King, for example) by seeing his ambassador or representative. The ambassador may be seen as someone who functions in the King's place and who offers you the King's blessing. In Persia, messengers and agents of the King were called the King's ears, and some agents of royalty have been called "the eyes and ears of the

King." Representative seeing occurs when you see or are seen by someone's representative.

Seeing through incorporation: Imagine you are in Puerto Rico but want to see the United States of America. You can see the United States by traveling to Florida or elsewhere in the United States, but there is another way to see the United States: That is if Puerto Rico became incorporated into the United States as the fifty-first state.

Seeing through interpretation: Consider a portrait of King Olaf I of Norway (who died in the year 1000). Can you be said to see King Olaf I in the portrait? In a strict sense, we might be strained to claim this, for the portrait was evidently made of a model that the people or the court thought might fit the actual or legendary King. But there is an ordinary sense in which such a portrait can stand in for the King. We have come to interpret the saintly martyr King in this portrayal and although we would not rely on this portrait to carry with us authentic information of the King's actual appearance, we may still have an ordinary, common sense event in which seeing the portrait is to see the King.

So far, all three modes of seeing may be at work in the Eucharist. Imagine that the Eucharist was instituted by Jesus in roughly the way it is depicted in a synthesized form from New Testament sources: On the night before Jesus was betrayed, he broke bread with his disciples and gave it to them, declaring this is his body, and imagine that he distributed wine identified as his blood. Imagine that he enjoined or commissioned that this rite be carried out in remembrance of him. Putting aside questions of Apostolic succession, let us imagine that what passes as the Eucharist throughout the history of Christianity is a repeated symbolic rite in which the words of Jesus are spoken blessing and identifying bread and wine as his body and blood which are then distributed to followers of Jesus.

Under these circumstances, we seem to have representative seeing. Priests, ministers, or others who preside in the rite and who distribute the bread and wine may be seen as agents or ambassadors of Christ. One would also have seeing by incorporation on at least two levels. Those who follow Christ are understood in Christian tradition to be adopted into or incorporated as the Body of Christ. In this sense, the priest or minister and even those receiving the sacraments are to be considered children of the Father through Christ. To see one another is to see a child of God and to see the Body of Christ in the world. This intensifies the first form of seeing: It is one thing to see the King by seeing a professionally trained ambassador, but another by seeing an ambassador who is the King's son or daughter (whom we may also understand to function as heirs).

There would also be a seeing by interpretation insofar as the Christian rites are interpreted as acts that imitate the initial institution of the rite by Christ. If, say, a child were only able to interpret the Eucharist as adults moving around a big silver chalice and dispensing juice, the child would no more see the Eucharist than he would see chess if all he could make out was a battle between a horse and castle.

There remains at least one other level of seeing that is worthy of note: *seeing as revelation or disclosure.* Imagine you love someone dearly who has commissioned that a letter of love be read to you. Is seeing the letter or hearing it a case of seeing or hearing the beloved or seeing or hearing his love? Isn't it possible that seeing or hearing the letter might even be a deeply moving experience in which the heart of the beloved becomes revealed and encountered? If you are reluctant to answer yes on the grounds that the spatial location of the lover is key, imagine that you are hearing or seeing the letter in the presence of the beloved but for some reason you cannot directly see him or hear his actual voice. So long as the lover has commissioned the letter and his love is thereby expressed in its content, doesn't the event of listening and even subsequently acting on the letter count as a disclosure, revelation, or encounter? Moreover, imagine that the lover has instructed you to participate in a representation of a last meal you had with him in which bread and wine are offered as in some way embodying or expressing his loving care for you. I suggest that under these conditions you would see the disclosure or revelation of the lover through these acts and terms. The Eucharist fits this pattern because in the Eucharist you not only have the loving will and testimony of Jesus conveyed (through Gospel and epistles), you have the act of love (the self-donation of Jesus embodied in the Eucharistic reenactment) displayed or made manifest. As for the spatial proximity of the divine lover (God the Father, Son, Holy Spirit), Christians affirm the omnipresence of God, and so there is no place where God is absent.

As noted earlier, this fourth kind of seeing (building on the earlier three) is not restricted to a visual sighting. In a Eucharistic service involving song, incense, eating, drinking and tasting, feeling (the sensation of passing the peace), and movement, wouldn't the whole event comprise a multilayered experience of the real presence of Christ?

Consider the opposite. Imagine you are a Christian but somehow isolated and not in the company of any practitioners of the faith and unable (because, let us imagine, it is illegal) for there to be any Christian worship. It is not possible to reenact through symbolic repetition Christ's self-donation and sharing of bread and wine. You cannot engage in any display or recognition of the incorporation of believers into the Body of Christ. There are no rites you can interpret of Christ's self-giving love, and there is no Scripture or any Christian rite whereby you may feel Christ's love. Although God's gracious presence may be manifested to you in terms of internal awareness and displayed through your solitary (but perhaps clandestine) Christian witness, you would be bereft of the great goods of Christ's presence as mediated and made evident in the sacraments and Christian rites.

Consider an objection: The account just given does not do enough to capture what most Christians have held to be special about Christ's Eucharistic presence. Couldn't all four modes of the disclosure of Christ's presence take place when witnessing an act of extraordinary compassion carried out in the name of Christ without any symbolic repetition in the Eucharist?

I believe the answer is "'yes," but this does not undermine the account. Foundational to the vast majority of Eucharistic theology, West and East, is the thesis that, in the Eucharist, Christians live out liturgically a series of acts that are protean and that should lead Christians to acts of compassion and justice that make the reality of Christ evident. The real presence of Christ in the sacraments remains distinctive because of its intentional reenactment of acts of Christ and its drama and romance of confession, reform, renewal, and so on. However, the place of Christian rites in a complete Christian philosophical theology of creation and ethics is intended to enhance the recognition of the need for and the reality of acting in accord with Christ's commission of love beyond church and ritual.[16] It should also be noted in winding up this section that modal sacramental realism is in the spirit of the liturgical renewal movement, with its focus on the whole rite rather than giving central stage to the elements of bread and wine themselves, but the account is compatible with traditional Roman Catholic or Orthodox teaching about the elements.

In summary, after offering a definition of religious and Christian rites, this chapter surveyed reasons for taking Christian rites seriously

---

[16] For a further exposition of rites and Christian identity, see my "Rites and Christian Philosophy" in *Ritual and Philosophy*, ed. Kevin Schilbrack (Oxford: Routledge, 2005).

and many of the goods and ills involved in Christian rites; replied to two philosophical worries about Christian rites; and advanced a model regarding how a Christian might claim to see and experience the real presence of Christ through the Eucharist.

FURTHER WORK

A philosophy of Christian rites can draw on many areas of philosophy for its elucidation and evolution, from the philosophy of language and meaning to the philosophy of time and history, to aesthetics. Some theologians have proposed that, in some way, the enactment of the Eucharist today can participate in the original Eucharist once offered by Jesus in the first century. Surely this will involve some philosophy of time and work on the concept of participation. In Christian ritual, there seems to be an interesting role for attention and intention. When does an authentic participation in a Christian rite require that the participant fully embrace every proposition uttered? For some, recitation of the Nicene Creed is more of a general way in which the practitioner intends that she or he be united with the Christian community but she or he may not believe, for example, that Christ's birth was virginal. Some philosophers think that actual propositional claims are made in the Creed that require assent in terms of truth for full participation in the rite, but others allow that the rites may only require that one hopes the claims are true or one is in solidarity with the believing community, or one accepts the creedal claims as metaphors or analogical language of God that is shrouded in mystery. Some recent philosophy of religion suggests that we should seek to see the world sacramentally or in some sense along the lines of the way the sacraments themselves may be seen as conveying the real, divine presence.[17]

Philosophical reflection on Christian rites also sets the stage for the cross-cultural study of rites. For example, are there important analogies or disanalogies between Buddhist and Christian rites in which it appears there is confession and reconciliation? This latter question is one that has broad interest, not just to those in religious traditions, but to secular thinkers who are seeking to garnish as much wisdom as possible as to how we might come to work through conflict and seek moral reform. These two tasks alone provide sufficient grounds for a comprehensive study of rites of reconciliation in Christian and non-Christian sources.

---

[17] See O. Davies, *The Creativity of God: World, Eucharist, Reason* (Cambridge: Cambridge University Press, 2004).

This is a task that may interest social scientists, but it is important, too, for philosophers who are also committed to thinking through the theory of justice, moral psychology, and the possibility of a comprehensive philosophy of religion.[18]

[18] I am grateful for some illuminating exchanges on the sacraments and prayer with Frances Howard-Snyder, Andrew Chigneel, Victoria Harrison, and C. Stephen Evans at a Sino-American Conference at Hong Kong Baptist University, and am indebted to Chad Meister for excellent proposals in the final editing of this chapter.

14 Revelation and miracles

THOMAS D. SULLIVAN AND SANDRA MENSSEN

Answers to four connected questions about revelations and miracles carry the gravest implications for both Christian and non-Christian revelatory claims. Stripped of nuances to be added later, the questions are: (1) Can belief in a revelatory claim be appropriate if no adequate case backs the content of the belief? (2) Can a case for a revelatory claim succeed without first establishing the existence of God? (3) Can a case for a revelatory claim succeed if it does not include appeal to a confirming miracle? (4) Are Christian revelatory claims vulnerable to Humean-type arguments against the credibility of miracles?

We, of course, cannot fully engage the questions in this brief chapter. We can, however, at least clarify the questions and the interconnections among them. We can also gain a sense of the value of and need for exploring more fully the content of Christian revelation from a philosophical standpoint.

However, before we take up these four questions directly, we must discuss some terms. We aim here not only to provide some context for our later discussion, but also to draw off some of the vapors clinging to the issues.

KEY TERMS AND CONCEPTS

Revelation and associated concepts

From the Latin *revelare* – to remove the veil – "revelation" has the general sense of uncovering something hidden. The general sense allows a wide range of candidates both for what does the revealing and for what is revealed, including (nonexhaustively) persons, things, processes, events, words, meanings, music, and works of art. "Revelation" in the narrower, religious sense restricts the domain of revealer and revealed. In theistic religions, a god, directly or indirectly, is either the revealer or what is revealed (or both). Nontheistic religions can be said to view received texts as revelation inasmuch as the sacred text discloses ultimate reality or offers means for overcoming the limits and sorrows of life. The sacred text may be seen as authorless, as in the Mimamsa school of Hinduism: It is insisted that there is no God, in an effort to elevate the intrinsic authority of the vibrant text.[1]

Theistic religions often endorse a distinction between "universal" and "special" revelation.[2] Universal revelation is God's revelation through the physical world sustained by God's continual activity. Scripture declares: "The heavens are telling the glory of God" (Psalm 19). Deist Thomas Paine, adamantly anti-Christian and scorning the authority of all religious Scripture, nonetheless agrees: "There is a Word of God; there is a revelation. *The word of god is the creation we behold:* And it is in *this word*, which no human invention can counterfeit or alter, that God speaketh universally to man."[3] In contrast to universal revelation, special revelation is God's intervention into the natural order, through (for instance) extraordinary communications to prophets, authors of Scripture, and religious communities, and through such manifestations of the divine as the Incarnation and Resurrection. Our main questions in this chapter bear on special, not universal, revelation.

It is by no means a straightforward matter to assign an intension and extension to "Christian." We might content ourselves with one or another statement drawn from Scripture, declaring that a Christian is a person who subscribes to John 3:16, say, or Hebrews 1:2. Any selection would look arbitrary to someone. Yet the problem can be avoided if an inquirer simply contextualizes the questions concerning Christianity, and makes precise reference to the Christian claims at issue. On occasion, however, we will find it useful to refer to "strong" Christian revelatory claims. These include, by stipulation, the substance of the high doctrines Scripture expresses in I Corinthians 15:1–28 and in the so-called *kerygmatic* sermons of Acts.[4] (Although our concern is ultimately with authentic revelations, we will focus here on *revelatory claims* that a revelation has really occurred.)

Propositional revelation differs from nonpropositional. In propositional revelation, what is revealed is *that* something is the case. In nonpropositional revelation, what is revealed is a person, or action, or thing.

---

[1] Ninian Smart, *World Philosophies* (London: Routledge, 1999), 45.

[2] The more common terminology is general and special. This terminology, however, unfortunately invites confusion given the distinction between general and special senses of the term revelation.

[3] Thomas Paine, *The Age of Reason*, Part I, chapter 9 (New York: Barnes and Noble, 2006), 33.

[4] Obviously, what pertains to the "substance" can be and is disputed, but the stipulation hopefully is sufficient to give meaning to "strong" Christian revelation.

Christians generally take nonpropositional revelation to be more fundamental: God reveals the innermost being of the divine in the person of
Jesus Christ and in all the great deeds leading up to the final disclosure.
Yet it certainly does not follow, as some standard sources seem to suggest, that revelation cannot involve God's communicating information
expressible in propositions. It would be strange indeed for Christians
to deny that God has revealed truths listed in Council statements and
creeds or, for instance, in the early teaching found in I Corinthians 15:3–
5, with its abundant "that" (*oti*) clauses: "For I delivered to you as of
first importance what I also received, *that* Christ died for our sins in
accordance with the Scriptures, *that* he was buried, *that* he was raised
on the third day" (emphasis added).

Miracles and wonders

The *locus classicus* for all modern and contemporary discussion of
miracles is Section X of Hume's *Enquiries Concerning Human Understanding*. Estimates of the value of Hume's argument vary, ranging from
John Earman's charge that Hume's essay is an "abject failure"[5] to Robert
Fogelin's spirited defense.[6] Experts are also at variance about what Hume
was trying to prove and how his arguments go. His definition of miracle, however, is easy enough to locate, and often quoted: "A miracle may
accurately be defined, as a transgression of a law of nature by a particular
volition of the deity, or by the interposition of some invisible agent."[7]

Despite Hume's assertion, though, the definition is *not* accurate.
Accuracy requires encircling a target concept, and it alone. Hume's definition is ambiguous. A "law of nature" may be understood as a universal
but contingent pattern in nature. A-type events are always, though not
necessarily, followed by B-type events. On a second understanding, a
"law of nature" is universal and necessary. Necessarily, A-type events

---

[5] John Earman, *Hume's Abject Failure: The Argument against Miracles* (Oxford: Oxford
University Press, 2000).

[6] Robert J. Fogelin, *A Defense of Hume on Miracles* (Princeton, NJ: Princeton University
Press, 2003).

[7] David Hume, *An Enquiry concerning Human Understanding*, Section X, "Of Miracles" (Chicago, IL: Gateway, 1956), 119n. Aquinas described a miracle in somewhat
the same terms as "outside the order commonly observed in things" (our translation of
praeter ordinem communiter obvservatum in rebus). See his *Summa Contra Gentiles*
III, chapter 101. Arguably, Aquinas's definition, making no mention of law, is to be
preferred because it is more general than Hume's, and neutral between the view that a
miracle is a violation of a norm, and a view such as Nancy Cartwright's, which maintains that our scientific knowledge bears on natures, not laws. See Nancy Cartwright,
The Dappled World: A Study of the Boundaries of Science (Cambridge: Cambridge
University Press, 1999).

give rise to B-type events (or in the case of nondeterministic laws, A-type events necessarily render probable B-type events). The first understanding is nonmodal; the second, modal. Hume's general epistemology and ontology commit him to the first, nonmodal definition, but it carries many familiar burdens, including the failure to distinguish between nomic (lawlike) and accidental generalizations. Despite Hume, it thus seems some kind of modal understanding is required.

All miracles are wonders, but not all wonders are miracles, not in any proper sense. Miracles make anyone wonder, because the cause, a supernatural being, is hidden from view. However, should something escape the understanding of the cause, even if the cause is natural, the event can make us wonder. If, for example, A-events and B-events are only contingently connected, why is there an invariable move from one to the other? If necessarily connected, why? The capacity for wonder varies with the individual. At one end of the spectrum, Walt Whitman wants to "stop and loiter all the time to sing...in ecstatic songs" over the "mere fact consciousness" ("Beginning My Studies" in *Leaves of Grass*). The eliminativist philosopher, on the other hand, having lost sight of the datum, moves on.

Ontological and epistemic foundations

Miracles can be foundational to Christianity in two ways. First, miracles are fundamental to the teaching. Everything rests on miracle claims, such as the claim that Christ rose from the dead. Call something fundamental to revelation in this way "ontologically foundational." By contrast, call something "epistemically foundational" to revelation if without it the *case* for revealed religion is inadequate. The Resurrection and the Incarnation are ontologically foundational, but not necessarily epistemically foundational. One might believe in the Resurrection on the testimony of the Christian Church, and believe the Church is reliable for reasons other than that its teachings have been certified through a miracle.

FOUR KEY QUESTIONS

Is a mature, informed adult's belief in a revelatory claim necessarily inappropriate if no adequate case backs the content of the individual's belief?

Many revelatory claims collide with what is known or contradict one another. Not all, then, can be true. It therefore might seem that the belief of a mature, informed adult is irrational, blind, or somehow inappropriate unless the person has an adequate case supporting his or her belief – an argument that the revelatory claim is *true* that is at least as strong as any argument the claim is *false.*

Perhaps it would widely be thought that this *is* required for certain idiosyncratic or outlandish revelatory claims. But even if an "adequate case" is required for *some* revelatory claims, is it required for all? Opponents of Christianity, from deists to atheists, respond "Yes," and conclude that Christianity is bogus because no case is convincing.

Some Christian theologians and philosophers think that *when it comes to central Christian claims* there is no need for a case, because Christianity is not a proper object for epistemological evaluation. Faith is one thing, reason another. Christianity is both absurd and most worthy of acceptance. Such is the standard reading of Tertullian and Kierkegaard.

However, one needn't go anywhere near this far to hold, reasonably enough, that a case for Christianity (a case as described earlier) can sometimes be dispensed with. A person could have some kind of direct experience of Christian truths, as might be thought to have happened to Paul on the road to Damascus. Alvin Plantinga has argued that Christian revelation might be known to be true through the instigation of the Holy Spirit, who moves the believer to accept the Christian ideas in appropriate circumstances.[8]

Yet even if Christian revelatory claims can be known to be true without a case, many Christians do not think they *know* God is triune; rather, they just *believe* that God is. They are never wracked with doubt about the claim, for example, that there are trees, but they sometimes do feel assailed by doubts about God's providence – say, particularly in the midst of trouble. It is perhaps for this reason that the Christian creeds begin with "I believe..." rather than "I know," and that Christian churches are willing to receive people who can attest to their believing what the creeds profess; no one is required to *know* the exalted mysteries are true.

In that case, one might look for a defense of the reasonableness of *believing* without an argument. The nineteenth-century writer John Henry Newman offers such a defense in his *Oxford University Sermons* and his *Grammar of Assent.* Newman observes that Christ called many who were incapable of making much of a case, if any, for following him. Yet they rightly responded, Newman continues, because their hearts

---

[8] Plantinga has worked out, in great detail, the theory that Christianity can be properly basic, requiring neither evidence nor argument, though objections to it – potential defeaters – can and should be rebutted. See Alvin Plantinga, *Warranted Christian Belief* (Oxford: Oxford University Press, 2000).

were well disposed and they acted on antecedent reasons.[9] This is not to say they stood in no need of spiritual healing; many were "dissolute," but the multitude who accepted him were well disposed insofar as they were prepared to receive "truths beyond this world, whether or not their knowledge was clear, or their lives consistent."[10] Still, Newman acknowledges a debt to reason: "When the Gospel is said to require a rational Faith, this need not mean more than that Faith is accordant to right Reason in the abstract, not that it results from it in the particular case."[11]

Newman's remark suggests an important qualification regarding the "case" that backs an individual's belief. At most, there is a need for an adequate case in the sense of a case in the abstract – a case someone could latch onto. Here, a comparison might be useful. As children, we are taught that we cannot divide by zero. Why not? It is by no means easy to say. But the belief in the propriety of the rule can be rational and right only if there is a way to rationalize the rule.

Can a case for a revelatory claim be adequate without inclusion of an argument for God's existence which, leaving aside revelation, renders God's existence more probable than not?

If dramatic miracles attesting to the truth of a revelatory claim are possible, then it is possible that a case for a revelatory claim might be adequate without including a probable argument for God's existence (an argument that abstracts from God's performance of the dramatic miracle).

However, the dominance of what might be called "standard natural theology" (SNT) suggests that despite this *theoretical* possibility that the answer to the question posed in our section heading is "Yes," the actual human situation is such that the theoretical possibility is irrelevant, at least for vast numbers of people. SNT begins by attempting to show, without any essential reliance on a putative revelation, that a god probably exists with something like the great attributes of omniscience, omnipotence, and infinite goodness (or at the very least, that it's not

---

[9] Newman so stresses the importance of antecedent reasoning he often sounds like a modern Bayesian theorist.

[10] John Henry Newman, *A Reason for the Hope Within: Sermons on the Theory of Religious Belief* (Denville, NJ: Dimension Books, 1985), 188.

[11] Newman, *Reason for the Hope Within*, p. 175. This aspect of Newman's general line is reminiscent in many ways of the tack taken by contemporary externalist epistemologists who contend that we need not be aware of what justifies our judgments in order for them to be, in fact, justified. By contrast, internalists insist that to be justified in our judgments we must be aware of the evidence that justifies them.

improbable such a god exists). Once that has been done, the idea is, an investigator can go on to consider miracles and putative revelations in light of available public evidence. Christian philosophers generally seem to assume that if SNT is not successful, then there is no hope of building a case for either miracles or revelation.

On the surface, the approach of SNT seems to make good sense. Unless there is a God, there can be neither a revelation from God nor a miracle the ultimate cause of which is God. First things first: Establish that there probably is a God, and *then* consider whether that God has vouchsafed a revelation, perhaps a revelation including miracles and miracle-claims.

However, it is a mistake to think a convincing philosophical case for a revelatory claim requires first obtaining a probable case for a good God. Notice an analogous point: We may have no way of finding out whether there is extraterrestrial intelligence except by listening to signals from outer space, as is done in the SETI program (Search for Extra-Terrestrial Intelligence). Scholars of classical literature may have no way of finding out whether Homer ever existed – whether there existed a single individual primarily responsible for the *Iliad*, let us say – without examining the content of the alleged composition; without scrutinizing its cohesiveness, the consistency and richness of its language, and so on. In both these cases, it is reasonable to look at one and the same time to see whether there has been a communication from a being of a certain sort, *and* whether the being at issue exists.

To be sure, there is *something* to the demand first to prove there is a God before going on to examine putative revelations, but nowhere near as much as usually is thought. After all, if a convincing argument were to show that the existence of a "mere" creator is not highly improbable, then a reasonable person could not categorically dismiss revelatory claims without examination. Happily, such an argument can be supplied. Here are the core premises of one such argument (it should not be conflated with the well-known kalam argument for a creator's existence):

(1) *It is not improbable* that the physical universe came to be (that is, had a beginning).

(2) *It is not improbable* that whatever comes to be has a cause distinct outside itself.[12]

---

[12] Heisenberg's uncertainty principle does nothing to overturn our claim at (2). That principle would undercut causality only if causes had to be determining conditions, but they need not be; instead, they can be nonlogical necessary conditions. For discussion see Richard W. Miller, *Fact and Method* (Princeton, NJ: Princeton University Press, 1987), especially pp. 60–64.

Hence, no one should confidently claim there is no creator – or even that it is highly improbable there is a creator. Our contention is that if one assigns a probability to the conjunction of the propositions that the physical universe came to be, and that whatever comes to be has a cause distinct outside itself, the probability is not going to be anywhere in the neighborhood of zero. Some would say that the propositions are inscrutable, and that if probabilistic language is to be used, the best way to represent the inscrutability is to assign to each hypothesis an interval $<0, 1>$. If that interval is assigned, then the probability of the conjunction is *not* in the neighborhood of zero.

We suggest, then, that even when the possibility of dramatic miracles is set aside, the answer to the question that constitutes the title of this section may still be "Yes."[13] If there is a place for faith, a space within us for the movement of God's Spirit, then it cannot be expected that any argument for an unqualified "Yes" will yield *knowledge* that the putative revelation is, indeed, a heavenly gift. Still, against the relentless criticisms of Christopher Hitchens, Sam Harris, Daniel Dennett, Richard Dawkins, and a host of quieter, less journalistic naysayers, due diligence may show the content of the Christian revelatory claim is best explained by positing a good God who has revealed. It is not true of all religion that it "poisons everything" (Hitchens) or that it is a "delusion" (Dawkins). The Christian philosophical theologian may reasonably hope to show that the best explanation of the putative revelation is that a good God has chosen to make it ours. This revelation assures us that God defeats evil through the cross and Resurrection. Exactly how, we do not expect to learn while in corruptible flesh, but if the line of argument so far marked out holds promise, Christian philosophers can find new material for reflection in areas of inquiry they have, perhaps half-consciously, left to theological students of revelation and their opponents.[14]

Can a case for theistic revelation be adequate without including a certified miracle?
Various positions on a question of considerable significance

It is unclear where nontheistic writers stand on this question. They generally require that a case be put forth for theistic revelation and argue

---

[13] Indeed, it may be that the *only* way of acquiring an adequate case for the existence of God is to examine putative communications, to take them as part of the relevant database for an "inference to the best explanation."

[14] See Sandra Menssen and Thomas D. Sullivan, *The Agnostic Inquirer: Revelation from a Philosophical Standpoint* (Grand Rapids, MI: Eerdmans, 2007). We attempt in this book to develop a line of argument demarcated in section 2.2 of the present chapter.

that the cases coming forward are inadequate. Seldom, however, do they speak directly to the issue of whether a certified miracle must be part of the case.

Distinguished Christians are divided over the matter. Given recent trends in apologetics, which emphasize the epistemic role of miracle, one might find it surprising that earlier thinkers gave less emphasis to that role. Although the Resurrection lies at the center of strong Christian revelatory claims, the Evangelists (most particularly Mark) portray Jesus as drawing people to himself by a personality dazzling and stupefying, creating awe and fascination. Apologists through the centuries have preferred to emphasize the content of the message and its power to heal and restore. For these apologists, miracles are secondary signs of the authenticity of the message.[15] About the wonder of the man, they never tire of speaking.

Some Christian thinkers have maintained that a case for a revelation could not be adequate unless it were accompanied by a certified miracle. That is the position of Richard Swinburne, one of the greatest philosophers of religion of our time, and it was the position of William Paley (whom Swinburne cites approvingly). However, Thomas Aquinas argued that people should have accepted Christ even if he had not performed miracles.[16] Other important Christian thinkers, including John Henry Newman, have explicitly asserted that a confirming miracle need not ground belief in revelation. Christians also may point out that one whose authority far exceeds that of any philosopher certainly sanctioned acceptance of the revelation without a confirming miracle: "Believe me, that I am in the Father and the Father in me; or else believe me for the sake of the works themselves."[17]

What would be the consequence of assuming a miracle is necessary to complete an adequate case for a revelatory claim? Swinburne draws the following inference: "Before we ever come to look at the details of its message and method of promulgation, there is, among the so-called great religions of the world, only one serious candidate for having a body of doctrine which is to be believed on the grounds that it is revealed, and that is the Christian revelation."[18] Furthermore, insisting that a miracle is necessary to validate a revelatory claim also puts a great deal

---

[15] Avery Cardinal Dulles, *A History of Apologetics* (San Francisco, CA: Ignatius Press, 1999), 25.

[16] See Aquinas's *Quodlibetal Questions*, Q. 2, A. 4. We thank Timothy Pawl and Faith Pawl for this reference.

[17] John 14:8 (RSV).

[18] Swinburne, *Revelation*, 2e. (Oxford: Oxford University Press, 2007), 126.

of pressure on the case for the epistemically foundational miracle. If a miracle is needed, then Christianity will depend much more on the credibility of the early witnesses than it will if it is first agreed that the Church or Scripture contains the assured revelation of God, and many people feel unable to assess the credibility of the early witnesses. Finally, the requirement of a confirming miracle condemns the judgment of such early Christians as Dionysius and Damaris, who, at Athens, came to a belief in Christianity,[19] though, as Newman observed, St. Paul did no miracle there.

Reasons to think any case on behalf of a revelatory claim is insufficient without a confirming miracle

It is not infrequently argued that God must have provided an epistemically foundational miracle confirming his revelation, because otherwise there is too much chance of deception. In response, it might be pointed out that God appears to be prepared to allow plenty of deception in this world about all kinds of matters, and surely must be allowing some, given that world religions differ on some particulars. The argument might be strong if everyone was damned who failed to believe the right religion, but that exclusivist idea carries a heavy burden of proof.

One would expect to find Swinburne offering a case for his contention that content-based evidence is insufficient to show the probable truth of the Christian revelatory claim, and that a revelation must be confirmed by a miracle. Unfortunately, however, it is hard to credit the line of reasoning he seems to propose on behalf of the contention. He says:

> [A] revelation may be expected to contain claims that we cannot possibly confirm by mere human reflection or ordinary historical investigation.... And clearly with respect to many of the purportedly revealed claims about which we can have some a priori or empirical evidence of the kinds described, that evidence is not going to be nearly sufficient to make those claims probable....
> So satisfying the test of content fairly well would not be sufficient to show some candidate revelation to be genuine; the mere fact that there is no very probable falsity in some purported revelation is not adequate for this purpose. We need also the second test of the method of expression [the test of miracle].[20]

---

[19] See Acts 17:34.
[20] Swinburne, *Revelation*, 111–12.

This informal argument, with its suppressed premises, is answerable. Notice that Swinburne has drawn attention to only two types of revelatory claims, when, in fact, there are more, at least abstractly considered. His first type – call it RC-1 – is the sort of claim that "we cannot possibly confirm by mere human reflection or ordinary historical investigation." The second – RC-2 – is the type for which there is evidence, but the "evidence is not going to be nearly sufficient to make those claims probable." What about claims – call them RC-3 – that could be made probable on the basis of some kind of evidence? Can it just be assumed without argument that this class is empty? If not, perhaps verified claims could serve as a springboard for certifying the entire set,[21] via an argument along the following lines: *This and that are true, so the Christian Church is plausibly enough the oracle of God, and hence the rest of the Church's message is true.*

Despite the inadequacy of this stretch of reasoning on Swinburne's part, though, the fact that he takes the position he does with regard to miracle suggests a meta-argument that is troubling for the Christian philosopher who wishes to deny the need for a confirming miracle. If the most thorough and exact philosophical defense of Christianity written in our time (Swinburne's), a defense ranging over more than half a dozen volumes and including detailed discussion of the content of the Christian revelatory claim, does not constitute, *in the author's own assessment,* an adequate case when the evidence for the Resurrection is deleted, how can it reasonably be assumed that such a case might nonetheless be constructed? Using the tools of modern probability theory and the resources of contemporary biblical and church history, Swinburne elaborates an insight one finds in earlier writers about the power of prior probability – the antecedent assumptions made about the likelihood of something occurring. In the words of John Henry Newman:

> The Word of Life is offered to a man; and, on its being offered, he has Faith in it. Why? On these two grounds, – the word of its human messenger, and the likelihood of the message. And why does he feel the message to be probable? Because he has a love for it, his love being strong, though the testimony is weak. He has a keen sense of the intrinsic excellence of the message, of

---

[21] What belongs to the entire set of Christian claims? Here, of course, we need to be careful. If the set is reduced too far, so that the revelatory claim is exceedingly weak, the strategy may not work because there is not enough to work from. If, on the other hand, the set is expanded incautiously to include propositions not essential even to strong versions of a revelatory claim, it will be easy to overturn the claim.

its desirableness, of its likeness to what it seems to him Divine Goodness would vouchsafe did He vouchsafe any, of the need of a Revelation, and its probability.[22]

Nevertheless, Swinburne holds that the content of Christian revelation is insufficient, absent a confirming miracle, to establish the probable truth of Christianity.

Reasons to think an adequate content-based case is available without appeal to miracle

Obviously, content-based evidence for the Christian revelatory claim, including evidence in Swinburne's multi-volume case for Christianity, Newman's *Grammar of Assent*, and other works, needs to be examined on its own terms and at length. Such evidence, judiciously weighed as part of a review that includes counter-evidence, provides the best reason for thinking an adequate case is available without appeal to miracle. We clearly can't undertake such a review here.

However, having just presented a "meta-argument" based on Swinburne's work in order to raise suspicion about the claim that a confirming miracle is not necessary, we present a response to that meta-argument grounded in positions to which Swinburne commits himself. The response, based on an old line of thought freshened by C. S. Lewis,[23] goes as follows:

(1) Jesus implied he was God.
(2) Either he was deluded about being God or not.
(3) If the former, he was crazy.
(4) If the latter, he was either God or wicked.
(5) Jesus was neither crazy nor wicked.
(6) So Jesus was God.

Swinburne accepts (1) and (5), presumably on the basis of the content of the Christian revelatory claim. In addition, despite some quick dismissals of some of the propositions in between (by individuals such as Graham Oppy and Peter Smith),[24] it is unlikely Swinburne would reject

---

[22] John Henry Newman, *Oxford University Sermons*, Sermon XI, "The Nature of Faith in Relation to Reason" (London: Longmans, Green and Co., 1918), 202–03.

[23] C. S. Lewis, *God in the Dock*, ed. Walter Hooper (Grand Rapids, MI: Eerdmans, 1970), "What Are We to Make of Jesus Christ?," 156–61.

[24] See Graham Oppy, *Arguing about Gods* (Cambridge: Cambridge University Press, 2006), 406–07, and Peter Smith, <logicmatters.blogspot.com> "Philosophy of Religion 4: Lord, Liar, Lunatic," March 30, 2008.

them. Perhaps Swinburne's own content-based evidence for Christianity is stronger than even he thinks.

Despite our inability here to survey the content-based evidence for Christian revelatory claims, we can also call attention to an important sort of evidence that may easily be excluded by an inquirer following along with Swinburne's argument, given his views – noted earlier – concerning non-Christian revelation. (His approach does not invite close scrutiny of non-Christian revelatory claims.) If it is plausible that there have been non-Christian revelations, that may increase the plausibility that there have been Christian revelations. Consider a parallel. Westerners disinclined to accept the sort of mystical experience reported by Proust might come to think of it as credible when they learn that it has many of the features of mystical experience reported by followers of Samkhya-Yoga who, in meditative states, experience themselves as eternal monads outside of space and time.[25]

Where might non-Christian revelations be found? In at least two places. First, in the myths. Of course no one believes in the gods of the ancient pantheon. Still, in these and other myths, might there not have been some divine inspiration? Both Socrates and Plato thought so. C. S. Lewis declares, "We must not be ashamed of the mythical radiance resting on our theology. We must not be nervous about 'parallels' and 'pagan Christs': they *ought* to be there – it would be a stumbling block if they weren't."[26] And again, "He is here of whom the corn king was an image."[27]

Second, in non-Christian theistic religions, how can anyone who accepts Christian revelation be certain no revelation is captured in Krishna's declaration of "the unheard of secret of God's love for man"?[28] Or the Quran's acceptance of Jesus as the Messiah born of God and the Virgin Mary?[29] Or the Zoroastrian doctrine that God is purely and utterly good, and that matter, created by God, is neither evil nor the source of evil?

Do Humean arguments turning on miracles refute strong Christian revelatory claims?

Earlier, we distinguished between a miracle being either *ontologically* or *epistemologically* fundamental to a revelatory claim. Therefore,

[25] R. C. Zaehner, *At Sundry Times: An Essay in the Comparison of Religions* (London: Faber and Faber, 1958), 48–49.

[26] Lewis, "Myth Becomes Fact," in *God in the Dock*, 67.

[27] Lewis, "The Grand Miracle," in *God in the Dock*, 84.

[28] Zaehner, *At Sundry Times* (referencing *The Bhagavad-Gita*, 18:65–66), 133.

[29] Zaehner, *At Sundry Times*, 157.

the credibility of a revelatory claim containing a story of a miracle need not depend on that miracle for confirmation of the entire revelatory claim. In some legitimate sense, baptism may be a miracle because in the natural course of events, waters do not wash filth from souls and initiate people into the divine life. Yet no one points to the miracle of baptism as the stunning confirmation of the reality of the Incarnation and all that has come with it. Rather, the apologetic starts elsewhere and *concludes* to the miraculous power of baptism.

Even so, arguments against miracles obviously threaten strong revelatory claims. If it could be shown that any miracle essential to the content of a revelatory claim is literally incredible – unworthy of credence – the revelatory claim would be falsified. Thus something should be said about whether arguments have been crafted that show miracles are unworthy of belief. The candidate arguments are almost invariably parasitic on Hume's essay "On Miracles," often viewed as constituting a decisive refutation of Christian claims. Hume argues that the testimony of witnesses of a reported miracle always is met by a contrary proof of the miracle not having happened. He certainly sounds confident enough about his main idea: "The proof against a miracle, as it is founded on invariable experience, is a *species* or *kind* which is full and certain when taken alone, because it implies no doubt, as is the case with all probabilities."[30]

However, this is one of the places where Hume misleadingly speaks of proof when he means something weaker. According to careful students of Hume's aims,[31] Hume was trying to show neither that miracles are impossible, nor that they never have occurred, nor even that we could never have reason to believe they occurred. Rather, what he was trying to show was (as Hume himself puts it) "that no human testimony can have such force as to prove a miracle, and make it a just foundation for any such system of religion."[32]

Now, although dangerous for faith, if this is all Hume sought to show, then a defender of a strong Christian revelatory claim might even agree with him, though, no doubt, with some qualms. After all, we argued earlier that testimony on the part of miracles is *not* a necessary foundation for any revelatory claim.

---

[30] Hume presents the argument in a letter to Hugh Blair, but it is resonant of much that is found in Hume's essay "Of Miracles." The letter is cited by Fogelin in *A Defense of Hume on Miracles*, p. 45.

[31] Erik J. Wielenberg, *God and the Reach of Reason* (Cambridge: Cambridge University Press, 2008), 126–27.

[32] Hume, "Of Miracles," p. 132.

Still, if a reason is sought for resisting Hume's arguments for being so skeptical about the testimony offered on behalf of miracles, we might begin by observing that Hume fails to attend to what Newman calls antecedent reasons or what Swinburne terms prior probability insofar as they bear on the riveting person of Christ, the profound *content* of the revelatory claim, or the telos of the Resurrection event. Thus Hume treats us to the imaginary tale of a Queen Elizabeth who rises from the dead after three days. Her resurrection would, indeed, be unworthy of credence: There is nothing about her person, her character, her ambitions, her self-descriptions, nothing about the telos of the event, nothing about an anticipated teaching that preceded the event, nothing about a teaching reverberating for centuries after the event, nothing that gives us reason to accept as real the resurrection we are to imagine being proclaimed.[33] All the evidence for her resurrection rests on testimony concerning the event, and that, indeed, may be too little. There is more than such testimony to lean on in the claims concerning a risen Christ, and whereas the testimony on behalf of Christ's Resurrection held firm under the most extraordinary affliction, it is hard to imagine witnesses stoned, racked, boiled, burned, and nailed upside down crying out "Elizabeth has risen."

[33] See our discussion in *The Agnostic Inquirer*, p. 93.

15 Prayer

HARRIET HARRIS

I. SURVEY AND CRITICAL ANALYSIS: MAKING AND NOT MAKING SENSE OF PRAYER

Herbert McCabe warns us off thinking that we need to get our ideas of God right before we establish whether or not to pray. It is the other way round, he says: The "way we understand God is as 'whatever makes sense of prayer.'"[1] This seems to be borne out in the negative, too; making no sense of prayer, because of logical, empirical, or moral objections, involves bewilderment at the idea or worship of God.

No account of prayer entirely makes sense of it, but the ways of not making sense, and the conclusions drawn from these ways, vary greatly. Philosophers and theologians have many different views, for example, on the point or pointlessness of prayer. We survey five ways of making and not making sense of prayer, turning on the question, "what is its point?"

1. Communing with God

Most accounts of prayer situate it within the context of relationship with God; its point being to commune with God. This is so of all the positions surveyed subsequently, except for atheist positions and those that see prayer only as expedient to moral training.

When prayer is understood as communing with God, it is sometimes said to be pointless. Prayer is "an absolute waste of time"[2] because it has no goals of effectiveness. It is simply for the sake of relationship with God, and with one another in God. Although it yields beneficial side effects of the kind noted in "therapeutic" models of prayer (see position 3, which follows), if we made sense of prayer in terms of utility and

---

[1] *God Matters* (London and New York: Mowbray, 1987), 217.

[2] McCabe, *God Matters*, p. 225; cf. Michael Hanby, "Interceding, Giving Grief to Management," in *The Blackwell Companion to Christian Ethics*, ed. Stanley Hauerwas and Samuel Wells (Oxford; Malden MA; Carlton, Victoria: Blackwell, 2004), 237–49.

effectiveness, we would misunderstand what is most important about it. In prayer, we collectively share in the interior life of the Godhead. Making sense of this is a theological matter, which we will take up in section II. Philosophically, it remains the case that prayer does have a point: to abide with one another and with God, and, also therefore, to resist the pull to walk away and do something more useful.

2. Praying for things in order to obtain things

Particular questions arise regarding prayers of petition and intercession, which, *prima facie*, are expected to have efficacy beyond enjoying relationship with God. This is where the main focus of philosophical questions about prayer fall, and therefore this section is the longest.

Petitionary prayer is prayer in which desires are presented to God. Intercessory prayer is made on behalf of others. At face value, both types of prayer seem to be impetratory, "impetrate" being a theological term meaning to obtain things by request. The conviction behind impetratory prayer is that God gives us some things not only as we wish, but because we wish and ask for them.[3] We therefore now consider the proposition that *the point of impetratory prayer is to achieve those things by prayer which God gives because of prayer.*

This proposition is challenging on several counts.

Immutability
(1) GOD'S IMMUTABLE WILL.

"If all things come to pass by the will of God, and his counsels are fixed, and none of the things he wills can be changed, prayer is in vain" (Origen, *Treatise on Prayer*, V.6).[4]

Having articulated this problem, Origen argues that God foresees our prayers and answers them according to our deserts, making arrangements accordingly in the divine disposition of all things (VI.4). Our prayers, or failures to pray, and the worthiness or unworthiness of those prayers, are amongst the factors God takes into account from eternity. This leads to a further quandary regarding God's foreknowledge, which Origen also raises, and which will be taken up subsequently.

Origen's line of response can be strengthened by Boethius's notion of God as outside time. Boethius casts all time as present to God's

---

[3] Freidrich Heiler, *Prayer: a study in the history and psychology of religion*, trans. and ed. Samuel McComb and J. Edgar Park (London: Oxford University Press, 1958), 253.

[4] *Origen's Treatise on Prayer; translation and notes with an account of the practice and doctrine of prayer from the New Testament times to Origen*, by Eric George Day (London: Society for Promoting Christian Knowledge, 1954).

eternal present, so that God does not *fore*know anything (*Consolations of Philosophy*, V.6).[5] This enables Aquinas to argue that God wills from eternity that whatever he wills to happen should happen at the time he wills that it should happen. Whereas God's will is eternal and therefore immutable, its effects are temporal and subject to change. The creation of things in time does not imply succession on the part of the Creator (*Summa Contra Gentiles* II. 19)[6], nor do responses to prayer: We pray "not that we may change the divine decree, but that we might obtain that which God has decreed will be obtained by prayer" (*Summa Theologiae*, 2a2ae 832).[7]

Aquinas thereby preserves intact the point of impetratory prayer; to achieve those things by prayer which God gives because of prayer. But he does not help us understand why God incorporates the prayers of creatures into the outworkings of divine purpose. Is it not pointless and inefficient to do so?

According to already-discussed position 1, the inefficiency of prayer helps to preserve its point. Although it is inefficient on God's part to include us as causes, God does so because the relationship wrought by prayer is good. For consistency's sake, position 1 could be modified to include *some* prayers having causal efficacy. We can then accommodate Pascal's insight that God has instituted prayer so as to confer upon his creatures the dignity of being causes.[8]

However, now we are considering two potential points to impetratory prayer: (a) to enhance our relationship with God by giving our prayers a causal role in God's plans for the world, and (b) actually to obtain things by those prayers. How do we make sense of (b) if the course of the world is set from all eternity?

Peter Geach argues that impetration requires "two-way contingency": that it be neither impossible nor inevitable that God should bring about the things requested.[9] Some philosophers think Aquinas fails to maintain two-way contingency by regarding all events as predetermined and therefore inevitable.[10] Yet, it is not inevitable in Aquinas's theory that God should bring about what is requested in impetratory prayer. First, not all impetratory prayers are answered, or answered in the way

[5] London: William Heinemann, 1918.
[6] London: Burns, Oates & Washbourne, 1923–1929.
[7] London: Eyre and Spottiswoode; New York: McGraw and Hill Book Company, with Blackfriars, 1963.
[8] Blaise Pascal, *Pensees*. trans. A. J. Krailsheimer (New York: Penguin, 1966), 320.
[9] P. T. Geach, *God and the Soul* (London: Routledge and Kegan Paul, 1969), Chapter 7.
[10] e.g., Vincent Brummer, *What Are We Doing When We Pray? On prayer and the nature of faith* (Aldershot; Burlington, CT: Ashgate, 2008), 40.

they are put. Second, the effect is ordained to follow from the prayer, so if the prayer were not offered, the effect would not come. Hence, Aquinas's theory accommodates two-way contingency, and the efficacy of prayer is maintained. This is the case even though those prayers that are offered are known from all eternity.

In this way, we have made sense of the point of impetratory prayer in relation to God's immutable will, both in respect to (a), the goodness of our relationship with God, and (b), actually obtaining those things that God has ordained to be obtained by prayer.

(II) GOD'S IMMUTABLE NATURE. However, the doctrine of immutability, as it was developed in Patristic times, refers not only to God's will but to God's nature. How can the immutability of Godself be defended, if God responds to prayers? Even if the divine response to prayers is preordained, there is still time before and time after the response is effected. God changes, for example, from one who has not to one who has made a covenant with Moses in response to Moses' prayer (Exod. 34:8–9).

In addressing this problem, Geach entertains the possibility that real change occurs in God's creatures, and only a "Cambridge-change" occurs in God.[11] Cambridge-change is where a predicate that at one time could be ascribed to an entity no longer can be ascribed to it. For example, a novel can progress from obscurity to the status of a classic, without any real change occurring in the novel itself. God can come to be worshipped by St Augustine, but the real change is in Augustine. Such real changes have two-way contingency, and may echo what Augustine himself expresses: that God "wishes our desire to be exercised in prayer that we may be able to receive what he is preparing to give."[12]

Some argue that a mere Cambridge-change retains too strong a sense of immutability. Brummer proposes that impetratory prayer does not make sense unless such prayer can bring about real change in both God and creatures, for then God can "*really* respond" to a contingent universe (p. 44).

Yet, if God desires that some things be brought about by prayer, so that the effects of God's will are timely and in relation to the prayers offered, what needs to be added to ensure that God is *really* responding? Brummer holds that prayer must "affect the *relation* between God and

---

[11] *God and the Soul*, pp. 71–72, 93, 97–99; P. T. Geach, *Providence and Evil* (London: Cambridge University Press, 1977), 18–19.

[12] Augustine, *Letters*, in *A Select Library of the Nicene and Post-Nicene Father*, ed. Phillip Shaff (Oxford: Parker & Co; Buffalo, NY: Christian Literature Company, 1886-), chapter 17; Vincent Brummer, *What Are We Doing When We Pray?*, 42.

the person who prays and therefore have a *real* effect on both" (p. 44). He shares with Eleonore Stump a conviction that being affected is a requirement of being relationally engaged, which is a requirement of being personal. In Brummer's eyes, the problem with settling for a Cambridge-change in God is that when both parties to a potential change are capable of personal rather than merely causal relations, then change will not be merely of the Cambridge type. A novel will not be affected by its rise from obscurity, but a person would be affected if lifted from obscurity to wide acclaim. Therefore, we cannot hold that the type of change applicable to a person raised from obscurity to wide acclaim is Cambridge-change. By analogy, within this line of thinking, an image of a deity would not be affected by praise or other sorts of prayer, but a personal deity would be. Therefore, a God who is personal and who receives prayers will be changed in a way that goes beyond the Cambridge criterion.

"Yes" and "no," defenders of immutability would say. God does not change as creatures do, but God does change for positive reasons – such as maintaining perfect goodness. Novatian, who makes an uncompromising defense of God's unchanging nature (*De Trinitate*, 4),[13] allows that God can be angry and indignant – but not in a corrupting way. Novation argues that God's anger maintains God's immutable perfection and passionate goodness, whereas Aquinas regards anger as more challenging for immutability than love and joy.[14] Whichever way immutability is conceived, the doctrine is intended to show God as unaffected by the passions that hinder creatures from loving perfectly.[15]

In its strongest form, immutability admits of "no temporal or spatial changes..., not even temporal or spatial 'merely Cambridge changes'."[16] Cambridge-change compromises God's eternality; that all things are present to God's eternal present. The doctrine of immutability sits within the tradition of negative theology, which tells us first what God is not: God is not subject to the changeable created order, and can neither diminish nor increase in goodness. These denials affirm that

---

[13] *The Trinity, The Spectacles, Jewish Foods, In Praise of Purity, Letters* / [by] Novatian; trans. Russell J. DeSimone (Washington, DC: Catholic University of America Press, [c1974]).

[14] Thomas G. Weinandy, *Does God Suffer?* (Edinburgh: T & T Clark, 2000), 106. Aquinas thought God could be said to be angry insofar as God may wish to punish someone, but that anger could not be fittingly attributed to God in ways that imply change in bodily states and therefore temporality. He believed God could have an analogue to the passions of love and joy, though without a bodily state. See Eleonore Stump, *Aquinas* (London: Routledge, 2003), 148–49.

[15] Thomas G. Weinandy, *Does God Suffer?*, 78–79, 97–110.

[16] Paul Helm, *Eternal God: a study of God without time* (Oxford: Clarendon, 1988), 19.

God is perfect in goodness, and no change or fluctuation can alter that (Weinandy, p. 110). Contrary to Brummer's fears, therefore, immutability does not render God aloof, static, and impersonal, but enables God to love us perfectly by being in no corrupting state of flux.

Let us push further, however, the complaint that an immutable God would not be personally, relationally engaged. The argument might be put that an immutable God could be no more relationally engaged than a dispensing machine set from all eternity to answer prayers at the point at which (some) prayers are offered. Creatures would not enjoy a relationship with such a machine, at least of the kind that the inducement to prayer encourages creatures to expect to enjoy.

Yet, could not an immutable God respond in ways that are fitting within the type of personal relationship believers expect – with love, forgiveness, pity, compassion – but in such a way that these effects of divine will emanate from an immutable God, whose love and goodness are not subject to emotional flux? Anselm's way of conveying this is to say that God is compassionate in terms of our experience, in that we experience the effect of compassion, but that God does not experience the feeling: "For when You behold us in our wretched condition, we experience the effect of Your mercy; but You do not experience any emotion. And so You are merciful because You saved us wretched creatures ... and You are not merciful because You do not experience compassion for wretchedness." (*Proslogion*, ch VIII).[17] Indeed, could not such a God show what is flawed in the analogy with a dispensing machine? A machine that dispensed answers to prayer, not being personal, would be able to respond to basic needs but not to higher personal needs. It could provide food, but not comfort. It could send company to the lonely, but could not work on a soul that remains lonely regardless how many people are around. An immutable God, arguably, is perfectly personal (because unaffected by negative passions), and therefore not to be likened to a mechanistic force.

Omni questions

The doctrine of immutability is intended to preserve God's perfect goodness (omnibenevolence), but if prayer cannot affect God's goodness, wherein lies its efficacy? Arguably not in supplementing the knowledge of an omniscient being, or the power of an omnipotent being, unless omniscience or omnipotence are modified:

> If what is requested in a petitionary prayer is or results in a state of affairs, the realisation of which would make the world better

[17] Jasper Hopkins, *A New Interpretive Translation of St Anselm's Monologion and Proslogion* (Minneapolis, MN: A.J. Banning Press, 1986).

than it would otherwise be, an omniscient, omnipotent, perfectly good being will bring about that state of affairs even if no prayer for its realization has been made.[18]

We will consider how far sense can be made of impetratory prayer in light of God's omni qualities. Because discussion of any one quality affects how the others are conceived, some of the material that follows could have been placed under more than one heading.

Omniscience

Two sets of questions arise regarding God's omniscience and impetratory prayer:

(i) an omniscient God already knows what we will ask.
(ii) an omniscient God has knowledge of the future.

(i) On already knowing what we will ask: Calvin recognized that prayer "seems in a sense superfluous," for "does God not know, even without being reminded, both in what respect we are troubled and what is expedient for us...?"[19] Prayer could even seem to evince a lack of faith, as though God would not know our needs, or would take no notice otherwise. Kant went further, asserting that "nothing is accomplished by" prayer, because prayer "is no more than a *stated* wish directed to a Being who needs no such information regarding the inner disposition of the wisher."[20]

However, that God already knows what we will ask is not a reason not to ask, for something important may be enacted in the asking. Calvin's view is "those very things which flow to us from [God's] voluntary liberality he would have us recognize as granted to our prayers" (*Institutes*, III xx 3). This is an epistemological counterpart to Aquinas's position that God ordains that some things be brought about by prayer. Indeed, Aquinas states that we pray "not in order to inform God of our needs and desires, but in order to remind ourselves that in these matters we need divine assistance" (ST 2a2ae.83.2). For both Aquinas and Calvin, prayer helps us appreciate what is the source of all good things. Calvin suggests that in order to cleanse us of indolence, God may be

---

[18] This argument is considered, and subsequently refuted, by Eleonore Stump, "Petitionary Prayer", *APQ*, 1979, reprinted in *Miracles*, ed. Richard Swinburne (London and New York: Macmilllan, 1989), 174.

[19] *Institutes of the Christian Religion* (Philadelphia, PA: The Westminster Press, 1960) III, xx, 3.

[20] Kant, *Religion Within the Limits of Reason Alone* (New York: Harper and Brothers, 1960), 182.

inactive toward us when we do not pray (*Institutes*, III xx 3). This has repercussions for our concept of God's goodness.

Brummer makes a stronger claim than Calvin: not that God withholds benefits in order that we learn to pray, but that God is unable to grant certain benefits unless we pray: "We acknowledge our personal dependence on God in a way which enables God to give us what he could not have given us without the acknowledgement" (p. 52).

This raises questions about God's omnipotence, as do the second set of problems arising from omniscience, which concern God's knowledge of the future.

(ii) Regarding God's knowledge of the future, Origen put the problem this way: "If God foreknows the future, and if this must needs come to pass, prayer is in vain" (Origen, *Treatise of Prayer*, V. 6). If omniscience includes foreknowledge, the future is set; it cannot turn out differently from what God knows.

We considered earlier that one response to this dilemma is to adopt a Boethian view of God as outside of time, and therefore as not *fore*knowing anything. Aquinas takes this route and maintains that all events being eternally present to God is consonant with our having free will. His point is not that prayer can change the course of events – for all events are ordered by God from eternity – but that the freely offered prayers of human beings have efficacy within the divine order. That God's eye is all-seeing does not impede the efficacy of freely offered impetratory prayers, in achieving those things God has disposed to be achieved by prayer.

A contrary stance is that God is not timeless but everlasting, and therefore contains duration and succession.[21] On this view, the future is future (rather than eternally present) for God as well as for us. Therefore, there is sense in praying to God to ask that it turn out in some ways rather than others. Because the future is not yet there to be known, God's knowledge of the future is limited.[22] Views then vary as to whether this limitation on God's knowledge of the future follows necessarily from the principle of creativity (as in Process theology), or whether it is self-limitation on God's part in order to keep the future open to our will and

---

[21] Brummer, *What Are We Doing When We Pray?*, pp. 47–51; Nicholas Wolsterstorff, "God Everlasting," in *Contemporary Philosophy of Religion*, ed. S. Cahn and D. Shatz (Oxford: Oxford University Press, 1982). For debate, see J. Sanders, "Why Simple Foreknowledge Offers No More Providential Control than the Openness of God," *Faith and Philosophy*, vol. 14 (1997), 26–40.

[22] Swinburne, Richard, *The Coherence of Theism* (Oxford: Clarendon, 1977), 175–78; William Hasker, *God, Time and Knowledge* (Ithaca, NY: Cornell University Press, 1989).

influence (Swinburne, Fiddes). Either way, the future is seen as open, and our prayers as able to affect its path.

Paul Fiddes is somewhat influenced by Process philosophy, but utilizes a triune rather than dipolar view of God. He situates time inside God, arguing that because relationship exists amongst the three persons of the Godhead, succession exists in God. This approach challenges Aquinas's position that "eternity lacks succession, since it exists all at once" (ST Ia.10.1). Fiddes argues because a "triune God is in eternal movement," in God there is "some kind of successiveness in which one thing comes after another, and so time is in God rather than God in time." He sees this as "the basis for God's creation of our time, in which (in Barth's phrase) 'God has time for us.'"[23] Here, there are echoes of Anselm: "For yesterday and to-day and to-morrow have no existence, except in time; but thou, although nothing exists without thee, nevertheless dost not exist in space or time, but all things exist in thee. For nothing contains thee, but thou containest all" (*Proslogion*, ch XIX). In Fiddes's view, this "panentheism" is key for intercession. It means that our love for others, expressed in intercessory prayer, is taken up into God's persuasive love for others, not because it adds to God's love, *qua* God's, but because God chooses to work through created love as well as divine love.[24] This has significant ramifications for divine omnipotence and omnibenevolence.

Omnipotence

We have arrived in two different ways – via Brummer and Fiddes – at a view that God somehow needs our prayers in order to bring about certain benefits. We shall revisit Fiddes's panentheistic view when we discuss omnibenevolence.

Brummer's argument, which, in this respect, he shares with Stump, is that sometimes God cannot act without our freely offered prayers, by virtue of the fact that God has created us as persons with whom to be in relationship. In order to maintain personal relationship (where personal relationship implies the free will of persons), there are some ways in which God cannot act toward us, and this puts limits around omnipotence. God cannot force us, without making the personal relationship into a causal one. God cannot oblige us, without damaging the personal relationship by constraining our freedom (Brummer, p. 53). God cannot

---

[23] *Participating in God: A Pastoral Doctrine of the Trinity* (London: Darton, Longman and Todd, 2000), 122.

[24] In correspondence with the author.

bring about "friendship magically, by means of his omnipotence, and yet permit people involved to have free will" (Stump, "Petitionary Prayer," p. 181).

Stump views petitionary prayers as a kind of "buffer" between ourselves and God, which prevent God from overwhelming us (p. 186). She draws an analogy with a caring teacher and a needy pupil. The teacher not only waits to be asked before stepping in to help, but also sometimes withholds help so that the pupil does not become overly dependent.

Stump then asks how we can make sense of intercession – prayers offered on behalf of others. If God responds to prayers for others, this could be seen as oppressively meddlesome. But if God withholds assistance unless asked, this throws into question God's goodness. Using the example of Monica's prayers for her son, Augustine, Stump suggests a middle position: God would have saved Augustine without Monica's prayers, but not in the same amount of time, or by the same process, or with the same effect (pp. 184–85). Arguably, however, a delayed or less efficacious salvation nonetheless compromises God's goodness.

Omni-benevolence

If God could save, or heal, or divert famine without being asked, would it not be best that God do so? Arguments on this point are bound up with positions taken on the problem of evil and the primacy of the goodness of creaturely freedom. Stump's position is that, out of God's goodness, God waits on us, and sometimes limits actions because of the goods that petitionary prayer protects with regard to our freedom and personal relationship with God. In any instance, God could be understood to be *either* preserving the goods of freedom and personal relationship that intercessory prayer protects, *or* acting in the interest of some other good: "If men do not always pray for all the good things they might and ought to pray for, then in some cases either God will not bring about some good thing or he will do so but at the expense of the good wrought and preserved by petitionary prayer" (Stump, p. 187). If one accepts this response, a question about the quantity of evil still remains: "Too much happens that's hard to believe is the result of an omni-being, too little that is plausibly an answer to prayer."[25]

Fiddes believes that Stump has not gone far enough: "Does God really say (in effect), 'I would have healed Mary if you had only asked

---

[25] Georges Rey, "Meta-atheism: Religious avowal as self-deception," in *Philosophers without Gods: Meditation on Atheism and the Secular Life*, ed. Louise M. Antony (Oxford University Press, 2007), 259.

me, but I waited for all eternity to hear your prayer and it didn't arrive, so I decided not to build this into my plan for the world'" (Fiddes, p. 138). Fiddes resists the notion "that the 'primary causation' of an event is a unilateral act of God, once human permission has been granted" (p. 138). He argues instead that "God always draws near to people with persuasive love, with or without us, and God's grace will be the major factor in transforming human life; but our intercessions still make a difference to what God achieves, though we be the minor partner" (p. 138). Following Timothy Gorringe,[26] he likens God to a theater director who moves amongst the actors, allowing freedom but knowing where to guide the steps and how to draw out the right impulses. Because God has perfect knowledge of us, God has a very strong, albeit only predictive, sense of the future. God also knows more potentialities than we know, and knows the power of God's own love. The future is open to the risk of our influencing it in wrong directions, and to our failures to pray, but the cross and Resurrection at the center of history show that God's love is stronger than the risks we pose.

God's goodness is maintained in Fiddes's account of impetratory prayer because omnipotence takes the brunt of the modifications. Unanswered prayers, for example, may not reflect an unresponsive God, but may be attributable to consequences we inherit of the actions and interactions of others, which God cannot override (pp. 147–48). God's action amongst persons is restricted to persuasion. An advantage of this notion is that divine persuasion can also be applied to the natural world, if, as in the Process vision of reality, all entities have a mental or feeling aspect. Perhaps notions such as collective consciousness, the selfish gene, societal organisation, and altruism amongst bacteria, capture something of this vision. Fiddes takes this vision metaphorically rather than as scientific description, but finds it resonates with a biblical understanding of God's relationship with the rest of the world, wherein God makes a covenant with every living creature (Gen. 9.10), and creation waits for God to set it free (Rom. 8.19–22) (p. 145).

On such a view, our impetratory prayers make us allies of God's persuasive action, and prayers for the environment, inner peace, and world peace are efficacious in the same way. The whole of creation is held within God's relational movements, and God chooses to need the prayers – the persuasive love – of created beings for the work of persuading and transforming creation.

---

[26] *God's Theatre* (London: SCM, 1991).

3. Petitionary and intercessory prayer have nonimpetratory value

Where philosophers cannot make sense of God in light of impetratory prayer, they struggle to find a point for it. Some reinterpret petitions and intercessions as nonimpetratory; as not obtaining things from God. Under such reinterpretation, prayer has no causal efficacy in relation to God. Indeed, there may even be no God. Prayer matters only for the effects it works within those who pray (and perhaps within those who know they are being prayed for). Such models of prayer are sometimes called therapeutic. Immanuel Kant, for example, regarded prayer as means for strengthening moral resolve. He thought it fitting to act within the spirit of prayer, the spirit being to perform our actions "as though they were being executed in the service of God" (even then he regarded as preferable an ability to fall in with the moral law without the aid of prayer).[27]

That prayer brings about a change in those who pray is a crucial aspect of the activity of prayer. The question is whether it is the only aspect. As a theist, the Wittgensteinian philosopher, D. Z. Phillips, argues that it is. He accords a kind of efficacy to petitionary prayer, but not of a Thomist sort, wherein God is the primary cause, nor in Fiddes's sense, wherein God is the senior partner.

> To say that the conversion of the world depends on the prayers of believers is not to suggest some kind of determinism, or quasi-physical cause and effect sequence, but rather, that the witness of believers to their love of God *is* the only power which brings men and women to God.[28]

The efficacy lies in the power of believers to live out the love of God. For Phillips, this is entirely dependent on there being a God, for the ultimate essence of prayer is our dependence on God: "The power of God works through the love of God, but since this love is given by God ... the dependence which seems to be dependence on the prayers themselves, leads one back to take account of dependence on God" (p. 128).

Phillips says that believers search for the causal efficacy of prayer (as we discussed under position 2 in this chapter) when they confuse dependence on prayer with dependence on God. He thinks that religious

---

[27] *Religion within the Limits of Reason Alone* (New York: Harper and Brothers, 1960), 181.

[28] D. Z. Phillips, *The Concept of Prayer* (London: Routledge and Kegan Paul, 1965), 128.

believers who ask God for things make a mistake insofar as they treat prayers superstitiously, as though the saying of the words will bring about the effect. A deeper understanding of prayer – a study of its depth-grammar – reveals that in petitionary prayer the believer is "asking that his desires will not destroy the spirit of God in him" (p. 122). So all petitionary prayer, when offered in a nonmistaken way, has the form "thy will be done."

Something akin to Phillips's stance has been taken by atheist philosophers who argue, rather like Kant, that prayer can be effective in moral training without the need for God to exist. In the middle of the twentieth century, T. R. Miles rejected "pseudo-causal prayer-language" as logically meaningless. He and Phillips were both influenced by logical positivism, and regarded impetratory prayer as meaningless because attempts to persuade God by prayer cannot be verified experimentally. However, he held that "performatory prayer language" can reflect a meaningful activity, in that prayers can bring about a change in the person praying, such as deepening the level of the person's dedication and commitment.[29]

Atheist versions of position 3 would struggle to make sense of the need people have to draw on strength outside of themselves,[30] unless they locate such need in self-delusion. Arguably, however, self-delusion is already part of such a position, and undermines the very efficacy aimed at in performatory prayer language:

> if one does not believe that there is a God who wills anything, to recommend that men should behave toward the world as if they did believe this because it is somehow good for them to do so and should reinforce this behaviour by engaging in rituals that used to be followed because men did believe this is to infer from one's theory of religion a rule of conduct which is, at best, a form of deliberate self-deception which would be rendered unsuccessful by the acceptance of the very theory it is based upon.[31]

4. Petitionary and intercessory prayer have no value

Some more recent atheist philosophers recoil from the errors of wasting one's time in prayer, and think that the efficacy of prayer can be

---

[29] T. R. Miles, *Religion and the Scientific Outlook* (London: Allen & Unwin 1959).

[30] Gordon Graham, *Evil and Christian Ethics* (Cambridge: Cambridge University Press, 2001).

[31] Terence Penelhum, "Petitionary Prayer," reprinted in *Miracles*, ed. Swinburne (London and New York: Macmillan), 1989, 156–57.

empirically denied. Daniel Dennett asserts that "we now have quite solid grounds (e.g., the recently released Benson study at Harvard) for believing that intercessory prayer simply doesn't work."[32]

Since 1998, studies have been run in the United States attempting to test whether intercessory prayer has beneficial effects, the assumption being that if prayer is efficacious, this can be tracked scientifically. The Benson study at Harvard, mentioned by Dennett and published in 2006, suggests that intercessory prayer actually made things worse for patients recovering from heart surgery.[33] However, there are philosophical and theological reasons for maintaining that such experiments cannot establish the efficacy or inefficacy of prayer.

First, a correlation could (perhaps) be reliably drawn between intercessions offered and the people prayed for making a better, similar, or worse recovery than a control group. However, it could never be established empirically whether the correlation were brought about by the efficacy or inefficacy of prayer. What would experimenters be looking for in order to make a claim either way? The joke about the man who stands on the roof of his house in a flood, praying to God to help him, nicely illustrates the difficulty. The man refuses help from a rescue boat and helicopter, because he is waiting for God to save him. Having refused other sources of help, he drowns, and meets God postmortem. "Why didn't you save me?" the man asks, to which God replies "I sent a boat and a helicopter. . . ." The inapplicability of observation and experiment to claims that prayer has or has not worked is what led logical positivists to say that causal language about prayer is meaningless. Logical positivists unreasonably tied meaning to empirical verifiability/falsifiability, but they rightly recognised that many religious claims, including those regarding answers to prayer, are not subject to scientific testing.

Second, experiments to test the efficacy of prayer need to regulate as far as possible the amount of prayer offered, in time and people, and the words used, if measuring can be conducted at all. The Benson study arranged that lists of those to be prayed for be posted "not later than 7 15 pm EST each evening, with intercessory prayer beginning by midnight for patients on the list." The intercessors agreed to "add the phrase 'for a

---

[32] Daniel Dennett, "Thank Goodness," in *Philosophers without Gods: Meditation on Atheism and the Secular Life*, ed. Louise M. Antony (Oxford University Press, 2007), 116.

[33] Herbert Benson, et al., "Study of the Therapeutic Effects of Intercessory Prayer (STEP) in Cardiac Bypass Patients: A multicenter randomized trial of uncertainty and certainty of receiving intercessory prayer," *American Heart Journal* 151, no. 4 (April 2006): 934–42.

successful surgery with a quick, healthy recovery and no complications' to their usual prayers" (p. 935). These conditions reflect mistaken religious practice (as D. Z. Phillips would have put it, pp. 113–14): Prayers are conducted like spells, as though efficacy resides in the words used rather than in the divine being addressed. An additional problem for measuring is that no experiment could factor in the general prayers for the sick that are offered on a continual basis in intercessions in liturgies around the world.

Third, it cannot be assumed that God will fall in with such experiments. If, indeed, a divine being is addressed in prayer, this divine being may resist being put to the test, and refuse to respond according to the "norm" – not that we would know what God's norm is anyway.

Nonetheless, some philosophers regard it as special pleading when religious believers claim immunity from empirical investigation. "Exceptionalism is the norm for religious faith," complains Jonathan E. Adler: "When bumper stickers, and religious leaders, proclaim that 'prayer works,' common sense ... asks for evidence of the most unobtrusive sort: How often does prayer help the ill recover compared to crossing one's fingers or wishful thinking?"[34] It therefore is worth offering four responses to the charge of special pleading.

First, most religious beliefs are not unfalsifiable. Their falsifiability is what refines them and makes people careful about their language of God. This is how negative theology arose, by which people say only what God is not – for example, God is immutable. Indeed, the doctrine of immutability helps to falsify claims that we can conduct experiments to test the efficacy of prayer because the fact that God is immutable entails that we do not enter into transactions with God through prayer. (The doctrine arose partly to distinguish Christian prayer from pagan attempts to make deals with God.) The falsifying of religious beliefs within the tradition of negative theology helps people avoid mistakes that are otherwise easy to commit.

Second, some religious beliefs are empirically falsifiable, in principle – such as that Jesus suffered under Pontius Pilate, was crucified, dead and buried, or that Moses led Israel out of Egypt – but to treat those that are not empirically falsifiable as though they are empirically falsifiable is to make a mistake. This mistake underlies Adler's complaint that religious believers refuse to apply chemical testing to the wine at the Eucharist. He thinks that believers think that "ritual can turn wine into

---

[34] "Faith and Fanaticism," in Antony, ed., *Philosophers without Gods*, p. 272.

blood,"[35] and so he makes exactly the mistake Phillips identifies, of treating prayer superstitiously as though the words and actions perform the trick. Believers do not think ritual turns wine into blood. They think (in some sense much debated amongst denominations) that God does this.[36] Chemical testing is no more relevant at the saying of the Eucharistic prayer than it is at the point where a printed rectangle of paper (that is, a bank note) actually becomes worth £50. Testing the paper for chemical change would reveal a lack of understanding of how banking systems work. It is the bank's promise, not a ritual at the bank, that makes it worth £50. Chemically, the paper is not worth £50. It has not, for example, become a particular weight of precious metal. But in another sense it is worth £50, and one can spend it on £50 worth of goods. Chemically, the wine at a Eucharist does not become blood, but in another sense (debated theologically amongst denominations) it does become the blood of Christ, and with effect: believers who consume it, along with the bread, are constituted as the body of Christ, with the responsibility to live as Christ's feet, hands, limbs, and mouths on earth.

Third, although the wine becomes the blood of Christ with effect, the claim that it does so is unfalsifiable. If people no longer treat a bank note as being worth £50, it ceases to have this currency and the signification no longer applies, whereas if people no longer live as members of the Body of Christ, the signification still applies in that God is a partner to the agreement. Christ is not made absent from the Eucharist by the unworthiness of believers. Rather, he is present in judgment and mercy. In this respect, the claim about wine becoming blood is unfalsifiable; it is made true by God's promise and act, which cannot be contravened. However, its unfalsifiability does not render it meaningless. On the contrary, Christ being persistently present is heavy with meaning. Yet, it will not be heavy with meaning for any who do not believe that God makes the agreement.

This attempt to respond to charges of special pleading hopefully will have shown why religious believers would not find it relevant to run empirical tests on many of their beliefs, and also why they find it reasonable to disentangle unfalsifiability from meaninglessness. However, it may only show that one is unlikely to understand the Eucharistic prayer without the kind of purchase one gets through participation.

[35] "Faith and Fanaticism," p. 272.

[36] Christians in almost all denominations receive the wine at Communion with the words "the blood of Christ." Not all believe in transubstantiation, but chemical testing would be no more relevant in the context of theories of transubstantiation than in any other theory of what happens at the Eucharist.

Therefore, it is worth showing our fourth point: that it is not special pleading to hold that participating in prayer is a necessary condition for understanding prayer. Participating is a necessary but not sufficient condition for understanding. This is true of most activities. Playing or listening to music is a necessary condition for having any understanding of music, but is not a sufficient condition for full or even sound understanding. In itself, taking part in an activity does not entail being able to give an account of the activity. Moreover, practice of an activity can rest on mistaken understanding, as when prayers are treated like spells. Dennett and Adler have misunderstood prayer, though so have some of the religious believers whose practice they have used as data.

5. Prayer as surrender

Prayer differs from other activities, however, in that, at various points, it involves surrendering our attempts to understand. This claim may seem to play into the hands of secular atheist complainants, but it only highlights their distance from the tradition of negative theology and the kinds of falsifiability attributable to religious beliefs within that tradition. We are "seduced by the promise of explanation," Rowan Williams writes, but prayer "is precisely what *resists* the urge of religious language to claim a total perspective: By articulating its own incompleteness before God, it turns away from any claim to human completeness."[37]

Position 5 regards the displacement of one's grasp of things as the essence of prayer. Within this position, the difficulties of understanding impetration are not qualitatively different from the dynamics of praise, which involves the "dispossession of the human mind conceived as central to the order of the world," or contemplation, wherein we acknowledge the inadequacy of words, images, and gestures to finish the job of religious speech (Williams, pp. 10–11). In this context, the point of prayer lies in it being a process of surrender, from which new understanding and new life (see subsequent discussion) come.

II. FUTURE DIRECTIONS FOR THINKING ABOUT PRAYER

Position 5 may look like "exceptionalism" to Joseph Adler, and a revelation of the depth-grammar of prayer to D. Z. Phillips. It may debunk the very attempts within philosophy of religion to make sense or nonsense of petitionary prayer, as discussed earlier under positions 2, 3, and 4. The question arises whether, ultimately, prayer and philosophy

---

[37] *On Christian Theology* (Oxford: Blackwell, 2000), 14, 13.

are opposed. Perhaps this anxiety is what led the Jewish philosopher Emmanuel Levinas to view prayer as "one of the most difficult subjects for a philosopher" and to insist that "the Judaism of reason must take precedence over the Judaism of prayer."[38]

Future directions for thinking about prayer will profitably take position 5 by the horns so that the experience of prayer as surrender and loss can be addressed philosophically.

The radical nature of not making sense: losing and finding oneself

Kant and Miles were able to see prayer as self-renunciation, but only on a moral plane. The negation of one's understanding takes self-renunciation deeper; one stops justifying prayer morally and, indeed, stops justifying it at all. The point, or pointlessness, of prayer resides not in terms of moral achievements or conceptual performance, but in discovering that "one's selfhood and value simply lie in the abiding faithful presence of God" (Williams, p. 11).

This way of thinking is to be located in the tradition that prayer is a kind of dying and rising.[39] The self dies and finds new life in God. As Thomas Merton expresses it: "God Himself, bearing in Himself the secret of who I am, begins to live in me not only as my Creator but as my other and true self. *Vivo, iam non ego, vivit vero in me Christus.*"[40]

In losing ourselves, we find God, or are found by God, at our center. This has implications for theological conceptions of the self,[41] and also for the efficacy of prayer. Williams writes: "To act from [our] centre *is* to give God freedom in the world, to do the works of God" (p. 12). All prayer, and not just impetratory prayer, is necessary in order for God to act, because all prayer is a surrender of the self and an act of making room for God.

The point of prayer, seen in this light, seems more active than that considered in position 1. While the point (or pointlessness) of prayer is to commune with God, it is to do so not purely for enjoyment, but for

---

[38] Emmanuel Levinas, *Difficult Freedom: Essays on Judaism*, trans. Seán Hand (London: Athlone Press, 1990), 269, 271.

[39] Cf. Herbert McCabe: "All our prayer is an abandonment of ourselves... because it is a sharing in Christ's abandonment of himself in death. In prayer we stop believing in ourselves, relying on ourselves, and we believe and trust in God. It is all a sharing in Christ's death... looking forward to that ultimate sharing in his death which is our own death in him, through which we rise in him to understand the Father in the Son, to pray the prayer which is the Spirit, to communicate with our Father in joy and love for eternity," *God Still Matters* (London: Continuum, 2002), 218.

[40] Thomas Merton, *Seeds of Contemplation* (London: Hollis and Carter, 1949), 23.

[41] See especially Sarah Coakley, *Powers and Submissions: Spirituality, Philosophy and Gender* (Oxford: Blackwell, 2002).

our good and the good of all the world. The value of prayer lies both in the relationship prayer forges, and in the freedom it brings to live in a God-directed way (with the ensuing benefits for self, others, and creation).

This raises the question, "Is God's action therefore to be identified directly only in the lives of those who pray (and indirectly in how they then live in the world)?" Or does the self-surrender that makes room for God in those who pray mean that God can also act in the lives of others and in the world? Fiddes's vision, whereby God chooses to work through created as well as divine love, goes some way toward making sense of how our sacrifices – and not only God's own sacrifice – can heal the world. There is plenty of scope for future work on the relation of personal sacrifice to the efficacy of prayer.

The God who knows us perfectly

Talk of losing ourselves and finding God at our center articulates an experience, in prayer, of a God who knows us better than we know ourselves. In the earlier discussion, we considered two ultimately incompatible metaphysical pictures: a Thomist vision of an eternal, immutable being, and Fiddes's panentheistic vision in which God holds time and the world within the relational movements amongst the three persons of the Trinity. It is important to acknowledge that both metaphysical pictures enable God to be present to the people and circumstances of prayer, and to have perfect knowledge of us. This is so in Fiddes's view because we are all held in God. It is so on a Thomist view because, as Stump explains, presentness or simultaneity is attributable to God's life and relationships: God's eternal reality is one of the "*relata* in a simultaneity relationship."[42] Stump says this enables us to make sense of Aquinas's claim that the eternal divine gaze views future events "presently" (*Aquinas*, p. 138).

The question is whether a God of eternality is able to be more present and knowing than a God who undergoes succession and changes with us. This invites more work on omniscience, developing the concept of the divine gaze, as Charles Taliaferro and Janet Martin Soskice have begun.[43] Following the defense of immutability provided earlier, the

[42] *Aquinas*, p. 137.
[43] Janet Martin Soskice, "Love and Attention," in *Philosophy, Religion and the Spiritual Life*, ed. Michael McGhee (Cambridge University Press, 1992), 59–72; Charles Taliaferro, "The God's Eye Point of View," in *Faith and Philosophical Analysis: The impact of analytical philosophy upon the philosophy of religion*, ed. Harriet A. Harris and Christopher J. Insole (Aldershot; Burlington, VT: Ashgate, 2005), 76–84.

divine gaze arguably would be partial and God's knowledge of us imperfect unless God's transcendent otherness were maintained, such that God is subject to none of the limits that constrain creatures.

Furthermore, without some articulation of transcendence, the divine gaze could cease to seem divine. Holding on to transcendence is important when considering what is meant by talk of God as our center, or as nearer to us than we are to ourselves; the hint that God alone can plumb the depths within us (Eckhart [*Sermon* 71]; Julian of Norwich [*Revelations of Divine Love* 56][44]; Augustine, *Confessions* X 8).[45] The question arises whether God is anything other than the depth within us. William James was interested in this question in relation to Augustine's *Confessions*.[46] Merold Westphal asks it of Levinas: If God is "the *he* in the depth of you,"[47] is God only the depth dimension of the human person, or, in Levinas' philosophy, the "trans-empirical moral significance of the neighbour"?[48]

To avoid this reduction, the otherness of God must be maintained: "The issue is whether God is a speaker ... who speaks to us with a voice that is neither ours, nor our society's, nor that of the widow, orphan and stranger ... whether God is an agent distinct from ourselves, our society, and our neighbour" (Westphal, p. 41). Notions of prayer as surrender could be brought in to help here because surrender implies throwing ourselves upon another. John Drury also combats the danger of reducing God to our own voice by conceiving of prayer as "studied receptivity."[49] The person praying is aware of the need to "take things in" (p. 23), which implies receiving from a source other than oneself. Indeed, Drury expresses this process in terms of self-surrender, quoting T.S. Eliot's *East Coker*:

In order to arrive at what you do not know

You must go by a way which is the way of ignorance.

[44] Meister Eckhart, *German Sermons & Treatises*, trans. with introduction and notes by M. O'C. Walshe (London; Dulverton: Watkins; Longmead, Shaftesbury: Element Books, 1979–1987); Julian of Norwich, *Revelations of Divine Love*, translated into modern English and with an introduction by Clifton Wolters (Harmondsworth: Penguin, 1966).

[45] *Confessions*, trans. and annotated by J. G. Pilkington, Edinburgh: T&T Clark, 1876.

[46] *Varieties of Religious Experience* (New York: Longmans, Green & Co, 1902).

[47] Emmanuel Levinas, "God and Philosophy," in *Collected Philosophical Papers*, trans. Alphonso Lingis (Dordrecht: Kluwer, 1978), 165.

[48] Merold Westphal, *Levinas and Kierkegaard in Dialogue* (Bloomington and Indianapolis, IN: Indiana University Press, 2008) 71.

[49] *Angels and Dirt: An enquiry into theology and prayer* (London: Darton, Longman & Todd, 1972), 23–24.

God speaking to God

Rather than reducing God to our voice within us, Christian theology ultimately understands prayer as God's Spirit speaking in and through us back to God (Gal. 4:4–7, Rom. 8:26–7, Eph. 2:18). It would be helpful for philosophical theologians to integrate this central conviction about prayer into philosophical discussions of prayer. After all, if in prayer, God speaks to God, most of the problems raised regarding impetratory prayer are changed. We no longer need to consider that we somehow inform God, or influence God, or empower God. God is the subject of prayer. However, we come back to the question of why God should choose to go via us. In reply, perhaps we can only say that God does so for the sake of our relationship with God, with one another, and with the whole of creation.

How far philosophers will explore prayer as God speaking to God partly depends on how Trinitarian they find it reasonable to be. In the context of a Trinitarian theology, prayer is the principal way in which we participate in the divine life. We pray by the Spirit, through the Son (whose spirit of sonship is within us, and whose prayers, as the risen Christ, support ours [Rom. 8:15, 34]), to the Father. Without some such theology, the notion of communing with God can barely be developed. Trinitarian emphases also help us avoid being transactional or individualistic in our accounts of prayer. Prayer is not for wrestling some good out of God, nor merely for conforming our lives to God's, but is for sharing in the life of God and with one another in God.[50]

Interfaith questions

By the end of this discussion, the view of prayer given is Trinitarian in its conception of communing with God, and Christological in its model of dying and rising. Some insights that receive Trinitarian and Christological expression in Christianity are articulated in other ways by practitioners of other faiths. The conviction behind this essay is that the deeper we go in the tradition in which we are rooted (in my case, Christianity), the more likely the depths discovered will speak to the depths of other traditions.[51] This mirrors what happens in prayer itself. Augustine said, "I know less of myself than dost Thou. I beseech Thee now, O my God, to reveal to me myself also, that I may confess unto my brethren,

---

[50] Kelly S. Johnson, "Praying: Poverty," in *The Blackwell Companion to Christian Ethics*, ed. Stanley Hauerwas and Samuel Wells (Oxford; Malden MA; Carlton, Victoria: Blackwell, 2004), 225–36.

[51] Cf. Nicholas Adams' account of scriptural reasoning, in *Habermas the Theology* (Cambridge: Cambridge University Press, 2006), 242.

who are to pray for me, what I find in myself weak" (*Confessions* X, 37). He found God plumbing the depths of his soul, and realized that what is revealed at the depths is what can best be shared with others. The depth within us, while being less accessible than our superficial levels, is not thereby less communicable, for deep speaks to deep.[52] Participating in a reality that transcends and embraces us, which Christians express in relation to a Triune God, finds echoes in prayer practices of other faiths, as does surrender of the self, for which, in Christianity, Christ is the type. Insights of practitioners of the many and various world faiths will also hold up mirrors for Christian prayer.

[52] Cf. McCabe, *God Matters*, 172–73.

16 Heaven and hell

JERRY L. WALLS

The doctrines of heaven and hell are climactic components in a dramatic narrative that elevates the meaning and significance of our lives to epic proportions. At the center of this drama is the eternal God, in whose image we were created for the purpose of knowing and loving him. As free actors in this divine drama, we may choose whether or not we accept his will for our lives, with consequences of monumental import. To accept his grace is to participate in the eternal joy and satisfaction that will result when his work of redemption is complete and his will is done on earth, as it is in heaven.[1] To reject his grace is to decline the role God intended for us and thereby to choose for ourselves eternal misery and suffering.

There are versions of the doctrines of heaven and hell in religions other than Christianity, but the uniquely Christian picture of God shapes these doctrines in a distinctive way. In particular, the Christian doctrine that the one God exists in three persons gives vivid expression to the claim that God is love in his eternal nature, and created us to share in the loving relationship of the Trinity. The Christian doctrines of the Incarnation, Atonement, and Resurrection of Jesus reveal the love of God for us and the extent of his desire to be in relationship with us.

This extraordinary framework of beliefs has not only defined the hopes, aspirations, and fears of individuals in Europe and America for the better part of two millennia, it has also been a dominant cultural force that has inspired many of the greatest works of art ever produced, both literary and visual. Despite this impressive pedigree, heaven and hell, along with the larger framework of orthodox Christian belief, have

---

[1] As N. T. Wright reminds us, the biblical emphasis is not on us going to heaven, but on heaven coming to earth. He notes: "This is the ultimate rejection of all types of Gnosticism, of every worldview that sees the final goal as the separation of the world from God, of the physical from the spiritual, of earth from heaven." *Surprised by Hope: Rethinking Heaven, the Resurrection, and the Mission of the Church* (New York: HarperOne, 2008), 104.

lost, ever since the enlightenment, the central role they once enjoyed in the thinking and imagination of the West. In 1989, citing what he saw as "irreversible changes" in our habits of thought, Harvard theologian Gordon Kaufman proclaimed, "I don't think there can be any future for heaven and hell."[2] Kaufman's pronouncement, however, may have been a bit premature, or perhaps merely out of touch with the world of Christianity beyond Harvard Divinity School. Just two years later, *U. S News and World Report* ran an article entitled "Hell's Sober Comeback," in which it observed that "hell is undergoing something of a revival in American religious thought," even among theologians.[3]

Indeed, the revival has also spread to philosophers, where hell has incited considerable debate in recent years. The larger context here is the resurgence of interest in the field of philosophy of religion in the past few decades, which has resulted in serious philosophical work on a number of distinctively Christian doctrines along with more traditional topics such as theistic arguments and the problem of evil. At the time of this writing, heaven is beginning to receive attention as well, but not to the same extent as hell. This is likely because of the fact that hell poses more obvious difficulties that require analysis and resolution than heaven.

TRADITIONAL ACCOUNTS OF HELL AND
CONTEMPORARY MODIFICATIONS

The problems posed by the doctrine of hell have been felt by believers for some time, and indeed, hell was among the first items of the Christian creed to fall into decline among those who were otherwise orthodox. For many believers, these problems are broadly moral in the sense that hell seems hard to reconcile with the love and goodness of God. Seen as such, hell is very much part of the traditional problem of evil, perhaps the most severe part of the problem, because it involves an eternal evil that will never be redeemed.

For the sake of focusing our discussion, we can summarize the traditional doctrine of hell in three statements.

1   Some persons will never repent of their sins and accept the grace of God and therefore will not be saved.
2   Impenitent sinners who reject the grace of God will be consigned to hell, a place of consummate misery that is the just punishment for sins they commit in this life.

[2] Cited by Kenneth L. Woodward, "Heaven," *Newsweek* (March 27, 1989), 54.
[3] "Hell's Sober Comeback," *U.S. News and World Report* (March 25, 1991), 56.

3   There is no escape from hell, either by repentance, or by suicide, or by annihilation.

Notice that 3 can be taken as either contingently true or necessarily true. It is contingently true if it is possible for sinners to repent, commit suicide, or otherwise annihilate themselves, but none, in fact, do so. It is necessarily true if it is impossible to repent, and so on, either because repentance is no longer metaphysically or psychologically possible, or because God would not accept it even if it were given.

In describing the misery of the damned, traditional theologians often distinguished between the pain of loss and the pains of sense. The former is the emptiness and frustration that naturally results from being separated from God, whereas the latter is physical pain, often believed to be caused by fire of agonizing intensity. The combination of such extreme suffering with hopeless despair of endless duration makes hell a truly terrifying possibility even to contemplate.

Many notable western theologians have attempted to make moral sense of the doctrine of eternal hell in terms of divine retributive justice that is visited upon fully deserving sinners. In particular, these theologians have argued that any sin against God is infinitely serious, and accordingly requires an infinite punishment if justice is to be maintained. Those who have defended hell along these lines include Augustine, Aquinas, Anselm, and Jonathan Edwards. Anselm put this point most vividly in the context of his famous argument for the necessity of the Incarnation, claiming that it would be better to let the whole world perish, indeed an infinite number of such worlds, than to do even the smallest thing against God's will. Edwards put a distinct twist on the argument by casting it in terms of God's infinite beauty, honor, and authority. These attributes place us under an obligation to return to him the proportionate amount of love, honor, and obedience, so if we fail in this obligation, we deserve infinite punishment.

Despite the ingenuity of these arguments and the stature of those who have made them, this approach to defending eternal hell has come under heavy fire in contemporary philosophy of religion. Indeed, there is a broad consensus in the current discussion that eternal hell cannot be defended on the grounds that it is a just punishment for sins committed in this life, which is a rejection of statement 2 of the traditional account of hell, spelled out earlier. The main difficulty, often called the proportionality objection, is that eternal punishment is radically out of proportion to any sins that finite beings could commit in a finite amount of time. Even the most infamous villains in history, who have done massive amounts of evil, have still done only finite harm and therefore do not deserve infinite punishment. Contemporary philosophers who have subjected the punishment model of eternal hell to searching criticism include Marilyn Adams, Jonathan Kvanvig, and Charles Seymour.[4]

In response to the perceived failure of the punishment model, philosophers have turned to other strategies to defend the doctrine of eternal hell. The most common move has been to appeal to libertarian freedom to explain how persons, of their own accord, may choose to be separated from God, and accordingly experience eternal misery as a result. This is the approach I have defended, along with a number of other philosophers.

The essence of this view, as stated by Richard Swinburne, is that damnation is "a loss of good, not an inflicted evil; and it is not so much a punishment inflicted from without as an inevitable consequence of a man allowing himself to lose his moral awareness."[5] In terms of the classic distinction noted earlier, this view highlights the pain of loss much more than the pains of sense. Indeed, Swinburne thinks the New Testament is unclear on whether hell includes pains of sense and suggests that perhaps annihilation is the ultimate end of those who reject God.

Kvanvig has defended a similar account, which he calls the "issuant conception of hell," because he believes hell should issue from the same attribute of God as the doctrine of heaven – namely, love. All of us, he points out, are recipients of divine love, and we must choose whether we will accept his offer to live in relation to him, or attempt to live independently of him. We cannot actually live independently of God, so to make that choice is, in reality, to opt for annihilation. However, not all who choose to live independently of God do so in a clear and settled way, and God, in his love, permits them to remain in existence. Kvanvig classifies his position as a "composite" view because it allows two possible final ends for the damned – either eternal separation from God or annihilation.[6]

Seymour's account of hell also relies heavily on libertarian freedom, as is apparent from the fact that he calls it the freedom view. However,

---

[4] Marilyn McCord Adams, "Hell and the God of Justice," *Religious Studies* 11 (1975): 433–47; Jonathan L. Kvanvig, *The Problem of Hell* (Oxford: Oxford University Press, 1993), 25–66; Charles Seymour, *A Theodicy of Hell* (Dordrecht: Kluwer Academic Press, 2000), 37–94.

[5] Richard Swinburne, *Responsibility and Atonement* (Oxford: Clarendon Press, 1989), 182.

[6] *The Problem of Hell*, 151–59.

in contrast to some who emphasize that damnation is freely chosen, he contends that it includes pains of sense as well as the pain of loss, as reflected in his basic definition of hell as "an eternal existence, all of whose moments are on the whole bad."[7] The centrality of freedom in his account is also evident in his rejection of traditional arguments that sins committed in this life could be sufficient to deserve eternal punishment. To the contrary, what keeps the damned in hell is their continuing choice to sin and rebel against God. In principle, sinners can repent and escape hell, so if they do not it is because of their own free choice to remain there.[8]

By way of summarizing this part of the discussion, it is worth highlighting that Kvanvig, Seymour, and I agree in rejecting 3, the third claim of the traditional view stated earlier. Kvanvig thinks sinners can escape hell by annihilation and he also holds, along with Seymour and me, that it is possible for sinners in hell to repent, and if they do so, they can be saved. Indeed, it seems likely that some, if not many, persons who have not received grace in this life will do so after death and be saved. My defense of this view hinges on the conviction that God truly desires to save all persons and he will give all persons "optimal grace," the fullest opportunity possible to be saved, and only those who persist in rejecting such grace will be finally lost.[9]

FREEDOM VERSUS UNIVERSALISM

Although the appeal to libertarian freedom provides resources to construct alternatives to the punishment model of hell, these revised accounts of the doctrine are not without their critics. Indeed, a number of philosophers are rejecting eternal hell in favor of the doctrine of universal salvation. These philosophers dispute not only claims 2 and 3 spelled out earlier, but number 1 as well.

The issue of universal salvation has been a part of the discussion in contemporary philosophy of religion at least since the publication of John Hick's classic work, *Evil and the God of Love*, in 1966. In that volume, Hick argued that universalism is a "practical certainty," but

---

[7] *A Theodicy of Hell*, 161.

[8] For an interesting critique of this general line of argument, see Kenneth Himma, "Eternally Incorrigible: The continuing-sin response to the proportionality problem of hell," *Religious Studies* 39 (2003): 61–78.

[9] Jerry L. Walls, *Hell: The Logic of Damnation* (Notre Dame, IN: University of Notre Dame Press, 1992), 83–105. See also Andrei A. Buckareff and Allen Plug, "Escaping Hell: Divine motivation and the problem of hell," *Religious Studies* 41 (2005): 39–54.

stopped short of dogmatic affirmation that all will be saved because of his belief in human freedom along with his view that free choices cannot be known in advance, even by God.[10]

More recently, advocates of the doctrine are asserting it with more certainty, contending that freedom is not an obstacle to universal salvation. One bold proponent of universal salvation is Marilyn Adams, whose defense of universalism is part of her larger work on the problem of evil. Among her more radical suggestions is that sin should be seen more as a metaphysical matter than a moral one. In this vein, she highlights what she calls the "size gap" between God and human beings. Failure to recognize the enormity of this size gap leads us to exaggerate the dignity of human nature, particularly our freedom, as something so sacrosanct that not even God may interfere with it. Allowing us the freedom to damn ourselves, Adams maintains, is not an appropriate sort of compliment for God to pay to the likes of us.

Those who defend the freedom view of hell tend to see God and human beings on the analogy of the relationship between parents and adult children, a view that treats us as God's moral peers, according to Adams. A more fitting model would be the relationship between a mother and an infant or toddler. In such a relationship, the infant has no significant freedom or responsibility, and a good mother will not hesitate to interfere if the toddler is about to hurt himself. Given this picture, human freedom obviously poses no difficulty for universal salvation. As Adams has colorfully put the point, if God needs to override our freedom and determine our choices in order to prevent some of us from damning ourselves, this is "no more of an insult to our dignity than a mother's changing a diaper is to the baby."[11]

Although Adams is certainly right to remind us of the inestimable size gap between God and us, we can hardly do justice to the biblical narrative if we do not also acknowledge that God has chosen to relate to us in a loving fashion that requires significant response on our part. It is striking that one of the chief biblical metaphors for the divine–human relationship is that of marriage, which suggests that God has privileged us to know him in a way that requires more from us in the way of love, trust, and obedience than a toddler could ever return to a mother. In view of this, it is highly doubtful that Adams can so easily dispense with human freedom in her bid to defend universalism.

---

[10] John Hick, *Evil and the God of Love* (San Francisco, CA: Harper and Row, 1966), 343.

[11] Marilyn McCord Adams, *Horrendous Evils and the Goodness of God* (Ithaca, NY: Cornell University Press, 1999), 157.

Another philosopher who has mounted a vigorous case for universalism is Thomas Talbott, who has argued at length for the doctrine on biblical, as well as philosophical, grounds.[12] What is interesting about his view is that he insists not merely that the doctrine is possibly true, or practically certain, but that it is necessarily true. It is the only position that is even possibly true for Christian theism. The heart of his case for this strong claim is that the notion of anyone choosing eternal hell is finally incoherent. There is simply no intelligible motive that would make any sense of anyone making such a choice because the result of choosing evil is greater and greater misery, and it is impossible to sustain this in the long run. Unlike Adams, Talbott has argued that God can save everyone without overriding freedom. Rather, he holds that all persons can be moved to repent freely, in the nondeterministic sense.

Talbott's position hinges on three crucial concepts, the first of which is his account of what is involved in choosing an eternal destiny. The essence of his account is that such a choice must be fully informed so that a person truly gets what he wants and never regrets the choice he makes. The choice must be one that is free from ignorance and illusion in such a way that the person making it fully understands what he has chosen and freely persists in it. With these conditions spelled out, Talbott thinks there is an obvious asymmetry between choosing the joy heaven offers as an eternal destiny as opposed to choosing the endless misery of hell. Although the motives for choosing heaven are abundantly evident, there are no intelligible motives for preferring hell.

This point is reinforced by the second concept crucial to Talbott's position – namely, that the New Testament picture of hell is "a forcibly imposed punishment rather than a freely embraced condition," and moreover, that it is a matter of "unbearable suffering."[13] Talbott particularly stresses this claim against those who defend the freedom view of hell and charges that those who do so are guilty of holding a view that "in effect takes the hell out of hell, at least as far as the damned are concerned."[14] By contrast, he is confident that his view puts the hell back into hell and thereby assures that eventually even the most hardened sinners inevitably will repent and embrace heaven as their final destiny.

---

[12] Talbott lays out his biblical as well as his philosophical case for universalism in *Universal Salvation? The Current Debate*, ed. Robin A. Parry and Christopher Partridge (Grand Rapids, MI: Eerdmans, 2003).

[13] Thomas Talbott, "Freedom, Damnation and the Power to Sin with Impunity," *Religious Studies* 37 (2001): 420.

[14] Talbott, "Freedom," 429–30.

The third crucial component of Talbott's case is a distinction he draws between the power to do something, on the one hand, and the psychological ability to do it on the other. He points out that in the standard account of libertarian freedom, it is assumed that an act is not within an agent's power to perform unless it is also psychologically possible for him. Talbott rejects this assumption, contending that an agent may have power to perform an action even if it is not psychologically possible for him. Talbott illustrates this distinction by pointing to examples of dramatic conversions, such as those of St. Paul or C. S. Lewis, in which "the final act of submission seems to occur in a context where the alternative is no longer psychologically possible at all."[15] Although St. Paul may have had the power to disobey Christ and reject his call, Talbott insists that such a choice was not psychologically possible for him, in light of the revelation he had received.

We now can state Talbott's position in relation to the three essential claims of the traditional view of hell stated earlier. Whereas he clearly rejects 1 and 3, he affirms a version of 2. Although he may not hold that the suffering of hell reaches the level of consummate misery, he asserts that it is a place of unbearable suffering that no one could freely choose forever. Indeed, to persist in evil is to experience "greater and greater misery,"[16] so it is inevitable that eventually everyone will repent and be saved.

Talbott's case for universalism is a challenging one, so let us examine it more carefully, beginning with his claim that hell is a matter of unbearable suffering. The notion of a forcibly imposed punishment that causes greater and greater misery eliminates any meaningful sense of freedom from the equation, and undermines Talbott's claim that all can be brought freely to repent. There is a limit to how much misery any finite being can bear, so if there is not a limit to it, freedom would simply be overwhelmed at some point as the pain increased and intensified. Where exactly this limit lies is, perhaps, something only God could know, but clearly there is such a limit.

This point is reinforced by a distinction Talbott himself has drawn between two kinds of compulsion, one of which he affirms and the other of which he repudiates. The appropriate kind of compulsion is illustrated by those dramatic sorts of conversions mentioned earlier, whereas the wrong kind is illustrated by St. Augustine, who was willing to resort to the sword to persuade certain heretics to return to the Church. As

[15] Talbott, "Freedom," 426.
[16] Talbott, "Freedom," 420.

Talbott puts the distinction: "A stunning revelation such as Paul reportedly received, one that provides clear vision and *compelling evidence,*
thereby altering one's beliefs in a perfectly rational way, does not compel
behavior in the same way that threatening with a sword might."[17] Conversion at the end of a sword is obviously much different than conversion
at the end of a persuasive argument or experiential encounter. Conversion at sword point is pretty clearly not a free choice, nor is it a rationally
or morally defensible way to change someone's beliefs.

Talbott's distinction here is a very sensible one, but ironically, it
poses serious problems for him in view of his claim that hell is a matter of ever increasing "forcibly imposed punishment" that is literally
unbearable for its recipients. Now, this very much agrees with the traditional view of hell to which he claims to subscribe, for it has typically
been thought to include physical punishment of a rather intense degree.
If this is not what he means, he should not pretend that he endorses
the traditional understanding of why hell is unbearable. However, if he
actually does support the view that hell includes unbearable physical
punishment, then he faces another sort of difficulty, for such punishment seems to be a paradigmatic example of the sort of compulsion he
repudiates as inappropriate. Indeed, even if the punishment of hell were
"only" psychological and emotional, if it induced repentance by ever
increasing misery that at some point became unbearable, it would still
accordingly constitute an unacceptable form of compulsion.

It might be thought that Talbott could avoid this criticism by appealing to his distinction between the power to do something and the psychological ability to do it. Perhaps, it might be suggested, sinners under
the pressure of ever increasing misery have the power to continue resisting God, even if, at some point, they are no longer psychologically able
to do so. This distinction, however, will not help Talbott's case because
finite beings have neither the power nor the psychological ability to
absorb ever increasing misery, whether it is physical or psychological.
Our capacity to absorb misery is limited and at some point, as misery
increases and compounds, we would be coerced to submit, or would be
completely disintegrated or destroyed.

Talbott has responded to these criticisms and, in doing so, has clarified his position in some important respects. In the first place, he has
now made clear that those who submit to repentance under the force of
ever increasing misery are not free in the libertarian sense in this choice
because they ultimately cannot do otherwise. The choices that are made

---

[17] Talbott, "Freedom," 427.

to reach that point are free in the libertarian sense, but ironically, once that point is reached, the only choice possible is to repent.

Second, and more importantly, Talbott has provided helpful explication of the "forcibly imposed punishment" and "unbearable suffering" that characterize hell. What has emerged from his explanation is that he, in fact, understands these terms in a sense that is significantly different than traditional punishment models of hell, despite what his earlier writings seem to suggest. To help us understand the sort of suffering he means to affirm, he turns our attention to the example, inspired by a well-known movie plot, of a married man who foolishly has an affair with an unstable woman. When the affair ends, she takes her revenge by murdering his family. The profound guilt, sorrow, and anguish this man would naturally experience would constitute an unbearable suffering that God could use to induce him to repent, and "insofar as God uses the man's suffering as a means of correction, or a means to repentance, we can again say that the man has endured a forcibly imposed punishment for his sin."[18] Talbott goes on to comment that precisely the good that remains in even the worst of sinners can be a source of "unbearable torment" when our actions go against the grain of that good.

These clarifications are very helpful for understanding Talbott's position but, unfortunately, they also raise further problems for him. Most notably, his explanation of what he means by unbearable torment will not underwrite his crucial claim that all sinners inevitably must reach a point at which repentance is unavoidable. This claim was defensible when we took him to mean that the forcibly imposed punishment of hell produces ever increasing doses of such misery that no finite being could bear it forever. However, his explanation of this punishment now makes it appear that he has removed the unbearable aspect of unbearable torment. Indeed, dare we suggest that he has taken the hell out of his previous picture of hell?

Consider his case of the agonized adulterer. Although it surely is true that he would be in grievous pain over his foolish choices if he has any conscience at all, is it inevitable that he would be moved to repent? No doubt, God could use his anguish to prod him in the direction of repentance and reform, but there is nothing about the case as described that makes this outcome certain. It is a well-known phenomenon that people sometimes respond to tragedy by becoming angry at God and walking further away from him. Rather than accepting responsibility for his actions and committing to change, he might become resentful

---

[18] Talbott, "Misery and Freedom: Reply to Walls," *Religious Studies* 40 (2004): 218.

and embittered if he thought God allowed the murder of his family as a punishment or a divine wake-up call.

As Talbott observed, we have the freedom, "expressed in thousands of specific choices to move incrementally in the direction of repentance and reconciliation or in the direction of greater separation from God, and that freedom God always respects."[19] If this is so, it is not at all clear why choices to move farther and farther in the direction of separation from God must eventually reach a point at which repentance is the only option. The natural consequence of such choices is to harden one's heart and deaden one's conscience and if this is the result, repentance is hardly inevitable. Unless Talbott wants to resort back to his claim that such choices would create ever increasing misery that simply could not be borne forever, this is the likely result of moving ever farther away from God.

What this means is that Talbott has a dilemma – indeed, a hell of a dilemma – on his hands. He must choose between his clarified, milder account of what he means by divinely imposed misery, on the one hand, or his claim that all sinners must finally reach a point at which repentance is the only choice possible. If he chooses the first, there is no convincing reason why sinners may not persist forever in sin and rebellion. If he chooses the latter, he will be embracing a form of compulsion he wants to repudiate as unacceptable. Only the latter choice, however, will allow him to sustain his case for necessary universalism. Otherwise, it clearly fails.

HEAVENLY ISSUES

Although heaven has not generated as much discussion from contemporary philosophers as hell, there have been some interesting challenges to the doctrine posed in recent literature that merit philosophical attention. Before I turn to these, however, I want to begin with an issue internal to the traditional doctrine of heaven that has recently generated discussion. The issue is whether and in what sense persons in heaven are free – particularly whether they are free to sin, an issue that leads to what James Sennett has called "the dilemma of heavenly freedom." The dilemma arises from holding, on the one hand, the traditional belief that heaven is essentially morally perfect, which rules out the possibility of sin, and on the other hand that persons in heaven retain libertarian freedom, which implies it is possible they could sin.

---

[19] Talbott, "Misery," 221–22.

Sennett's proposed resolution holds that persons in heaven have only compatibilist freedom and are thus unable to sin because they have fully perfected characters. However, he preserves an important place for libertarian freedom (and the free will defense in theodicy) by arguing that libertarian free choices must play a significant role in the formation of perfected characters.[20] Although I am inclined to agree with Sennett's solution, I would argue there is a place for libertarian freedom in heaven because there is still a range of significant choices to be made within the limits of a perfected character.[21]

Let us turn now to the three challenges to heaven, beginning with what I will label the incompatibility objection, which proceeds from the argument against universal salvation I advanced in the previous section. Suppose universalism is false, and at least some persons will not be saved, but will be lost forever in eternal misery. If this is true, the objection goes, the saved in heaven could not experience perfect joy, for their happiness would at least be compromised if not undermined. This argument, which goes back at least to the nineteenth century theologian Friedrich Schleiermacher, has been revived in the current discussion and is usually advanced by proponents of universal salvation. Universalist Eric Reitan, for instance, defends the argument in an essay the title of which poses the question quite starkly: "Eternal damnation and blessed ignorance: is the damnation of some incompatible with the salvation of any?"[22] Obviously, he thinks the answer to his question is yes, so, in short, eternal hell is incompatible with heaven.

This argument clearly takes for granted not only that the saved would be aware of the damned, but that they would care about them. Indeed, precisely because the saved are perfected in love, they would truly empathize with the lost in their misery and deeply desire their salvation. Various responses have been offered to blunt the force of this argument or to challenge its assumptions. Some have suggested that the saved are not, in fact, aware of the lost, that they are in a state of "blessed ignorance" either because they are so caught up in bliss or because the memory of the lost has somehow been obliterated. Others have suggested that the saved see the lost with such moral clarity that their happiness cannot be disturbed by the lost. They understand that the lost have freely chosen their fate and, indeed, would like to infect the joy of heaven with their misery, but they refuse to allow them to

---

[20] James Sennett, "Is There Freedom in Heaven?" *Faith and Philosophy* 16 (1999): 70–78.
[21] Jerry L. Walls, *Heaven: The Logic of Eternal Joy* (New York: Oxford University Press, 2002), 61–62.
[22] *Religious Studies* 38 (2002), 429–50.

blackmail heaven or to spoil the happiness they perversely refuse for themselves.[23]

A second objection to heaven I will call the "dubious history argument." This objection, in the spirit of Nietzsche's suspicious account of the "genealogy" of Christian morality, is drawn from some recent accounts of the history of the doctrine that cast its origins in a dubious light. These historical treatments of heaven (and hell) contend that the doctrine was formulated by people with disreputable motives. J. Edward Wright, for instance, has tried to show that Jewish and Christian pictures of heaven were often inspired by the self-aggrandizing desire to believe God favors one's group over others. He admits the doctrine provides the positive benefit of hope for members of the group that sees itself as favored, but thinks it also created "a dangerous sense of superiority over outsiders by dehumanizing or demonizing them."[24]

It is undoubtedly true that some visions of heaven have been at least partly inspired by the sort of unsavory motives Wright identifies, but there is more to the story, even as told by him. In the very earliest days when the idea of life after death was conceived in Judaism, it was derived first and foremost from a deeply rooted faith in God's goodness and justice.[25] Life after death makes rational sense of how God's character and power can be ultimately vindicated despite the challenge that evil and injustice pose in this life. The fact that the deepest roots of belief in heaven are profoundly moral provides powerful resources to respond to those who would dismiss the doctrine because of its allegedly dubious origins.

The third assault on heaven I will mention is "the boredom argument," an objection that is not only poignant but also has a particularly jaded, postmodern feel to it. This objection to heaven has been famously formulated by Bernard Williams in an article entitled "The Makropulos Case: Reflections on the Tedium of Immortality."[26] The title of his essay is tediously telling: Williams believes the hope of eternal happiness is an incoherent one because no matter what delights may await us, they would eventually lose their luster and we would grow cold and indifferent. Earlier generations have looked to heaven in hopes that boredom

---

[23] C. S. Lewis develops this argument in *The Great Divorce* (San Francisco, CA: Harper, 2001), 129–37.

[24] J. Edward Wright, *The Early History of Heaven* (Oxford: Oxford University Press, 2000), 202. See also pp. 137, 157, 163, and 177.

[25] Wright, *The Early History of Heaven*, 158, 191–92.

[26] This essay is reprinted in *The Metaphysics of Death*, ed. John Martin Fischer (Stanford, CA: Stanford University Press, 1993), 73–92.

could be cured, but the tragic truth is that there is no cure. The emptiness and dissatisfaction that haunts this life would ultimately infect heaven as well, so the best we can hope for is to die shortly before the horror of not dying becomes overwhelmingly evident.

Although a number of responses to the boredom argument have been offered, this challenge awaits a full-scale answer.[27] I am inclined to think the heart of the issue is whether the idea of God is coherent – particularly the idea that God is an ecstatically happy being who has existed from all eternity and will continue to do so. If such a God exists, it is rational to hope he has the creative ability to share his eternal joy with us, even if our ability to conceptualize this in our current condition is imperfect and shadowy at best.

Whatever we believe about the matter, once the dream of heaven has invaded our hearts and stirred our imaginations and hopes, it is hard, if not impossible, to retreat from it without a shattering sense of disappointment. Heaven holds out the hope that our deepest longings for fulfillment and happiness can be satisfied not only for a period, but forever. To discard this dream and embrace a timely death as the best we can do is not merely a prudential compromise, but a profound surrender of hope. Only the reality of heaven can prevent our lives from ending with such a whimper.

---

[27] Garth Hallett surveys several of these solutions in his essay, "The Tedium of Immortality," *Faith and Philosophy* 18 (2001): 279–91. Also, in response to this issue, Charles Taliaferro makes a helpful distinction between time-enclosed goods and non–time-enclosed goods in his "Why We Need Immortality," *Modern Theology* 6, no. 4 (1990): 367–77.

Select Bibliography

Abraham, William J., *Canon and Criterion in Christian Theology* (Oxford: Clarendon, 1998).

Abraham, William J., *Crossing the Threshold of Divine Revelation* (Grand Rapids, MI: Eerdmans, 2006).

Adams, Marilyn McCord, *Horrendous Evils and the Goodness of God* (Ithaca, NY: Cornell University Press, 1999).

Adams, Robert M., "Has It Been Proved that All Real Existence Is Contingent?" *American Philosophical Quarterly* 8 (1971).

Adams, Robert M., "Divine Necessity," in *The Concept of God*, ed. Tomas V. Morris (Oxford: Oxford University Press, 1987).

Annas, Julia, *The Morality of Happiness* (Oxford; Oxford University Press, 1993).

Anselm, *Cur Homo Deus?* in *Anselm: Basic Writings*, trans. Thomas Williams (Indianapolis, IN: Hackett Publishing, 2007).

Anselm of Canterbury, *Why God Became Man*, in *Anselm of Canterbury: The Major Works*, ed. Brian Davies and G. R. Evans (Oxford: Oxford University Press, 1998).

Aquinas, Thomas, *Summa Contra Gentiles* (Notre Dame, IN: Notre Dame University Press, 1975).

Augustine, *On the Free Choice of the Will*, trans. Thomas Williams (Indianapolis, IN: Hackett Publishing, 1993).

Augustine, *The Trinity*, trans., with an introduction and notes, by E. Hill (New York: New City Press, 1991).

Aulén, Gustaf, *Christus Victor: An Historical Study of the Three Main Types of the Idea of the Atonement*, trans. A. G. Hebert with a foreword by Jaroslav Pelikan (New York: Macmillan, 1969).

Barth, Karl, "The Unity and Omnipresence of God," in *Church Dogmatics*, vol. 2, chapter VI, #31, 1, trans. T. H. L. Parker, et. al. (Edinburgh: T. & T. Clark, 1957).

Basinger, David, "Why Petition an Omnipotent, Omniscient, Wholly Good God?" *Religious Studies* 19 (1983): 25–41.

Boethius, *A Treatise against Eutyches and Nestorius*, trans. H. F. Stewart, E. K. Rand, and S. J. Tester in *Boethius* (Cambridge, MA: Harvard University Press, 1973).

Boff, Leonardo, *Trinity and Society*, trans. P. Burns (Maryknoll, NY: Orbis, 1988).

Brower, Jeffrey E. and Michael C. Rea, "Material Constitution and the Trinity," *Faith and Philosophy*, 22: 57–76.

Brown, David, "Anselm on Atonement," in *The Cambridge Companion to Anselm*, ed. Brian Davies and Brian Leftow (Cambridge: Cambridge University Press, 2004), 279–302.

Brummer, Vincent, *What Are We Doing When We Pray? On Prayer and the Nature of Faith* (Aldershot; Burlington, CT: Ashgate, 2008).

Brunner, Emil, *The Christian Doctrine of Creation and Redemption*, trans. Olive Wyon (London: Lutterworth, 1952).

Calvin, John, *Institutes of the Christian Religion*, vol. 1, book II, 16.1 (Philadelphia, PA: Westminster Press, 1960).

Carson, Thomas L., *Value and the Good Life* (Notre Dame, IN: Notre Dame Press, 2000).

Coakley, Sarah, *Powers and Submissions: Spirituality, Philosophy and Gender* (Oxford: Blackwell, 2002).

Corcoran, Kevin, ed. *Soul, Body, and Survival* (Ithaca, NY: Cornell University Press, 2001).

Craig, William Lane, *God, Time, and Eternity* (Dordrecht: Kluwer Academic Publishers, 2001).

Danielou, Jean, *Bible and the Liturgy* (Notre Dame, IN: University of Notre Dame Press, 2002).

Davis, Stephen T., Daniel Kendall and Gerald O'Collins, eds. *The Trinity: An Interdisciplinary Symposium on the Trinity* (Oxford: Oxford University Press, 1999).

Dix, Gregory, *The Shape of the Liturgy* (London: Continuum, 2005).

Draper, Paul, "Pain and Pleasure: An Evidential Problem for Theists," *Noûs* 23 (June 1989): 331–50, reprinted in *The Evidential Argument from Evil*, ed. Daniel Howard-Snyder (Indianapolis, IN: Indianapolis University Press, 1996), 12–29.

Dulles, Avery, *Models of the Church* (Garden City, NY: Doubleday, 1974).

Farmer, H. H., *The World and God* (London: Nisbet, 1936).

Fiddes, Paul, *Participating in God: A Pastoral Doctrine of the Trinity* (London: Darton, Longman and Todd, 2000).

Findlay, J. N., "Can God's Existence Be Disproved?" in *New Essays in Philosophical Theology*, ed. A. Flew and A. MacIntyre (New York: Macmillan, 1955).

Flint, Thomas, *Divine Providence: The Molinist Account* (Ithaca, NY: Cornell University Press, 1998).

Franks, Christopher A., "The Simplicity of the Living God: Aquinas, Barth, and some Philosophers," *Modern Theology* 21 (April 2005): 2.

Furnish, Victor Paul, *Theology and Ethics in Paul* (Nashville, TN: Abingdon, 1968).

Ganssle, Gregory E. and David M. Woodruff, *God and Time: Essays on the Nature of God* (New York: Oxford University Press, 2002).

Gracia, Jorge J. E., *How Can We Know What God Means? The Interpretation of Revelation* (New York: Palgrave Macmillan, 2001).

Hanson, R. P. C., *The Search for the Christian Doctrine of God: The Arian Controversy 318–381* (Edinburgh: T & T Clark, 1988).

Hare, John E., *The Moral Gap* (Oxford: Clarendon Press, 1996), chapter ten.

Hartshorne, Charles, *Man's Vision of God and the Logic of Theism* (Chicago: Willett, Clark, & Co., 1941).

Hasker, William, *God, Time, and Knowledge* (Ithaca, NY: Cornell University Press, 1989).

Hasker, William, *Providence, Evil, and the Openness of God* (London: Routledge, 2004).

Helm, Paul, *The Providence of God* (Downers Grove, IL: InterVarsity Press, 1994).

Heyduck, Richard, *The Recovery of Doctrine in the Contemporary Church: An Essay in Philosophical Ecclesiology* (Waco, TX: Baylor University Press, 2002).

Hick, John, *Evil and the God of Love* (London: Palgrave Macmillan, 2007).

Hitchens, Christopher, *God is Not Great: How Religion Poisons Everything* (New York: Twelve/Hachette Book Group, 2007).

Howard-Snyder, Daniel, ed., *The Evidential Argument from Evil* (Indianapolis, IN: Indiana University Press, 1996).

Hubbard, Moyer, *New Creation in Paul's Letters and Thought* (Cambridge: Cambridge University Press, 2002).

Hughes, Christopher, *On a Complex Theory of a Simple God* (Ithaca, NY and London: Cornell University Press, 1989).

Hume, David, *Enquiry Concerning Human Understanding*, sec. X, "Of Miracles" (Indianapolis, IN: Hackett Publishing Company, 1993).

Jantzen, Grace, *God's World, God's Body* (Philadelphia, PA: Westminster, 1984).

Jensen, P., "Forgiveness and Atonement," *Scottish Journal of Theology*, 46 (1993): 141–59.

Kirmmse, Bruce H., "The Thunderstorm: Kierkegaard's Ecclesiology," *Faith and Philosophy* 17 (2000): 87–102.

Leo the Great, *The Letters and Sermons of Leo the Great, Bishop of Rome*, trans. Charles Lett Feltoe, in *A Select Library of Nicene and Post-Nicene Fathers of the Christian Church*, Second Series, vol. 12, ed. Philip Schaff and Henry Wace (Grand Rapids, MI: WM. Eerdans Publishing Company, 1976).

Leftow, Brian, "Swinburne on Divine Necessity," *Religious Studies*, forthcoming.

Leftow, Brian, *Time and Eternity* (Ithaca, NY: Cornell University Press, 1989).

Lewis, David, "Do We Believe in Penal Substitution?" *Philosophical Papers* 26 (1997): 203–09.

MacDonald, Scott, ed., *Being and Goodness: The Concept of the Good in Metaphysics and Philosophical Theology* (Ithaca, NY: Cornell University Press, 1991).

Mannion, Gerard and Lewis S. Mudge, eds., *The Routledge Companion to the Christian Church* (New York and London: Routledge, 2008).

Mavrodes, George, *Revelation in Religious Belief* (Philadelphia, PA: Temple University Press, 1988).

Meadors, Edward, *Idolatry and the Hardening of the Heart* (London: T & T Clark, 2006).

Menssen, Sandra and Thomas D. Sullivan, *The Agnostic Inquirer* (Grand Rapids, MI: Eerdmans, 2007).

Moltmann, Jürgen, *The Trinity and the Kingdom*, trans. M. Kohl (San Francisco: Harper & Row, 1981).

Morris, Thomas, *The Logic of God Incarnate* (Ithaca, NY: Cornell University Press, 1986).

Moser, Paul K., *The Elusive God: Reorienting Religious Epistemology* (Cambridge: Cambridge University Press, 2008).

Newman, John Henry, *An Essay in Aid of a Grammar of Assent* (Notre Dame, IN: University of Notre Dame Press, 1992) and *Fifteen Sermons Preached Before the University of Oxford* (Notre Dame, IN: University of Notre Dame Press, 1997).

Olson, Roger E. and Christopher A. Hall, *The Trinity* (Grand Rapids, MI: Eerdmans, 2002).

Padgett, Alan G., *God, Eternity, and the Nature of Time* (New York: St. Martin's Press, 1992).

Phillips, D. Z., *The Concept of Prayer* (London: Routledge and Kegan Paul, 1965).

Plantinga, Alvin, *God, Freedom, and Evil* (New York: Harper and Row, 1974).

Porter, Jean, *Nature as Reason: A Thomistic Theory of the Natural Law* (Grand Rapids, MI: Eerdmans, 2005).

Porter, Steven, "Rethinking the Logic of Penal Substitution," in *Philosophy of Religion: A Reader and Guide*, ed. W. L. Craig (New Brunswick, NJ: Rutgers University Press, 2002).

Quinn, Philip L., "Kantian Philosophical Ecclesiology," in Philip L. Quinn and Christian Miller, *Essays in the Philosophy of Religion* (Oxford: Oxford University Press, 2006), 255–78.

Rogers, Katherin, *Anselm on Freedom* (Oxford: Oxford University Press, 2008).

Rusch, William, ed., *The Trinitarian Controversy* (Philadelphia, PA: Fortress, 1980).

Russell, Jeffrey Burton, *A History of Heaven* (Princeton, NJ: Princeton University Press, 1997).

Sanders, John, *The God Who Risks: A Theology of Divine Providence*, rev. ed. (Downers Grove, IL: InterVarsity Press, 2007).

Sarot, Marcel, *God, Possibility and Corporeality* (Kampen: Kok Pharos, 1992).

Saward, John, *Sweet and Blessed Country* (Oxford: Oxford University Press, 2005).

Schilbrack, Kevin, ed., *Thinking through Rituals: Philosophical Perspectives* (New York: Routledge, 2004).

Segal, Alan F., *A History of the Afterlife in Western Religion* (New York: Doubleday, 2004).

Segal, Robert, ed., *The Myth and Ritual Theory: an Anthology* (Hoboken, NJ: Wiley-Blackwell, 1998).

Stump, Eleonore and Norman Kretzmann, "Absolute Simplicity," *Faith and Philosophy*, vol. 2, 1985.

Stump, Eleonore, "Petitionary Prayer," *APQ*, 1979, reprinted in Richard Swinburne, ed., *Miracles* (London and New York: Macmillan, 1989).

Swinburne, Richard, *The Coherence of Theism*, rev. ed. (Oxford: Oxford University Press, 1993), 241–90.

Swinburne, Richard, *Responsibility and Atonement* (Oxford: Oxford University Press, 1989).

Swinburne, Richard, *The Resurrection of God Incarnate* (Oxford: Oxford University Press, 2003).

Swinburne, Richard, *Revelation: From Metaphor to Analogy*, 2nd ed. (Oxford: Oxford University Press, 2007).

Taliaferro, Charles and Stewart Goetz, "The Prospect of Christian Materialism," *Christian Scholar's Review* vol. XXXVII, no. 3 (Spring 2008).

van Inwagen, Peter, "The Possibility of Resurrection," in *Immortality*, ed. Paul Edwards (New York: Macmillan, 1992), 242–46.

van Inwagen, Peter, *The Problem of Evil* (Oxford: Oxford University Press, 2008).

Volf, Miroslav, *After Our Likeness: The Church as Image of the Trinity* (Grand Rapids, MI: Eerdmans, 1998).

von Balthasar, Hans Urs, *Prayer*, trans. Graham Harrison (San Francisco, CA: Ignatius Press, 1986).

Wainwright, Geoffrey, *Doxology: The Praise of God in Worship, Doctrine and Life: A Systematic Theology* (Oxford: Oxford University Press, 1984).

Wainwright, William J., "God's Body," in *The Concept of God*, ed. Thomas Morris (New York: Oxford University Press, 1987).

Wainwright, William J., *Religion and Morality* (Aldershot: Ashgate, 2005).

Walls, Jerry L., *Heaven: The Logic of Eternal Joy* (New York: Oxford University Press, 2002).

Walls, Jerry L., *Hell: The Logic of Damnation* (Notre Dame, IN: University of Notre Dame Press, 1992).

Weigel, Peter, *Aquinas on Simplicity* (Oxford and New York: Peter Lang, 2008).

Weinandy, Thomas, *Does God Change? Studies in Historical Theology*, vol. 4 (Still River, MA: St. Bede's Publications, 1985).

Wesley, John, "On the Omnipresence of God," in *The Works of John Wesley*, vol. 4 (*Sermons IV: 115–151*), ed. Albert C. Outler (Nashville, TN: Abingdon Press, 1987).

Wolterstorff, Nicholas, *Divine Discourse: Philosophical Reflections on the Claim that God Speaks* (Cambridge: Cambridge University Press, 1995).

Wolterstorff, Nicholas, "Divine Simplicity," *Philosophical Perspectives*, vol. 5 (1991).

Wright, N. T., *The Resurrection of the Son of God* (Minneapolis, MN: Fortress Press, 2003).

Zagzebski, Linda Trinkaus, *Divine Motivation Theory* (Cambridge: Cambridge University Press, 2004).

Zizioulas, John D., *Being as Communion: Studies in Personhood and the Church* (Crestwood, NY: St. Vladimir's Seminary Press, 1985).

Zizioulas, John D., *Communion and Otherness: Further Studies in Personhood and the Church*, ed. Paul McPartlan (Edinburgh: T & T Clark, 2006).

Index